"Jay's life is an amazing journey! He has proven that no challenge in life should be an excuse for not trying to achieve your dreams. This book is a must-read for anyone living with diabetes! Educational and motivating!"

—**Dr. Etie S. Moghissi**, MD, *Associate Clinical Professor of Medicine, UCLA Board of Trustees, American College of Endocrinology*

"Jay's Finish Line Vision *message is an inspirational mix of personal stories and excellent leadership advice. A sample of the evaluations from the managers and supervisors hearing him speak at our leadership conference were: 'Great comments on determination! … Thought provoking! … Great motivator! … Great research and personalized stories! … Absolutely loved him! … Glued the whole hour! … Awesome—Inspiring— Enjoyed it! … Bring this guy back!'"*

—**Scott Lange**, *Oklahoma Department of Transportation*

"Jay's Finish Line Vision *message is a great motivational boost from somebody with his experience who has such a gift. Our employees could not thank us enough for having him speak! Jay, please continue your mission changing the lives of individuals through your passionate message!"*

—**Dr. Paul Hobaica**, MD, *medical director, Arthrex Corporation*

"Jay's Finish Line Vision *message will have a long-term impact on any person who hears it. He will challenge, motivate, and encourage you in a way most speakers can't."*

—**Mike Swaim**, CPA, *Swaim Brown Wealth Management*

"'A great story ... Wonderful speaker! ... Truly inspirational! ... An unqualified success! ... Perfect fit with the theme of our sales meeting! ... I'm going to take what I learned back home, as a sales executive and a father.' These are just a few of the comments we had after Jay presented Finish Line Vision at our annual meeting. Everyone was energized by his message and able to take something away that will help them be a better, more focused associate for Security Benefit. It was a pleasure to have him speak to our leadership and sales team and give a unique perspective on endurance, perseverance, and discipline."

—**Kurt Auleta**, *VP Sales Operations, Security Benefit, Inc.*

"As a racing driver with type 1 diabetes, I know firsthand how it can affect every single minute, hour, and day of your life. But Jay has turned a negative into a positive. In Finish Line Vision, *Jay shows his passion for helping others overcome any obstacle—whether it's diabetes, a tough business decision, or any other challenge. This book is a great guide for anyone wanting to do that!"

—**Charlie Kimball**, *IndyCar Series driver*

"Finishing an Ironman triathlon in nine hours, forty-seven minutes (9:47) is exceptional for any triathlete. It is absolutely amazing for one like Jay who has type 1 diabetes. Jay's story shows what it took to make that happen, and that dreams can become reality when a big goal is aligned with a big commitment level."

—**Dr. Rick Kattouf II**, *fitness & nutrition expert, triathlon coach,* www.teamkattouf.com

"Jay delivered his Finish Line Vision *message at our leadership development retreat. The staff described it as 'Amazing! … Inspirational! … Loved listening to him! … Jay Hewitt was sensational! … Motivating! … Best speaker yet!' It touched every discipline and leader in Greenville Health System and challenged us all. The ability to continue moving forward despite obstacles is truly what differentiates leaders and makes us successful. Thank you again for such a powerful message!"*

—**Michael Riordan**, *president and CEO, Greenville Health System*

"Jay shared his Finish Line Vision *message at our annual conference. Our members described it as 'Amazing! … Perfect topic! … Great motivation! We all need finish line goals … Speechless! … Knocked it out of the park! … Awesome and inspiring!' He seamlessly tied his message to the banking industry and that made it even more personal and impactful. We could not have asked for more—fantastic job!"*

—**Rob Braswell**, *president and CEO, Community Bankers Association of Georgia*

"As a runner, swimmer, and cyclist myself, I feel qualified to say that anyone who completes an Ironman triathlon is simply incredible. As a physician who has devoted my professional life to helping patients with diabetes, I know the factors required to manage type 1 diabetes every day. Training for and completing an Ironman with type 1 diabetes is beyond my comprehension—it is Herculean! Mr. Hewitt has been enshrined in our Diabetes Hall of Honor and I have described his story, standing in front of the plaque to honor him, countless times. His story speaks volumes to those we encourage to engage and embrace their diabetes."

—**Dr. David M. Harlan**, MD, *chief, Diabetes Division, UMass Memorial Medical Center*

FINISH LINE
VISION

Find Your Passion. Overcome Your Obstacles. Fuel Your Life.

FINISH LINE
VISION®

JAY HEWITT

Advantage®

Published by Advantage, Charleston, South Carolina.
Member of Advantage Media Group.

ADVANTAGE is a registered trademark, and the Advantage colophon is a trademark of Advantage Media Group, Inc.

Printed in the United States of America.

10 9 8 7 6 5 4 3 2 1

ISBN: 978-1-59932-218-6
LCCN: 2017946900

Cover design by Katie Biondo.
Layout design by Megan Elger.

This publication is designed to provide accurate and authoritative information in regard to the subject matter covered. It is sold with the understanding that the publisher is not engaged in rendering legal, accounting, or other professional services. If legal advice or other expert assistance is required, the services of a competent professional person should be sought.

Advantage Media Group is proud to be a part of the Tree Neutral® program. Tree Neutral offsets the number of trees consumed in the production and printing of this book by taking proactive steps such as planting trees in direct proportion to the number of trees used to print books. To learn more about Tree Neutral, please visit **www.treeneutral.com**.

Advantage Media Group is a publisher of business, self-improvement, and professional development books. We help entrepreneurs, business leaders, and professionals share their Stories, Passion, and Knowledge to help others Learn & Grow. Do you have a manuscript or book idea that you would like us to consider for publishing? Please visit advantagefamily.com or call **1.866.775.1696.**

To my mom and dad. I am so proud to be your son;
thank you for your endless support and love.

To my wife, Anna, and Janna, Ainslie, and Thomas.
You make me so proud to be your husband and father. I love you each
so much and will always help you reach your finish lines.

TABLE OF CONTENTS

FOREWORD

I've known Jay Hewitt for quite some time now. I would go on training rides with him while I was training for the Tour de France. He would ride a few hours with me and then hop off the bike and go for a run and sometimes even do a swim before he met me. I always wondered what drove him to work so hard at a sport that was not his work. I realize now that he was not only trying to pursue his personal goals, but he was trying to prove a point to anyone who has diabetes or an illness where doctors say your life will change forever. He turned his diagnosis into a lifelong mission not only to get by with this disease but to prosper and live life to the fullest. At first I didn't even know he had diabetes. He was just another athlete trying to accomplish his goals. But he had a vision, he set goals, and he never strayed from them. That was what most impressed me then. Then to find out later that he had type 1 diabetes, I was even more impressed with him.

As I got to know Jay better I realized his desire to succeed and accomplish his goals was very similar to the best athletes in the world. He had what we call tunnel vision and what he calls finish line vision. Not only in his athletic endeavors was he like this but in his profession as well. He has advised me through many challenging times, and I consider him a great man.

Jay's finish line vision is a tool that I used myself on many occasions. When I won the 2009 national championship in my hometown in Greenville, SC, I had broken my collarbone three weeks before that in the Tour de France. I suffered the last five stages with a broken collarbone, but I wasn't going to let that stop me from finishing the tour. Then I made it my goal, my vision, not to let this setback stop me from winning my third national championship. After five hours of a grueling hot race over some very hilly terrain it came down to the finish line, but I ended up beating the best cyclists in the country in front of my hometown. The feeling doesn't get any better than that. Not letting any doubt enter my mind throughout that period and staying focused, keeping my finish line vision, is what helped me achieve that goal.

Jay's book is a guide to all on how to get back up after you get knocked down and keep going until you reach your finish line—no matter what the circumstance.

—George Hincapie
Five-time US Olympian
Three-time US Road Cycling National Champion
Sixteen-time Tour de France finisher
Author of the book, *The Loyal Lieutenant: Leading Out Lance and Pushing Through the Pain on the Rocky Road to Paris*
(George Hincapie with Craig Hummer, Harper Collins, 2014)

"Autobiography is only to be trusted when it reveals something disgraceful. A man who gives a good account of himself is probably lying, since any life when viewed from the inside is simply a series of defeats."

—GEORGE ORWELL, 1944

Wow. I cannot believe I am here.

That was the feeling I had listening to the Swedish national anthem playing as I stood at the start of the ITU Long Distance Triathlon World Championship, staring out as the sun rose over the frigid waters of a massive lake in northern Sweden. It was eerily calm and serene. Yet tens of thousands of spectators lined the water's edge and the grandstands surrounding the transition area, standing quietly at attention, waiting anxiously to erupt in raucous cheers and wave the flags of their homeland. In a few minutes I would plunge into that lake in a violent charge of several hundred of the best long-distance triathletes in the world—the fittest humans on the planet. Each of them wore the name and colors of their country on their jersey: Australia, Germany, Denmark, France, Great Britain, and many more. I wore USA on my racing skinsuit, representing the United States of America in my first year on the US national team. Each of these athletes was also ready to punch, kick, and pound me underwater for two and a half miles, all in the spirit of friendly competition, and then bolt out of the water like a cold shower to cycle seventy-five miles and then run eighteen miles to the glory of the finish line.

Ah, the finish line. Now that is always a magical place. Whether it is a long-distance triathlon, a high school or college graduation, or a moment in your career or personal life, it is a place you want to be one day. It is hard to get there. And that is what makes it great.

At this point I had been racing triathlons for just four years. I didn't even know what a triathlon was four years ago. *Isn't that something with a horse and a pistol and sword fighting or something like that?* No, that's a pentathlon. *Okay, good, because I don't have a horse. Oh, wait, I know what a triathlon is, it's that thing they do in the Winter Olympics with cross-country skiing and shooting a rifle, right?* No, that's a biathlon. *Throwing spears, pole vaulting, and running around a track?* Nope, decathlon. *Fund-raising on the telephone?* Telethon. *Singing and dancing?* Just stop. *Well, which one of all these #*%& "thlons" is a triathlon?!* Move on.

The life of a long-distance triathlete, or Ironman triathlete, is one of suffering, suffering and pain that you must embrace in miles and hours of training alone and in the intensity of the long race. It is also a life of balancing, balancing three very different sports—swimming, cycling, and running—to see who can perform them all the best while balancing and overcoming the obstacles that each athlete faces in their life and on race day and the limitations of their body. It is designed to test your speed, power, and endurance and your determination, discipline, and pain threshold.

Why would someone sign up for something like this?

Because it is similar to challenges and success in life, that's why. Whether you are a student or working professional, a mom or dad, an athlete or an artist, or a person battling a health condition, you have to work hard and balance obligations and overcome different obstacles to achieve success—to reach your finish line.

I had not lived a life as an elite endurance athlete. I found myself in this place staring out at those cold waters only because of a major obstacle that I had encountered thirteen years earlier—an obstacle that was thrust upon me without warning and no fault of my own. I was diagnosed with type 1 diabetes when I was twenty-three years old in law school. Since that day it had been thirteen years of injecting insulin with a syringe four or five times a day, pricking my finger to check my blood sugar up to ten times a day, wearing insulin pumps attached to my body, and being visited by paramedics after frightening episodes of insulin overdoses and hypoglycemia, rendering me unconscious and in a seizure.

Now here I was, representing the United States as one of the best triathletes in the world. But I never would have been here if I did not have diabetes. It was the challenge that confronted me, then motivated me, then helped me achieve things that I never would have thought possible—things in athletics, my working career, and my personal life.

Do you have a finish line in your life? Do you have a goal that you want to achieve, a dream that you want to live and experience, but you know the road to get there will be long and hard? It is intimidating and scary, with a lot of unknowns and doubts. There are obstacles in your way and you are afraid that you might fail, and failure intimidates us all … but you still dream of that moment—your finish line moment. How do you get there?

That's what this book is about: achieving your goals, even better, achieving your dreams, and visualizing your dreams and going after them.

Finish Line Vision® is the motivation that comes from visualizing your success, imagining yourself experiencing that moment. It comes from my life as a long-distance triathlete, but it has applied to other stages of my life as a student, an attorney, a business professional working behind a desk sixty hours a week, a keynote speaker, and a dad and husband.

I will take you on a journey and tell you my story, my successes and my failures, but also provide research on the neuropsychology of achievement and examples of high achievers in history. Some of them you may know, some you may not, but we will discover the secrets of their success. We will learn about health, fitness, and nutrition and about diabetes, a growing epidemic affecting 30 million people in America and over 420 million people worldwide. I promise you that if you apply these principles, learn from these successes and failures, work hard, and persevere … you will reach your finish line.

Now, let's get you there.

CHAPTER 1

DIABETES ATTACKS MY LIFE

Topic: Encountering Obstacles

I woke up in the hospital's emergency room.

I had tubes in my nose, an IV in my arm, and other equipment hooked up to me. A doctor, an endocrinologist, was standing at the foot of my bed, but I did not know she was an endocrinologist. I did not even know what that was. She was just a doctor in a white coat. I was so weak I could not lift my head.

"Hi Jay. I'm Dr. McFarland," she said quietly when I opened my eyes.

I blinked and looked at her, trying to figure out where I was and what had happened to me. *Why am I in the hospital? Have I been in a car accident? What day is it? Why am I too weak to sit up? What are all these things attached to me? Something is really wrong.* I heard some other minor discussion that I was too weak to engage in.

Then she told me.

"Jay, your blood sugar is dangerously high." The machine next to me pumping oxygen hummed and beeped, and the sounds of other staff in the ER murmured in the background. Blue fabric curtains hung around my bed, separating us from the rest of the emergency room.

"You have diabetes."

She was a gentle, soft-spoken, middle-aged woman and no doubt had had this conversation with many patients and families before. After contemplating this for a moment, I asked her some questions.

"Diabetes? What do you mean?" I said quietly. I watched her face.

I never knew anyone with diabetes. I thought it was some kind of blood disease, a disease where people had to inject themselves with syringes all the time. I think I had seen a great uncle, my grandmother's brother, one time years ago with big syringes and vials in his house, and it kind of freaked me out. Maybe he had diabetes. He was dead now. There was no history of diabetes in my close family—not in my parents, grandparents, brother, sister, cousins, aunts, or uncles.

She told me a little about diabetes. It sounded serious.

Is she telling me everything? Fear started building in me. I was hearing all of this alone. Laying there in the ER, this sounded bad. Something was wrong with *my blood*. I was going to have to test my blood every day and take injections with a syringe—shots, needles, multiple times a day—for the rest of my life.

While I don't think she laid all of the potential long-term health complications on me in that first conversation in the ER—blindness, foot or leg amputations, kidney failure, and dialysis—she did let me know that this was serious, very serious. And I knew it because my brain and body had been going through hell for the past month, and I woke up here.

"Am ... am I going to die?" I asked. That may sound like a silly question, but when you are weak and stripped of all pretenses of stability, laying helpless in an emergency room, you don't mince words or have the strength to dance around the subject. *How serious is this? Just give it to me straight. Bottom line.*

"No," she said, with a reassuring slight smile, "you're not going to die. Not now." She paused, and her expression changed as she looked deep into my eyes. "But your life is going to change."

The machines in that ER hummed and beeped, and the oxygen tubes wheezed, filling my nose. Her words sunk in.

How is my life going to change? What does this mean for me? Am I now going to be the "sick" guy, the one who can't do things others can? I could hear doors closing in my head. Nope, can't do that with diabetes. Slam! Can't do that either. Slam! *What girl is going to want to date me, marry me, live their life with a weak, sick husband who has to take shots all the time or who gets his leg amputated? I won't be the pillar of strength who takes care of a family. Somebody might have to take care of me.*

"What do we do? Is there a cure?" I couldn't think of anything else to say. Looking back now, I realize that this was my personality coming out with these questions. Identify the problem. Assess the problem. Fix the problem.

There has to be a cure. This is 1991. All I have to do is get the right medicine, the right treatment, and they can kill diabetes in me like they kill cancer cells. Send it into remission and hope it never comes back. Do surgery and take it out. Then I won't have to deal with it every day for the rest of my life.

She hesitated, with a slight sigh, as if she had answered this question many times before and wished she had a different answer.

"No," she said quietly, pausing. "There's no cure. Not today."

After that, she may have said other things, but I didn't pay attention. A medical record signed by Dr. McFarland on February 1, 1991, states, "Patient was admitted with acute onset diabetic ketoacidosis today and was admitted into intensive care. The condition on admission was serious/critical." I still have a copy of that handwritten record.

She left my bedside, parting the thin screen and closing it behind her, preparing to have me admitted into ICU. I rolled my head over while anxiety knotted my stomach. I fought back a tear in my eye. I lay there alone—thinking, wondering, worrying. *How did I end up here? How is my life going to change?*

HOW DID I END UP HERE?

Three months before I woke up in the hospital I was nearing the end of my first semester of law school. I was twenty-three years old. That first semester I would go to class three to five hours a day and then read cases that afternoon and evening. I would read hundreds of pages of archaic legal opinions on contracts, torts, constitutional law, property law, and wills and estate planning, outlining the arguments and holdings of the opinions so that I'd be prepared to discuss them if the professor called on me the next day. I thought, *First semester of law school is miserable, so it's normal to feel miserable, right?* Winter arrived in November with cold, dark, gloomy, wet weather and stressful first semester final exams in December, and I was not exercising much—just reading, studying, and no doubt stressing.

When I came back from Christmas break in early January 1991, for several weeks I felt like I was developing a cold: a general run-down feeling, a sore throat, gradually feeling weaker. I had no appetite and started losing weight. As it got worse I thought I maybe just had the flu. Soon I could not even walk the short distance with my heavy bookbag (law books in those days were about two inches thick before tablets and laptops and today's digital tools) from my car across the large parking lot without stopping to rest against a car. I rested on each landing walking up the stairs to my classes on the third floor. I was fit, 6'3" and 175 pounds, and a good athlete, but now I could hardly walk. My throat was so sore and burned with a dry irritation that I would stop at the Wendy's across from the law school to get a Frosty ice cream and, since I was in the South, of course I got a sweet iced tea (one part tea, five parts sugar) just for some temporary relief.

I did not know it, but I was just poisoning myself.

I did not have time to be sick. If I missed even one class, much less a whole day, I would fall behind, and the professor could target me the next day like a predator drone strike. I shared an apartment with my twenty-five-year-old brother who was also in graduate school at the University of South Carolina. We had different classes and studied, often not seeing each other for days. No one spotted the signs of my body losing weight, severe thirst, pale skin, and dark eyes, or at least no one commented. But everyone looks pretty bad in dreary January of the first year of law school, pale with no sleep. And no one around me knew what diabetes was or what the symptoms of severe high blood sugar looked like.

During these January days of weakness and simply trudging through like a zombie, I do remember one person commenting that my breath smelled "fruity." I now know that is a symptom of ketoacidosis. Ketoacidosis is a severe medical condition. You can smell it on a person's breath due to acetone, a by-product of the decomposition of acid, making breath smell like fruit or nail polish remover. It is essentially a chemical breakdown occurring in the body. The body needs glucose to fuel muscles and cells all over the body: the brain, lungs, arms, and legs. Glucose comes from digesting carbohydrate foods like bread, potatoes, pasta, rice, and fruit and less-healthy sugary foods like candy, cookies, ice cream, and sugary drinks. The body digests carbohydrate in the stomach and releases it as glucose for the bloodstream to carry throughout the body as fuel for the cells. Diabetics often use the term "blood sugar" and "blood glucose" interchangeably because they mean the same thing. Sugar is just one form of carbohydrate, like beer is just one form of alcohol. Sugary sweets, bread, and pasta are all forms of carbohydrate that raise your blood glucose level, just like beer, wine, and liquor are all forms of alcohol that raise your blood alcohol level. You can't just eliminate one.

Insulin is essentially a bridge or gatekeeper hormone produced in the pancreas specifically to transfer glucose out of the bloodstream and into the hungry cells. After you eat something, the pancreas detects glucose in the blood and releases insulin that instantaneously transports the glucose out of the blood and into the waiting cells all over the body. If there is no insulin, or not enough insulin, the glucose remains stuck floating around trapped in the bloodstream like debris clogging a river, while the body's cells go hungry and wither from lack of glucose.

When the pancreas stops producing insulin completely—like it did for me and all people with type 1 diabetes—the liver eventually starts to break down fatty acids and protein stored in the body as its only source of fuel. That started happening in me in those January days when I felt run down and weak, like I had the flu. Breaking down fatty acid creates excess acid dumped into the blood, which is already overloaded with excess glucose. The blood is both the river of life and the sewer of waste. The excess acid and excess glucose float around and clog up the blood, like fresh food and sewage stuck in your house plumbing system. One thing you need but can't access (glucose), because you don't have any insulin—the other you don't want (acid). You need both of them out of your bloodstream.

So then the body's super filters, the kidneys, kick in to filter the blood, but they can become overloaded trying to clear out all of the excess glucose, sending it to the bladder and causing you to have to urinate multiple times an hour, even though you are not drinking any fluids. This leads to dehydration as the body keeps trying to flush the excess glucose out of the bloodstream and out of the body. You become constantly thirsty. The body essentially goes into preservation mode, consuming itself in fatty acids for fuel, as it cannot metabolize anything you eat because the pancreas quit producing insulin.

A final product of burning fats at a rapid rate are acid chemicals called ketones. If the ketones are produced at a rate faster than they can be burned, they too need to be excreted so even more fluids are lost through the urine, while the blood accumulates more and more ketone acids. The individual can develop a condition called diabetic ketoacidosis or 'DKA' which is often a medical emergency. Symptoms include abdominal pain, rapid breathing with a "fruity" smell to breath, nausea and vomiting (which causes further fluid loss). If fluid losses grow too great,

*and the blood ketone acid levels get too high, individuals can
lapse into a coma, and some die.*

—Dr. David M. Harlan, MD Chief of the Diabetes Division
and Co-Director of the Diabetes Center of Excellence at the
University of Massachusetts School of Medicine and UMass
Memorial Healthcare.

Other symptoms of diabetic ketoacidosis—prolonged (i.e., several days of) extreme high blood sugar—are dry mouth and thirst, excessive urine production, and feeling bloated and weak with a constant headache. As the condition progresses over several days, breathing becomes labored, with a deep, gasping character, and it leads to lethargy, confusion, hallucination, and eventually coma and death.

In January 1991, for several weeks trudging back and forth to classes and studying, I was experiencing, or was about to experience, all of these symptoms (except coma and death).

After a few weeks of fighting a losing battle against this "cold," still unaware of what I was dealing with, getting weaker and weaker, I drove one hundred miles from law school in Columbia, SC, to my childhood and parents' home in Greenville, SC, for the weekend. I thought maybe some home cooking and motherly care would help. Unbeknownst to me and my well-intended family, more carbohydrate-rich food meant more glucose dumped and trapped in my blood, feeding myself more poison. Before heading back that Sunday I watched part of the Super Bowl on January 27, 1991, which was also my father's birthday. I'm sure I ate some birthday cake (more sugar) and Super Bowl party food (more carbohydrates) even though I was nauseous and still not feeling any better. I remember that short drive back to school because I had to stop twice in ninety minutes to go to the bathroom, even though I had not drank much of anything. *I never had to stop in a short drive like this. Now twice every forty-five minutes? What is going on?*

The next day, Monday, January 28, I was weaker and more nauseous. Tuesday was even worse. I finally resigned myself to the fact that I had to see a doctor. My student health insurance policy required me first to visit the school's infirmary. My body was deteriorating daily as my blood sugar level climbed higher and higher. I had lost about twenty pounds in a month. My weight dropped from 175 pounds down to just over 150 pounds. I was pale and gaunt looking. My shirts were hanging on me, and my pants would not stay up no matter how many loops I tightened my belt.

After class on Wednesday, January 30, I had a brief but cloudy visit with a physician in the school's infirmary (or perhaps a medical resident, I don't know, I was pretty delirious) with lots of questions trying to diagnose my symptoms. He probably asked lots of questions about diabetes and other potential conditions, and I'm sure I probably denied any knowledge of diabetes because there was no history of it in my family. I didn't even know what it was. It was late in the afternoon. He said they needed a fasting blood test (i.e., no food in my system), so I had to return the next morning to give blood without eating anything the previous eight hours. *Ugh. Blood test. A big needle. I hate needles. Okay, I'll be back tomorrow morning.*

I was miserable that night—weak, unable to sleep, getting up every hour to pee and throw up. The next morning, I remember being so weak I could not hold my arm up long enough to shave my face. I followed instructions not to eat breakfast so that I could give a fasting blood test. But my throat was so dry and sore I drank some cold orange juice with ice. *That didn't count, right? I was still fasting. I had not eaten anything.*

I went back to the infirmary as instructed to give the blood sample, struggling to walk from the parking lot, feeling like my head was full of water and going to explode. They told me, "Sorry, we can't do the blood test. That orange juice counts. We need a fasting blood test. No food, no fruit juice." They told me I had to come back tomorrow morning.

I found out later that drinking orange juice is a great way for diabetics experiencing *low* blood sugar to make their blood sugar *come up*. Look at the nutrition label for a bottle of "all natural, fresh-squeezed, just-off-the-tree 100 percent pure orange juice." I never had. The ingredients and packaging may say "100 percent pure orange juice, no sugar added." That should mean it has no sugar, right? Wrong. If you look at the nutrition label for eight ounces it will probably say it contains about twenty-six grams of *carbohydrate* coming from about twenty-two grams of sugar. That "sugar" was not added by the manufacturer. It was added by nature in the form of the natural sugars sucrose, fructose, and glucose found in fruit. Now look at the nutrition label of a twelve-ounce can of Coca-Cola and you will see it contains thirty-nine grams of carbohydrate, all from thirty-nine grams of sugar added by those folks in the Coca-Cola plant with their secret recipe. Whether it comes from a glass of Coca-Cola or a glass of orange juice, they both have *carbohydrate* and will therefore raise a diabetic's blood sugar. Now I know why they could not have me drinking orange juice right before I took a fasting blood test. It would skew the test.

The next twenty-four hours was the worst day and night of my life. I barely remember any of it. I lay in bed all day, dry heaving and vomiting, with a piercing dull headache. That night I hallucinated and heard voices and sounds and saw visions, like trains barreling though my skull spewing psychedelic rainbow flashes behind them. I can only imagine what a hit of LSD does to your brain. This was hell. I was nauseous, crawling to the bathroom and hanging on the toilet to vomit and dry heaving since I had not felt like eating anything that day, burning my throat with each heave. I also had to pee constantly but could barely hold myself up to sit on the toilet. I stumbled and crawled back to my bed. I dropped in and out of sleep or consciousness. I know now that I was close to lapsing into a coma as my body tried its last measures to survive the onslaught of glucose and acid piling up in my blood for weeks, while the rest of my body, including lungs, heart, and muscles, was deprived of nutrients—all because I did not have any insulin to save me.

The next morning my brother found me in the apartment. I was delirious and semi-conscious. I kind of remember talking to him and hanging on to his shoulders as he dragged me from his car up the sidewalk to the infirmary, like a teammate carrying an injured player off the field. I collapsed at the infirmary and passed out. They transported me to the hospital emergency room by ambulance.

A LIFE CHANGE

This book is about how my life changed after that day, February 1, 1991, and how I struggled to manage my diabetes but ultimately used it as motivation to make it the best thing that every happened to me. If you are facing an obstacle in your life, whether that is a serious chronic health condition or something else in your life or business, *Finish Line Vision* will hopefully be a guide and motivation to overcome your obstacle. I will also show you how to achieve not just goals in your life but also dreams and how to use your obstacles as motivation to achieve them.

But first, let me share a little about how I got to that point.

CHAPTER 2

GETTING CUT IS BETTER THAN A PARTICIPATION TROPHY

Topic: Overcoming Obstacles

I discovered at an early age that I liked being in front of people.

The first time I did anything significant in front of an audience I played the lead role of Tom Sawyer in a middle school play. I guess the drama teacher thought I was pretty good at convincing other kids to paint the white picket fence for me. I even acted in a professional production of Shakespeare's *A Midsummer Night's Dream* at the local theater. People actually *paid* to watch that one.

I took piano lessons for about five years until I figured out a way to bust over that wall. My teacher was Ms. Davidson, a nice lady who gave lessons in her home. My last year I did not practice much (okay, any), because I was more interested in sports than piano. At my final recital I was in the middle of butchering one of my two songs, a mushy slow one that I never liked anyway, when I finally just stopped and looked at the audience of horrified moms, dads, grandparents, and other nervous kids. I paused. I could not remember another note so I just bailed out and announced, "I'm sorry folks. Ms. Davidson didn't teach me the rest." Then I launched into my next song with great enthusiasm, a fast upbeat one (and played it flawlessly I might add). The audience hesitated and then roared with laughter. When I finished they gave me the loudest ovation of the night. Just like the advice Russell Crowe received before he entered the Roman Colosseum in the movie *Gladiator*: "Win the crowd, and you'll win your freedom." *Are you not entertained?!* At the juice and cookies reception after the recital, Ms. Davidson told my parents and me, "I think it might be time for Jay to stop taking lessons."

I won my freedom.

But I did learn a lesson that night. When things go bad, think on your feet (or your piano bench) and don't give up. Just bluff a little and play the song you know best. I would learn that it works in a piano recital, in a triathlon race, or in business. Keep going.

I was born in Greenville, South Carolina, and have lived there most of my life. It is a beautiful town in the upstate of South Carolina just at the base of the Blue Ridge Mountains, a southernmost section of the Appalachian Mountains.

When I was a child in the 1970s and early 1980s, Greenville and upstate South Carolina were nearing the end of the cotton textile era. The infamous baseball player "Shoeless Joe" Jackson got to the major leagues playing for a textile mill club team in Greenville. He still holds the major league record for rookie batting average of .408 set in 1911 and ranks third all time in career batting average, ahead of legends like Ted Williams, Babe Ruth, Lou Gehrig, and Joe DiMaggio. Jackson helped the Chicago White Sox win the World Series in 1917, but when they lost in 1919 he was one of eight members of the team accused of throwing the series, even though his batting average had improved and he had no errors. A Chicago jury acquitted him, but the commissioner of baseball still banned all eight players for life. Thus, the minor league baseball team and stadium in Greenville cannot even mention his name. The small wooden millhouse he lived in is now a museum, relocated to sit across the street from the stadium, like a little boy who can't get a ticket into the ballpark. The pain of Shoeless Joe was immortalized in *Field of Dreams* staring Kevin Costner, a movie that has made plenty of grown men cry.

Today South Carolina has a thriving high-tech manufacturing economy, unlike other areas of the country where labor unions dominate. Union has always been a bad word in the South. If South Carolinians were willing to fire on Fort Sumter in 1861 to secede from "the Union," it should be no surprise that their grandchildren and great-grandchildren don't want labor unions. BMW North America opened a giant automobile manufacturing plant on the border of Greenville County in 1994, its only facility in the United States, employing over ten thousand people. There are a lot of BMWs driving around my hometown now.

I went to public school for twelve years in Greenville, first grade all the way through high school graduation. When I entered the first grade in 1973, Greenville County public schools had been racially integrated for just three years. I appreciate my parents sending me to public school with kids of all races and backgrounds for all of my childhood education. I grew up playing sports, sitting in class, and being friends with kids of all races and economic status. Those distinctions never mattered to me and they still don't. I respected anyone who worked hard to overcome their obstacles and achieve sitting and learning in the same classrooms that I did.

MY FIRST FAILURE

I played many sports growing up, but I was not an endurance athlete, like a runner, swimmer, or cyclist. Odd, I know, that I ended up racing Ironman triathlons and on the US national triathlon team—more on that later.

I played youth football for many years and even played in the Shrine Bowl of the Carolinas invitational game as a defensive end. I was always tall for my age, usually the tallest in my classes in elementary and middle school. But as I approached high school my tall, lean body made knocking down a jumper more fun (and less painful) than knocking down a person. And that jumper wasn't looking to pulverize me like a giant right tackle wanting to pound me into the turf. So in high school I switched to basketball. It was a big public high school—several thousand students—with a rich basketball tradition, becoming state champions the year before I arrived. Big crowds, lots of competition, honor, and excitement—I wanted to be a part of that.

I tried out for the high school freshman team and made it. I wasn't the best player on the team, but I got a lot of playing time and liked the honor of competing. The next October I tried out for the junior varsity (JV) team as a sophomore. I was fifteen years old.

I got cut. I remember the embarrassment of that day, the feeling of rejection. I felt like every kid in the high school knew it.

"Hey, didn't you play on the freshman team last year but got cut from the JV team this year?" I was humiliated. I knew some of the guys who made it were better, but I felt like I deserved one of the slots.

That was my first valuable life lesson at age fifteen—dealing with failure and rejection. Some results are often based on the subjective decision of a coach, a judge, a boss, or a customer—whether you make the team or get playing time, win the motion, get the promotion, or get the sale. You have to deal with those decisions even though you think they were wrong. Life is not always fair. How you respond to rejection determines whether you succeed in the long run. Give up? Or learn from it and keep trying?

A year passed and I tried out for the varsity team my junior year. What I lacked in talent I would make up with desire and work ethic. But the numbers were still stacked against me—all thirteen players from last

> **Some results are often based on the subjective decision of a coach, a judge, a boss, or a customer—whether you make the team or get playing time, win the motion, get the promotion, or get the sale. You have to deal with those decisions even though you think they were wrong. Life is not always fair.**

year's JV team moving up to varsity, several seniors returning from last year's varsity team, some sophomores who were good enough to be considered for varsity, and then a handful of other guys like me just trying to make the team.

The day came for the list to be posted.

Why does there always have to be a list? I walked into the lobby of the gymnasium alone, during class because I did not want others around me. My heart thumped, pounding in my chest like an unbalanced washing machine. In October 1983, the list was old school, typed on paper with thirteen names, pinned to a corkboard inside the trophy case above the school's basketball championship trophies—"J.L. Mann High School Varsity Boys Basketball Team 1983–84." I nervously scanned the names with a frenetic blur, hoping mine was going to jump out at me. I looked … and looked … and looked, down the list.

It wasn't there. I got cut again, just like last year. The air rushed out of my lungs, like someone had jumped out of that trophy case and slugged me in the chest. I walked out of the lobby and slinked back to my class, trying to disappear into the school, into the mass of kids.

This one hurt pretty bad. I was sixteen now, not a kid anymore, and able to stand up to my own defeats and disappointments. I was crushed and embarrassed. But I had to acknowledge that the guys who made the team were good, several already being recruited and receiving college scholarship offers. The whole school knew who made it and who didn't. It was all on that list. I felt like my name was posted on another list beside it that read "Losers Who Got Cut." If getting cut my sophomore year was a painful lesson, I didn't really need another lesson my junior year. More failure. More disappointment. More humiliation.

WHAT DO I DO NOW?

Most people don't realize a significant moment in their life when it is happening. I didn't. Looking back now years later I realize that getting cut from my high school basketball team (twice) was a significant point in my life at ages fifteen and sixteen. Now I'm glad it happened. I had to learn how to deal with disappointment and rejection all on my own, not with a team. It was all on my shoulders and I could not blame it on anyone else. How would I respond to adversity? Do I give up—embittered and dejected—feel sorry for myself, look for someone to blame? Or do I keep trying, fight, and attack it?

> **Most people don't realize a significant moment in their life when it is happening.**

Resentment and anger started to motivate me. That year I jealously watched games from the stands, and those emotions fueled my determination to work on my game, waiting for tryouts the next year to prove that I deserved to be on that team. It made me mad. Revenge is a powerful motivator and so is a dream. I had both. *I'll show them. You just gave me motivation. You cut the wrong kid.* Years later that same revenge was directed at my diabetes and later at my goal to race the Ironman triathlon. They cut the wrong kid, and diabetes would attack the wrong guy.

In his book *How Bad Do You Want It: Mastering the Psychology of Mind Over Muscle*, renowned endurance sports journalist Matt Fitzgerald researched how top athletes are able to overcome physical limitations and handle repeated failure and change, generating mental strength to achieve success in sports. Yes, these athletes are talented, and some have genetic advantages that can make them good, even great (height, size, body dimensions). But what makes some better than others? Mental strength is more important than their talent or body. Trying for something and failing and trying again and failing again. Fitzgerald writes, "Failing repeatedly is like walking on a bed of hot coals toward a wall that keeps receding as you approach it—a Sisyphean nightmare." Sisyphus was a figure in Greek mythology punished to roll a boulder up a hill, but each time the boulder rolled back down the hill, condemning him to an eternity of repeated failure and unending frustration.

I felt that frustration and repeated failure trying to make my high school basketball team.

DEVELOP ANGRY RESOLVE

This cycle of frustration causes an athlete, or any person in life, school, business, or any endeavor, to feel either defeated or determined. Which response you choose will determine whether you give up and quit or become even more motivated to try a different way. It can become an angry resolve. In the book *Bounce: Living the Resilient Life*, psychologist Robert Wicks calls this "sweet disgust"—a healthy fed-up state of mind that fuels positive change and relentless determination to fight back with anger. This angry resolve increases motivation and the maximum intensity of perceived effort (i.e., pain) an athlete in sports or a person in life is willing to endure to reach their finish line.

I have found that angry resolve is helpful in all aspects of life, not just sports. If you have just received bad news—been diagnosed with a health condition, lost your job or a promotion, gone through a divorce—how do you respond? Do you feel defeated and shrink and give up? Or do you develop determination to come back and succeed? It is normal to retreat temporarily to process the disappointment, but slowly that anger and resentment can start to build motivation rebound. Use that emotion in a healthy way. Channel it to show them they messed with the wrong guy or girl.

DEALING WITH CRITICS

The fall of my senior year arrived. Time for varsity basketball tryouts again. This was my last chance. I had failed twice. Do I try again? The football team was undefeated and ranked number one in the state and would eventually play in the state championship game that year. Those same athletes would switch to basketball, and everyone expected the basketball team to contend for a state championship as well.

To a seventeen-year-old walking the halls of high school I felt like everyone was looking at me with a mix of snickering or pity. I'm sure that few of the other students were actually thinking about me. But it feels that way when you're young or trying something public. I heard a wise observation many years later: At twenty you worry about what everyone thinks about you. At forty you don't care what anyone thinks about you. At sixty you realize that no one was really thinking about you.

At twenty you worry about what everyone thinks about you. At forty you don't care what anyone thinks about you. At sixty you realize that no one was really thinking about you.

I didn't care what the critics said. I was willing to risk that embarrassment. I wanted to make that team. This was my last chance. I wanted to wear that jersey and run out on the floor at games. Whenever I hear critics, I am reminded of a quote from the speech President Teddy Roosevelt gave at the Sorbonne University in Paris in 1910.

> *It is not the critic who counts, not the man who points out how the strong man stumbles or where the doer of deeds could have done better. The credit belongs to the man in the arena, whose face is marred by dust and sweat and blood. Who strives valiantly, who errs and comes up short again and again, because there is no effort without error and shortcoming. Who knows great enthusiasms, the great devotions, who spends himself in a worthy cause. Who at best knows the triumph of high achievement, and who at worst, if he fails, at least he fails while daring greatly, so that his fate will never be with those cold and timid souls who know neither victory nor defeat.*

I stepped into that arena a third time. I practiced hard and tried out for the varsity team again. When the list was posted my heart pounded so strong that I almost could not see from the blood pulsing in my eyes.

Then I saw my name, Jay Hewitt. It was on the list. I made it.

I remember the pride putting on that team jersey the first time, running out onto the court in front of the whole school for pep rallies and crowds at games. I remember other students looking up to me in the halls, and I remember playing in the state final four playoffs later that season. It was the same feeling I would have almost twenty years later when I put on the Team USA triathlon jersey the first time I raced in Europe for the US national team at the Long-Distance Triathlon World Championship. Several players eventually quit my high school basketball team later that season because of lack of playing time. I was disappointed and frustrated too, wanting to play more, but we had a great team and lots of great players. But I was never going to quit. *I suffered for this jersey. I earned it. You are never going to get it off me.*

Mark Twain said, "Twenty years from now you'll be more disappointed by the things you *didn't* do than by the things you did." I'm so glad I kept trying to make that basketball team, refusing to give up. It helped me, hardened me, and taught me to work hard and handle failure. Use failure as motivation to prove that you are stronger.

Find your angry determination. I would need that when diabetes entered my life six years later.

Twenty years from now you'll be more disappointed by the things you *didn't* do than by the things you did.

STRUGGLE CREATES SUCCESS

Struggling can be good. Rejection can be good. Failure can be good. It teaches you to work hard, to understand that you have to earn success—a spot on a team, an award, a grade, a job, a paycheck.

I do not like participation trophies for kids. Yes, young kids in elementary school deserve a jersey and souvenir, but as they get older, save the trophies for earned distinctions—most improved; best defender; first, second or third place, just like Olympic medals. Give them a medal only if they complete a challenging race or pass a fitness test. Some youth sports leagues do not even keep score. Not keeping score was okay for my four-year-old daughter's soccer games. The glory of just kicking the ball was enough as they all chased each other around the field. But older kids understand winning and losing even if no one is keeping score. Whether its kids participating on a sports team, a dance team, or a debate team, every kid at some point in the season needs to be singled out for one or two moments of personal accomplishment to demonstrate the value of hard work and earned achievement.

In their fascinating book *The Triple Package*, authors Amy Chua and Jed Rubenfeld, both professors at Yale Law School, studied why certain cultural groups succeed in America. Mormons have astonishing business success. Cubans in Miami climbed from poverty to prosperity in one generation. Nigerians earn doctorates at stunningly high rates. Indian and Chinese immigrants have much higher incomes than other Americans, and Jews have the highest of all. Why do these groups succeed more than others or more than most native-born Americans?

Chua and Rubenfeld contend that one of the reasons is that, since the 1960s, Americans have been taught that self-esteem—feeling good about yourself—is the key to success. By contrast, in all of America's most successful subgroups, those members tend to feel insecure, inadequate, and that they have to prove themselves. Those feelings motivated them to work hard to succeed.

The authors contend that the self-esteem movement erodes one of the traits for success—impulse control. Rising affluence in America since the Great Depression contributed to this and promoted instant gratification. Most Americans born since the 1950s have never really suffered like immigrant groups from around the world. Chua and Rubenfeld assert that "comfortable people have no pressing, life-threatening reason to exercise discipline and restraint. It's hard to live like you're in the Depression when you grow up in the suburbs with two SUVs."

Insecurity has caused Americans to succeed in the past. In the 1960s insecurity created by competition with (and threats from) the Soviet Union drove America to invest in science and technology. But that competition and threat evaporated when the Berlin Wall came down in 1989. By 2009, according to a 2010 joint report by the National Academy of Sciences, National Academy of Engineering, and Institute of Medicine, Americans were spending more on potato chips than the government spent on energy research and development.

Insecurity can fuel motivation. Desperation and deprivation drive determination. Challenge creates change. Chua and Rubenfeld contend that is why some in America have little motivation to work hard to overcome and succeed or make changes, because someone or something is always going to take care of them. Obesity and type 2 diabetes have reached epidemic proportions in the US, yet the government Supplemental Nutritional Assistance Program (SNAP, formerly known as the food stamp program) pays for cookies, soda, and ice cream and has no nutritional restrictions requiring healthy food, even though it is ironically called the "nutritional assistance" program. The United States Department of Agriculture (USDA), which administers the program, reported that in 2011 $1.3 billion in SNAP funds was spent on sweetened drinks, desserts, salty snacks, candy, and sugar, accounting for twenty cents of every dollar spent on food items. If SNAP regulations changed to no longer pay for these unhealthy foods, users would be forced to eliminate them from their diet (or pay for them with their own funds) and eating habits would change. Rather than paying for these unhealthy foods, imagine the benefits if the federal government spent these same 1.3 billion taxpayer dollars every year on research grants to cure diabetes or grants for rails-to-trails bike and running paths, parks, green spaces, gymnasiums, and other healthy alternatives, particularly in low income, impoverished areas where SNAP program users reside.

Government programs provide health insurance paid for by others with taxes and higher premiums. Religion says everything is God's plan and all you have to do is pray and he will provide and you will be happy one day in heaven. A column in the *Washington Post* by religion writer Cathleen Falsani criticized prosperity gospel as an "insipid heresy" that "turns Christianity into a vapid bless-me club, with a doctrine that amounts to little more than spiritual magic thinking: If you pray the right way, God will make you rich."

The American civil tort system also promotes this mind-set. As a lawyer I once represented a sofa manufacturer after a house fire. The plaintiff had been smoking and drinking on the sofa all night and passed out drunk. Cigarette embers ignited papers and bags of takeout food and eventually the upholstery of the sofa. After lengthy litigation the sofa's insurance company settled the claim, fearing the jury might accept the plaintiff's argument that it was "the sofa's fault" after a large verdict was rendered against a different sofa company. I once defended another case where the plaintiff had lost his leg in a motorcycle accident. The plaintiff understandably claimed that he needed the money for medical bills and future expenses. But after the case was settled his lawyer told me that rather than save the money for medical care, the plaintiff used the money to buy a new motorcycle. I recently saw a notice on a shopping cart in Target that stated, "Warning. Always buckle child in seat. 250 pounds max." It is bad enough that someone may contend that the store is at fault when their child falls out because "You never told me I should buckle in my own child," but a warning not to place a *child* over 250 pounds? We have children in America weighing 250 pounds?

By eliminating participation trophies I'm not contending that we should exalt winners with praise while we ignore other members of the team. There are unhealthy extremes on both ends. The deification of top high school athletes in football and basketball being recruited for college is an example of unhealthy adulation and stardom on winners at a young age.

Praise a child for their effort, not for their talent or results. "I'm proud of how hard you worked." "I'm proud of you for keeping going even when you were behind." When things go wrong a person that has been praised for talent will become frustrated and quit, wondering why their talent was suddenly not good enough. A person praised for effort will bounce back and keep using that effort. Hard work beats talent when talent doesn't work hard.

> **Praise a child for their effort, not for their talent or results.**

> **Hard work beats talent when talent doesn't work hard.**

When my daughter was eight I suggested that she and her friend do a kids triathlon. They did not practice or train intensely, but they were excited. Neither had done any competitive swimming, cycling, or running. The race was hard for them, but their elation at the finish line was magic. They were very interested in how they placed. It would have been destructive to their effort not to know. They wanted validation for their effort. Incidentally, my daughter placed close to last. She had to walk much of the 1.5-mile run because (unbeknownst to us) she was developing a cold that day. I told her I was more proud of her for not giving up than had she won. She was excited to enter her next triathlon just seven months later and improved dramatically. You may not be the fastest, but you will be faster than those who quit or never started.

My wife did pageants for several years as a teenager. At twenty-two she won the title of Miss South Carolina USA and was top ten in the 2003 Miss USA national pageant. Even though she won the state title and was

> **You may not be the fastest, but you will be faster than those who quit or never started.**

eventually judged one of the top ten in the nation, she lost a lot of pageants before that. The award for first, second, and third is purely a subjective decision of the judges, but in the legitimate pageant systems it is usually obvious which contestant worked hard to be fit, articulate, and carry herself with poise and confidence. While I understand that some pageants have a bad reputation and some pageant moms/parents are excessive (okay, ridiculous), I have seen how they teach a girl or young woman to win or lose with grace and dignity, standing on a stage all alone with no teammates or anyone else to blame or even talk to. Boys rarely face a solitary challenge like this, and I applaud these girls and young women for doing it.

In any competition the goal is to have fun, yes, but fun is accomplishing something you never thought possible. Fun is breaking a long losing streak. Fun is making a team after you got cut the previous year. Fun is making a shot after you have missed it ten straight times. Fun is breaking your personal record in a race or making it to the finish line at all. Tell a kid he did a great job catching that ball with a defender right on him, scoring that goal after being blocked the first time, or dancing that routine better than ever before. He or she will cherish those moments of individual accomplishment a lot more than that participation trophy.

In academics, fun is qualifying for the school's honors program after failing to make it the previous year. I remember qualifying for my elementary school's advanced reading program in the third grade. I was no literary prodigy. It was just a thirty-minute session a few times a month when I would get pulled out of class into a little room with some other kids and read and talk about different books, supposedly harder books than the rest of our class. It made me feel smart. I wanted to earn it and deserve it and have more of those moments. That feeling of academic accomplishment was implanted in me at age eight, and I still remember it today!

In the second grade my daughter did not qualify for a similar academic program at her public school. Her standardized test scores and grades were not good enough. She was disappointed, but I noticed that she started assuming that the kids who qualified must just be the "smart kids" and therefore she was not one of them.

"What do you think we should do?" my wife asked me.

"We should encourage her to try again next year," I said. "This can be a valuable learning experience. Tell her we believe in her and know she can do it."

"I'm going to look for ways to prepare for those tests," she said. "Sometimes it's just knowing how to take the test, being familiar with the testing format."

She asked teachers for suggestions and eventually found some tests on a site ironically called testingmom.com, which indicates that some moms probably feel just as tested by this process as the kids. We didn't even know if we were testing the right material, but our daughter knew we would help her if she would do the work.

Our daughter took the standardized tests again at the start of the third grade. She placed well but again not well enough to qualify. She watched each week as four kids from her classroom left to spend time in a different class. She was disappointed. I could tell she felt defeated, like perhaps she was not good enough. We continued to reassure her that she was good enough and encouraged her to keep her grades up. She took the test again at the end of third grade. When the letter came from the district announcing her qualification, it felt like she had just been accepted to college. She was thrilled. She understood at age eight what it felt like to not make it and then to work hard to make it. We praised her for her perseverance and determination. Her pride was even greater now.

My childhood was not difficult. I had two loving parents, a stable home, and few obstacles. I realize that many children grow up with devastating obstacles. The beautiful autobiography of Supreme Court Justice Sonia Sotomayor, *My Beloved World*, chronicles her life growing up in poverty in the Bronx as the child of immigrants, the death of her alcoholic father at a young age, and having type 1 diabetes and giving herself insulin shots since age eight. But she says she had "stubborn perseverance" to overcome the obstacles in her life, eventually graduating summa cum laude from Princeton and Yale Law School and being appointed to the United States Supreme Court in 2009.

Stubborn perseverance, angry resolve, sweet disgust—it can create healthy motivation to make your high school basketball team or the United States Supreme Court.

Use it to overcome your obstacles and achieve your goals. I would need this advice myself when a bigger challenge soon entered my life.

CHAPTER 3

COLLEGE, US SENATE, AND LAW SCHOOL

Topic: Backstory

After high school I spent four great years at Wake Forest University in Winston-Salem, NC. Wake Forest is a small, private university of only 3,500 undergraduate students with rigorous academic requirements. The classes are small, but the opportunities of the university are big. My parents think the only reason I went there was for ACC basketball games against Duke and North Carolina. They are partly right.

My senior year at Wake in the fall of 1988 I spent a semester in Washington, DC, as an exchange student at American University studying government and politics. It was a great time to be in Washington. President Reagan was just finishing his second term and Vice President George Bush and Michael Dukakis were in the final months of the presidential election. At the time I was pondering a future in public office. I wanted to make a positive influence on people, and I enjoyed public speaking. I thought politics was the only way to do that. I did not know that twenty years later I would find professional speaking was an even better way to do it, without the divisiveness of politics.

I got an internship with the US House of Representatives working for a little-known member from Wyoming: Dick Cheney. Of course, I did not know that in a few months newly elected President Bush Sr.

would appoint him to be secretary of defense, and in a few years he would be vice president under President George W. Bush. I could tell in 1988 that Representative Cheney was on his way up, and I liked his calm, competent demeanor. Spending time with him reminded me a bit of my father.

I graduated from Wake Forest with honors, and in the summer of 1989 I spent two months traveling through Europe with a backpack and a Eurail train pass. I trekked through nine countries—England, Holland, Belgium, France, Germany, Austria, Switzerland, Italy, and Greece—staying in youth hostels with college students and budget travelers from all over the world. It was great to explore a little bit of the world on my own, carefree and adventurous. I did not have diabetes at this point in my life so I didn't have to worry about much other than scrounging up a meal every now and then and finding a cheap place to sleep.

I did not speak any of the languages other than some pretty weak German that usually just got me in conversations that I didn't under-stand when I was just trying to order a beer. I didn't have much money and had saved some by working jobs in the summer to pay for this trip. I toured Europe for about ten dollars a day, eating a lot of cheese and bread and drinking a little (okay, a lot of) beer from each country. It was the least I could do to honor the local culture. When in Rome ... or Germany ... or England ...

WORKING FOR THE UNITED STATES SENATE

From 1989 to 1990 I spent a year working on the staff of US Senator Strom Thurmond in his Washington office. Senator Thurmond was a political icon, eighty-seven years old at the time. Regardless of your political views, liberal or conservative, Republican or Democrat, having that firsthand access to one of the longest-serving members of the Senate was a privilege and an education. He was a walking piece of American history like other political legends such as Democrat House Speaker Tip O'Neill, Senators Joseph McCarthy and Edward Kennedy, and US presidents.

At first I was Senator Thurmond's personal assistant, which meant I tagged along with him to receptions, committee meetings, and appointments and drove him around the city. It was a great opportunity to watch politics work behind the scenes and meet famous people. Generally, my job was to keep him on schedule; listen to conversations he had with senators, constituents, and anyone else who stopped him; and report back to the appropriate staff member in our office what someone had requested or what he had agreed to do. I was a professional eavesdropper, standing discretely over his shoulder at receptions and in the halls of Congress. One of my most important jobs was to help him bring chicken fingers from receptions back to our office staff members working after hours. I always put them on a little plate or napkin, but he would stuff them in his suit coat pockets.

Senator Thurmond was like a grandfather wanting to take care of his grandkids back in the office and the people of South Carolina. He was governor of South Carolina in 1946 and ran for president in 1948, winning four states in the general election. Six years later in 1954 he was elected to the United States Senate as a write-in candidate, defying the South Carolina Democratic Party that controlled the state and had endorsed a different candidate. Thousands of people wrote his name on the ballot the same way you write in your friend's name for high school homecoming queen, and he won election to the US Senate.

He eventually switched to the Republican Party and served forty-eight years in the Senate until 2003, the entire second half of the twentieth century. He retired at the age of one hundred as the longest-serving and oldest senator in US history. He knew every US president from Dwight Eisenhower to George W. Bush. In 1989 and 1990, spending hours with him riding in the car, sitting in his office, and walking the halls, I asked him questions and stories about them all: Eisenhower, John F.

Kennedy, Lyndon B. Johnson, Nixon, and Reagan. He knew them like you and I know our office coworkers and neighbors. Picking him up at his condo and taking him to his health club early in the mornings I saw how he did push-ups and sit-ups and exercised in his late eighties to stay fit and mentally sharp. He prided himself on his health and ... stamina. He was married to Nancy Moore, Miss South Carolina 1965, whom he married when he was sixty-six and she was twenty-two. Then he had four children with her, the last born when he was seventy-three years old, perhaps one of the most impressive feats of his remarkable life.

At the time I was there, he was the ranking member on the Senate Judiciary Committee, which confirmed all federal judges and members of the Supreme Court, and on the Senate Armed Services Committee, which received briefings on military actions around the world.

One day Senator Thurmond sent me to Marine Corps Base Quantico for a weapons shot. I'm sure the marine officers expected someone from our office with much more authority to preview and be impressed with these weapons so Senator Thurmond would vote to fund them. But the marines got me instead, and I made the most of it. I shot so much heavy artillery that day you would have thought I was starting a war. I blew up bunkers of railroad ties and cars and shot automatic weapons. It was awesome. I told the senator we definitely needed to keep funding those weapons. *Semper fi!*

I went with him to the White House a few times for meetings with President George H. W. Bush. He even got me a coveted seat in the gallery of the House Chamber to watch and listen to President Bush's State of the Union address in January 1990. Seated in the House Chamber that night, a seat harder to get than to a Super Bowl, Final Four, or game seven of the World Series, were the justices of the US Supreme Court, military leaders, and every member of the US House and Senate. I knew these people made decisions and history, and I was humbled to be there. I could have lobbed a wad of paper and bounced it off President Bush, but it might have been the last thing I ever did, or it at least would have given me a night in the holding cell under the Capitol.

My time with Senator Thurmond taught me to make adjustments to get the job done when someone was depending on me. One afternoon I picked him up from a physical at Bethesda Naval Hospital (now called Walter Reed National Military Medical Center). I was to drive him to Washington (now Reagan) National Airport for a flight. He sat in the front seat of my college two-door car that had also transported buddies for burgers and road trips. The Internet and cell phones didn't exist so he read from his briefcase and we listened to NPR; he didn't care much for my 1980s favorites Run DMC, Van Halen, and Guns N' Roses (on cassette tapes!).

It was approaching 5 p.m. and DC rush hour traffic was jammed. Nothing was moving. As the minutes passed, and Senator Thurmond just chatted away with me, I let him know that we might not make his flight. He looked around and pointed to the lane next to him, which was closed for construction and wide open, with nothing blocking it but a few orange cones and barrels.

"Geaux theya. Right theya. Jus geaux!" he said in his deep South Carolina low country accent.

I just received authorization from the senior member of the Senate Judiciary Committee and Armed Services Committee to defy local traffic laws. So I did. I figured he'd pull rank on any state trooper that tried to stop me. Or maybe you have immunity if you are carrying a woman in labor or a United States senator late for a flight.

A hard rain began to fall. We arrived at the airport and screeched up to the curb. I left my car sitting there. I might have even left the doors open. Airport security was a little more slack in 1989. I was already prepared to face Virginia Highway Patrol when I came back, so airport security would just have to get in line.

Senator Thurmond colored his hair, a blondish, reddish, orangish, unnatural color that most of us in the office knew about, but it was best not to broadcast to the public. But as we finally got to his gate, the color was starting to run down his cheek from the rain, so I offered him a napkin quickly.

"Good job! Fine job! You did a fine job!" he said to me loudly at the gate (Senator Thurmond wore hearing aids) as he patted my back and smiled broadly, thanking me as he always did. He gave me a few instructions to give to staff people back at the office. Then he calmly turned and shook the hand of the gate agent waiting for his ticket, who of course already knew who he was.

"How ya doin' young lady? Nice to see you. Strom Thurmond. What's your name?" Then he ambled down the jetway and disappeared.

I turned around and faced the people watching all of this, smiled, and gave a "thank you, carry on, nothing else to see here" wave. Then I walked slowly back to my car to face whatever forms of law enforcement waited on me there. I didn't hang around for them.

After a few months of being Senator Thurmond's personal assistant, unfortunately his senior staff realized that with my college degree and law school aspirations, I might have been a little overqualified for that job. They moved me to an office position as legislative correspondent where I monitored legislation and handled requests from constituents. I made $17,000 a year. It was worth it to live in poverty for a year to learn and observe. My meager salary meant I also was able to qualify for a student loan to law school. Even though they could, I did not want my parents to pay for law school. My dad had paid for four years of private college for three kids. I wanted to do this on my own.

LAW SCHOOL STRESS

Then came the torture and stress of law school in the fall of 1990 at the University of South Carolina. The first year of law school is psychological warfare—in class three to four hours a day, studying five to six hours a day. Not much exercise, just go to class, study, and if you have time, maybe nap for a few hours at night.

Law school professors torment you with the Socratic method of teaching. They don't lecture material while you sit passively, taking notes and listening like in college. They don't teach; they interrogate you in front of your classmates. They surprise you with questions in front of seventy-five other students in the class all hiding behind their desks, humiliating you if you have not read the lengthy cases, many of which are two hundred years old and written in archaic legal jargon that is essentially a foreign language. They cross-exam you until you break.

"Mr. Hewitt, what was the holding in the 1823 decision of *Gibbons v. Ogden*? What did the appellant argue? How does the federal government's authority to regulate interstate commerce affect a state's right to issue a patent license? Has the court addressed that question since then? In what case? Mr. Hewitt, did you even read the material?"

This badgering may be to prepare you to think on your feet when judges are peppering you with questions, but I think it really is just a way to torment law students. Whether it has a purpose or is just an intellectual hazing tradition, first-year law students are humiliated and humbled in order to see who will give up. They see who can take the public pressure and handle the workload because the practice of law can be difficult.

Law school can affect your way of thinking and your health, as I would soon find out. There is never one right answer. There are always different sides, different interpretations, dissenting opinions, and conflicting authority from a different case or law to argue. Even though the constitution or statute may be written in plain English, ten courts and three administrative panels may have interpreted it thirteen different ways. The facts of each case are different, and you must argue if the case law precedent applies—or the federal statute, state statute, US Constitution, a provision in the contract, or one of the millions of regulations—or distinguish those facts to argue why it doesn't apply.

I loved this intellectual challenge. I also loved the constitutional law and federal versus state law issues, having just come from Washington, DC. Law school forces you to become analytical and, indeed, argumentative. The profession even uses the word "argue" in hearings, briefs, and appellate opinions—what is the plaintiff's argument? The state's argument? The defendant's argument? No wonder lawyers are viewed as argumentative to the outside world. You must look for flaws in every position and holes in every case, poised to shoot down a conflicting point of view and be able to prove every point by backing it up with case law and supporting authority or sit down until you can. One positive aspect is that it requires you to sit silently and patiently while the opposing side presents their case—even though you of course think everything they are saying is baloney. In court you can't jump in and interrupt and talk over each other like television talk shows. When the opposing side is finished, the judge gives you your chance to present your side. It is (usually) a civil back-and-forth voicing and dissecting of each other's positions. In life you begin to expect others to do this point-counterpoint volleying, and it's difficult not to expect that from others in your life after doing it in class or work all day. This is one of the reasons you will find that lawyers will always ask you to support your position and opinion rather than just blather on. Law school and the profession demand it.

This constant mental jousting is one of the reasons researchers have discovered that law students and lawyers suffer from dangerously elevated levels of mental distress. I did not like to study in the law school library, because just being around other law students spread negative energy and stress like secondhand smoke.

One study was conducted on the entering University of Virginia Law School class in 1990, which was coincidentally the same year I entered law school just a few hundred miles away at the University of South Carolina. In his 2002 book, *Authentic Happiness*, University of Pennsylvania Professor of Psychology Dr. Martin Seligman, PhD, reports that he and researchers gave that entering class an optimism-pessimism test and then followed them throughout the next three years of law school. The researchers were amazed to find that in sharp contrast to other fields of work, the pessimistic law students on average did better in law school than their more optimistic classmates. Pessimism is seen as a *benefit* for lawyers because seeing potential problems and troubles, the dark side of every possible outcome, every possible catastrophe in every transaction, is what the job requires to prepare for it or find the culprit after it happens. You start seeing the glass as half empty and thinking about how to sue or prosecute somebody for causing it.

The American Bar Association (ABA) recognizes the dangers of stress and negativity in the legal profession. A 2016 seminar by lawyer and PhD in psychology Dr. Larry Richard was published on the American Bar Association (ABA) website. A survey of fifteen thousand lawyers revealed 19 percent reported anxiety, 23 percent reported stress, and 28 percent suffered from depression. Dr. Richard concluded that much of this is due to negativity required by the legal profession.

"To be a good lawyer, you must ask your client what is *wrong* with this, not what's right with this. What could go wrong in the future, rather than what are the potentials for good?" Dr. Richard reports that lawyers average in the ninetieth percentile for skepticism and that skepticism and pessimism are learned character traits. The longer you spend in a skeptical environment, the more skeptical and pessimistic you become. Another often-cited study by Johns Hopkins University entitled "Occupations and the Prevalence of Major Depressive Disorder," published in 1990 in the *Journal of Occupational Medicine*, found that of twenty-eight occupations studied, lawyers were 3.6 times more likely to suffer from depression and mental distress than the other occupations.

I am not citing this research to bash lawyers. I am one of them. This is not a criticism but rather a confession. The law is a wonderful profession and vitally important to maintaining order and liberty in a civilized society. I eventually practiced law for twenty years, and I worked with hundreds of lawyers in my career, many of them wonderful, engaging people. But I saw the mind-set of most lawyers firsthand and experienced it. Depression and mental distress is a problem that is well known in the legal profession.

Pessimism and a negative outlook may make you a good law student and lawyer, but it does not make you a very happy or healthy person. Couple that with stress and competitive pressure to outperform hundreds of other very bright, intellectually intense people to get a good grade on a subjectively graded exam (i.e., there is not a single right answer like math or science), a good class rank, a spot on a law review journal, and a job (i.e., classmates are not colleagues or teammates, they are competition) and you have a simmering pot of anxiety.

I remember one day feeling extremely stressed during the fall of my first semester of law school. I was standing in the parking lot of a local deli in the early evening waiting to eat with one of my classmates, David Gray. It was late October as I stood waiting on him, the evening air still very warm and humid in Columbia, South Carolina. It was at least eighty degrees out, but I was shaking and trembling.

I thought, *Why am I trembling? It's not cold.* I had a knot of anxiety in my stomach constantly that first semester.

I nagged myself with anxious thoughts and pressure. *I have to study. I have to do well on my final exams. These other students are very bright. They are reading and studying more than I am. Everything is riding on these first semester exams—grades, class rank, invitations for law review, first summer clerkship jobs.*

Oh, you think you can make me quit? Just watch. I proved that in high school trying to make the basketball team. Law school grades are determined by one three-hour final exam for each class at the end of each semester. You prepare for five months for one test in each class at the end of the semester. Have a bad day on test day? Too bad.

I discovered years later that this is not unlike racing an Ironman triathlon. You prepare for months for just one race, and you have to bring it all together and perform on that one race day because you can't do another Ironman distance race next week or next month like shorter triathlon races or other sports. Your body needs recovery time, but I disregarded that one year as we will see later.

Thus, the first five months of law school is a lot of pressure to make good grades for a summer job that leads to jobs in the future. There is no warm-up period. It starts day one. The first semester of law school is stressful and difficult.

My life was about to get a lot more difficult.

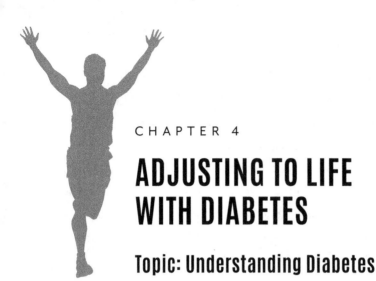

CHAPTER 4

ADJUSTING TO LIFE WITH DIABETES

Topic: Understanding Diabetes

I spent the weekend after February 1, 1991—the day I was diagnosed with diabetes—in the hospital receiving an IV drip of insulin to slowly, gradually bring my blood glucose level back down to normal. They gave me a quick primer on diabetes and nutrition, and then I was dismissed out the door with a box of syringes, a couple vials of insulin, a prescription to buy a blood sugar meter, and test strips. For something that would be with me for the rest of my life, fifty or sixty years if I was lucky to live that long with it (unless they cure it), it is ironic that I was out of the hospital in forty-eight hours.

Good luck. Count your carbs. Take your shots. Don't overdose. Have a nice life.

INSULIN: A TREATMENT, NOT A CURE

Insulin was discovered in 1921 as the key for blood sugar control by a Canadian surgeon, Frederick Banting, who teamed with a medical student lab assistant Charles Best. They discovered insulin as the treatment by removing the pancreas in laboratory dogs, noting the rise in the dog's blood glucose levels, and later injecting the dog with a crude extract from the removed pancreas, causing the blood sugar levels to decrease.

Prior to that, children dying from diabetic ketoacidosis, experiencing the same symptoms I had been feeling, were kept in large wards, often with fifty or more patients in a ward, mostly comatose. Their weak, pale bodies of skin and bones were slowly shriveling and deteriorating as if starving, even though food could not help them. Grieving family members were often present, awaiting the inevitable death.

In January 1922, a fourteen-year-old boy who lay dying in the Toronto General Hospital was given the first injection of insulin extracted from a fetal calf pancreas. But the extract of calf insulin was so crude and impure the boy suffered a severe allergic reaction, and further injections were cancelled. Over the next ten days biochemist James Collip, working with Banting and Best, worked day and night to improve and purify the cow pancreas extract, and a second dose was injected on January 23, 1922. This injection was successful. It wasn't perfect, but the boy began to slowly improve. Insulin was discovered as the treatment for diabetes. Prior to that, every patient died. In 1923, Banting was awarded the Nobel Prize in Physiology or Medicine, and he shared his cash prize with his assistant, Best.

Since that time, for decades, humans with diabetes were injected with a crude form of insulin extracted from animals until the first genetically engineered synthetic "human" insulin was created in a laboratory using E. coli in 1978, only thirteen years before I was diagnosed. Gradually, in the 1980s biosynthetic human insulin began to take over as the treatment method, but I still caught the tail end of injecting animal insulin when I was diagnosed.

Insulin is not a cure but just a treatment. A cure would be my pancreas producing my own insulin again naturally, where I do not have to inject it manually into my body. Type 1 diabetes does not go into remission. It does not go away.

TYPE 1 VERSUS TYPE 2 DIABETES

In the days, weeks, and months after that I adjusted to life with type 1 diabetes. Type 1 is often called "insulin-dependent" diabetes because you must inject insulin to survive. They still called it "juvenile diabetes" in 1991 when I was diagnosed because this form of diabetes usually happens in kids. Type 2 diabetes is sometimes called "adult onset" diabetes because it usually happens in older adults and more recently in adults of all ages with

> **Type 1 is often called "insulin-dependent" diabetes because you must inject insulin to survive.**

sedentary lifestyles, obesity, and unhealthy diets. With type 2 diabetes the pancreas still produces insulin, it is just not utilized properly or effectively. People with type 2 diabetes usually can control their blood sugar with oral medication, and certainly with a healthier diet and exercise to lose weight, without or before having to take regular injec-tions of insulin. According to the World Health Organization, in 2017 over 422 million people worldwide have diabetes and over 95 percent of those have type 2 diabetes. The numbers keep growing, mirroring an increase in the prevalence of obesity and overweight people. Diabetes is a major cause of blindness, kidney failure, heart attacks, strokes, and lower limb amputation. While they

> **Type 2 diabetes is sometimes called "adult onset" diabetes because it usually happens in older adults and more recently in adults of all ages with sedentary lifestyles, obesity, and unhealthy diets.**

have different names and are consid-ered different types, the goal and challenge with both type 1 and type 2 is the same—to manage your blood sugar. The lessons in this book can help with that.

When I was diagnosed in 1991 it was not the primitive years of diabetes treatment, which involved peeing on strips to detect sugar in urine or boiling huge gauge needles for injecting insulin. But my first blood sugar meter required me to jab my fingers with something resembling a sewing needle for a big drop of blood and wait forty-five seconds for the meter to give me a reading. Now meters require a much smaller drop of blood and only five seconds, but it is still finger pricks multiple times a day. My first ten years of living with diabetes in the 1990s there were no tools like insulin pumps, continuous glucose monitors, or disposable insulin pens to inject insulin like we have today.

STRESS AND DIABETES

After multiple discussions with leading diabetes experts over the years, including Dr. Ron Kahn, the former president of the world-renowned Joslin Diabetes Center in Boston, MA, I am pretty sure that the extreme stress that I was under (or put myself under) in the first six months of law school may have contributed to the onset of my diabetes. I probably caught the usual wintertime cold, a minor virus that my immune system would normally attack and kill after a few days. But the stress may have caused my immune system to attack the wrong cells in my body. Diabetes is an autoimmune disease, which is one in which the body's immune system attacks healthy cells. I prefer to call it a condition because a "disease" sounds like something that you contract or catch, like a virus or bacteria that infects your body. Diabetes just happens to your body. It is not contagious.

In his book, *Cheating Destiny*, James Hirsch, a former reporter for *The Wall Street Journal* and *The New York Times*, discusses the battle of living with type 1. He has had type 1 since he was fifteen, and his son was diagnosed at age six. Ironically or perhaps for that reason, his brother, Dr. Irl Hirsch, MD, is one of the country's leading diabetes scholars at the University of Washington Medical School. In *Cheating*

Destiny, James Hirsch poignantly describes how the immune system gets confused and ambushes the beta cells in the pancreas.

"What makes this disease so infuriating is that the immune system exists for only one reason: to protect the body, to shield it from foreign substances, viruses, and other harmful organisms. But in diabetics, the immune system attacks the very cells that it is supposed to defend, like palace guards storming their own garrison or Secret Service agents turning on their president. The [type 1] diabetic body endures an act of rank perfidy."

It's the ultimate act of betrayal. I could imagine my dying beta cells looking at armed attackers from my immune system and killing them, uttering the famous Latin words of dying desperation "et tu, Brute?"— purportedly the last words of Roman Emperor Julius Caesar as he was being stabbed to death, recognizing his friend Marcus Brutus as one of the assassins betraying him.

My beta cells were gone. The insulin factory closed.

LIVING WITH TYPE 1 DIABETES

Diabetes was a blow to my self-confidence as I realized that my body was not invincible. I had lived twenty-three years of "normal" life, eating and drinking whatever I wanted, doing whatever I wanted without worrying about anything affecting my body. I had always been a healthy person, but I certainly enjoyed ice cream, pizza, burgers, and fries like everybody else and never once worried about its effect on me. I was young, athletic, and fit. I did not need to worry about it.

Now I had a chronic, incurable medical condition. It required constant daily management, calculating carbohydrates in everything I ate. I carried around meters and test strips, hiding syringes and a vial of insulin in my bookbag and pockets, injecting myself in the bathroom stall like a heroin addict, shooting up whenever I ate something and every morning and every night. I injected myself with a needle five to six times a day when before that I had probably only had five shots in my entire life and certainly had never given one to myself.

This was going to be my life, every day, from now on. I did not get depressed, but I was definitely shaken. Diabetes was not going away, ever. I would have to think about it every hour, every meal, every day. *What is my blood sugar doing? Am I confused because my blood sugar is low … or am I just confused? Did I inject too much insulin for that meal I just ate … or too little? Should I eat some crackers to keep my blood sugar up before I go to class … or maybe not because last week that made it go too high and I felt nauseous and bloated? If I eat three crackers will that raise it enough? Will five crackers make it go too high? Saltine crackers don't raise it as much as graham crackers.*

LOW BLOOD SUGAR, HIGH BLOOD SUGAR—A DAILY BATTLE

Trying to avoid low blood sugar and high blood sugar is a daily battle and balancing act. It's like having a constant conversation with yourself. Low blood sugar (hypoglycemia) caused by injecting too much insulin can start out simply as confusion. Thinking is clouded and brain function is distorted, like you have had too many tequila shots (er, not that I have ever done that) and can't put thoughts together or read words on a page or see across the room.

Sometimes you do not realize it is happening. According to UMass Chief of Diabetes, Dr. Harlan, "Individuals with diabetes can be 'lulled' into the nerve/brain dysfunction, just as one can sit in a comfortable easy chair to read and not realize they are falling to sleep. Symptoms when the brain and nerves have insufficient energy to function include blurry

Low blood sugar (hypoglycemia) caused by injecting too much insulin can start out simply as confusion.

vision, confusion, and if sufficiently severe and prolonged, loss of consciousness, seizures, and even (in rare instances) death."

If low blood sugar happens while driving a car, it is very dangerous. I have been there, struggling to think clearly. *Where am I going? Is that light red or green? Does red mean stop ... or go? Red means stop ... red means stop. Okay. Think, Jay! Think! Do I turn into this lane ... or that one?* But fortunately I have always been able to keep myself together long enough to realize that I was having low blood sugar and stop the car.

Gradually but quickly the symptoms get more severe. It could take fifteen minutes or thirty minutes depending on how much insulin you have injected, what type of insulin, and when you injected it. It also depends on the carbohydrates you have eaten—what kind, when, and how much? If you injected fast-acting "meal time" bolus insulin thirty minutes ago, that insulin is kicking in and will continue to drive your blood sugar down quickly. If you took it several hours ago, it is nearing the end of its effect on your body. It also depends on whether you have any carbohydrate in your stomach that has not been digested yet to settle the low blood sugar storm from insulin taking over your body.

> **As the blood sugar continues dropping your hands start trembling and jerking and your lips start quivering. Your brain's cognitive function gets disabled and clouded so you do not even realize that you are having low blood sugar.**

As the blood sugar continues dropping your hands start trembling and jerking and your lips start quivering. Your brain's cognitive function gets disabled and clouded so you do not even realize that you are having low blood sugar. That is the real danger of it. It disables your brain and your body at the same time, so you don't realize what is happening or that you even need help, and your brain can't control your body to help yourself even if you could realize it. You're in trouble and don't even know it or how to correct it.

Hypoglycemia eventually causes violent trembling, shaking, and sweating, making one unable to hold or grasp anything. Spotting the building storm in yourself is important and possible if you know what signs to look for. It's like being on a small boat on a calm day on the ocean when a storm approaches in the distance. You see the dark clouds far off, hear the low thunder, sense the drop in temperature, notice the wind increasing, and see the waves picking up. *Uh-oh. Something seems different. I detect something changing. Better go in.* If you detect these signs and know what to look for in yourself, you can get to shore and stop the storm from happening by getting some carbohydrate in you. But if you don't, you'll be in the storm soon and you don't know how rough it's going to be, and you could eventually be helpless and unable to get to shore. You may even go down unless someone rescues you with some carbohydrate.

I learned very soon after I was diagnosed that as soon as I felt any of these symptoms I should check my blood sugar by pricking my finger and dropping blood on the blood glucose meter, but the meters in the 1990s were often inaccurate. They took forty-five seconds to give a reading while I stood there slightly confused. Sometimes I would prick my finger and forget to put the blood on the meter or put it on the meter and walk away and never look at the reading, confused and disoriented. You also must have your meter and a supply of strips with you wherever you are, which requires constant planning and preparation. Test strips are expensive and my student health insurance would pay for only a small number. If I tested more than once or twice a day my supply would run out and I had to buy more on my dime or just be ignorant of my blood sugar, guessing all the time.

Family, friends, and coworkers around you can spot these low blood sugar signs. Your mood may change, becoming irritable, cranky, and confused. But of course, temporary episodes of confusion and irritability can happen to anyone for a lot of other reasons, so it is a delicate relationship that friends and family must practice not to constantly harass the person with diabetes to check their blood sugar.

The real danger is when it happens while sleeping—you can't detect it yourself, and no one is watching you to spot it. That is why parents of kids with type 1 diabetes get up in the middle of the night to check their child's blood sugar, pricking the child's finger for blood at 2 or 3 a.m. If it is low, they must wake the child and convince him or her to drink juice or eat some sort of carbohydrate snack. This nightly duty is like those difficult first months of a newborn baby's life, when sleep-deprived parents are up every night to breastfeed, change diapers, and care for the newborn. But with a child with diabetes, this nighttime ritual lasts many years depending on when the child is diagnosed. When does a parent stop this nightly routine? Most parents say they stop when they notice many, many months of an older child not having low blood sugar at night and they have developed a routine prior to bedtime to eat and prevent nighttime lows. Today continuous glucose monitors now provide some alarms as well, but as a parent when you've seen your child convulsing and thrashing with hypoglycemia, you don't want to always just trust technology to alert you.

Fortunately, I suffered only a few severe low blood sugar episodes in law school in the early 1990s. I was very vigilant, or paranoid, about looking for signs of it happening to me. Given my constant requirement to read or study in school, one of the easiest signs for me to spot has always been difficulty reading sentences or comprehending them. Of course, at times I had difficulty comprehending archaic legal opinions without low blood sugar, so it was a challenge to distinguish the cause of my confusion. I spent a lot of time checking blood sugar thinking, *Am I confused because my blood sugar is low … or because I just can't understand what this means?*

I remember one severe low blood sugar episode about a year after I had been diagnosed. I injected myself with insulin before leaving my apartment with my friends to eat dinner. Mealtime fast-acting insulin in the early 1990s took at least thirty minutes to start working in my body and one to two hours before it would peak. I was using a mealtime insulin called Humulin R. I would sometimes try to time its start by injecting it about thirty minutes before I expected to have my meal in front of me, especially if I already had high blood sugar at the time I took my insulin. But every person is different and the body often absorbs it quicker or slower in the same person on different days. Today's fast-acting insulin starts working much faster (ten or fifteen minutes), which allows someone with diabetes to inject just a few minutes before the meal or even just as the plate of food is placed in front of you and you estimate the amount of carbohydrate in it.

I was already noticing how exercise lowered blood sugar levels and makes your body more sensitive to insulin, so you need less of it and it works faster.

But this particular evening there was a delay leaving the apartment and I had gone for a short run that afternoon. I would do runs of about three or four miles or play basketball a few times a week and I was already noticing how exercise lowered blood sugar levels and makes your body more sensitive to insulin, so you need less of it and it works faster.

My injection of insulin started working too fast that evening. I started shaking and trembling in the car on the way to dinner with my friends David Gray and Keith Padgett. Fortunately, I was not driving. David stopped at a gas station and got a can of Coke and helped me hold it, pouring it down my throat as I shook and trembled. Within a few minutes I was recovering, and thirty minutes later we were at the restaurant where I had to figure out if I needed to inject more insulin for what I was about to eat.

HYPERGLYCEMIA—HIGH BLOOD SUGAR

High blood sugar (hyperglycemia) is also an unpleasant feeling, albeit not as immediately dangerous. High blood sugar can happen in thirty minutes to one hour after eating—the approximate time it takes to digest carbohydrate and convert it to glucose for the bloodstream—and can last for several hours. For meals with a lot of fat the digestion takes longer and the high blood sugar occurs later, sometimes four hours after eating. I've noticed that with pizza and some Mexican and pasta dishes. My blood sugar will be normal, even low, an hour after eating but dangerously high three or four hours later. High blood sugar can happen daily, even multiple times a day, if you miscalculate the carbohydrate content of food or your insulin dose or mistime your dose.

High blood sugar makes you feel bloated, with a headache and stomachache. You feel tired and weak. Although your brain function is not impaired like with low blood sugar, your body generally feels like you have the stomach flu for several hours until you can get insulin to start bringing your blood sugar down. You can take a correction bolus of fast-acting insulin, but you have to be careful not to overdose impatiently, frustrated that your blood sugar will not come down. Frustrated repeated correction dosing of insulin (i.e., "angry bolus-ing") will cause severe low blood sugar in an hour or two when all that insulin finally kicks in. It's like being cold and putting more and more wood onto smoldering embers, frustrated that the fire will not start and warm up, and then when it catches, all of that wood

High blood sugar makes you feel bloated, with a headache and stomachache.

Frustrated repeated correction dosing of insulin (i.e., "angry bolus-ing") will cause severe low blood sugar in an hour or two when all that insulin finally kicks in.

starts burning hotter and hotter with a raging intensity, and you can't get the wood off the fire now. Then you have to throw water on the fire (eat carbohydrate) and hope you don't overdo it and start the maddening roller coaster of overreacting to highs and lows.

I have found that a good way to speed up and start the correction bolus of insulin is by doing light exercise, even just walking around—anything to get the blood pumping a little, rather than just sitting and waiting. That is similar to blowing on the smoldering embers to help get a fire started. It requires patience, which is hard when you feel miserable.

To avoid high blood sugar in law school I loaded up on "sugar-free" foods in the grocery store and diet drinks, hoping I could still enjoy some "normal"-tasting foods. Some of those were big mistakes. One day I was excited to find sugar-free chocolate in the grocery store. I love chocolate. I ate almost the whole bag in a grand rebellious "take that diabetes!" fit of victorious gluttony. But after an unusual number of trips to the toilet that day, I read the label on the bag: sweetened with sorbitol. "Excessive consumption may have a laxative effect." Indeed it may.

Diabetics must look at the *carbohydrate* content on a food label, not just the sugar.

Sugar free does not mean carbohydrate free. A piece of bread may not have any sugar in it, but it is loaded with carbohydrate. Diabetics must look at the *carbohydrate* content on a food label, not just the sugar. Eating with diabetes can be confusing and can even seem contradictory—healthy foods can still raise your blood sugar. Eating a breakfast of plain (no sugar added) yogurt and fresh fruit is healthy, much healthier than a sugary cinnamon bun or donuts. But with diabetes the yogurt and fruit can raise your blood sugar

Eating with diabetes can be confusing and can even seem contradictory—healthy foods can still raise your blood sugar.

just as much as the bun and donuts. So you can't just eat "healthy"—you have to always check the carbohydrate content of your "healthy" meal and adjust your insulin and activity to match it.

LIFE AS A LAWYER WITH TYPE 1 DIABETES

I graduated law school in 1993 near the top of my class and had job offers from several large firms in South Carolina. I began working as a young associate for a big firm with about fifty lawyers in Greenville. My life was pretty stable, and the future was bright with a good job and income at one of the most prestigious large law firms in the state that had been around since the 1940s. I kept my diabetes private except for those who needed to know. I did not want others to see me as weak or sick. I was single, living alone, and working long hours in the above ground salt mine of a large law firm. I billed my hours, recording everything I did every six minutes so the firm could bill those six minutes to a client. A young associate does not have time to do anything but research and draft memos for briefs, prepare pleadings and discovery, and review documents for hearings and trials. Senior lawyers would appear at my office door and toss in legal hand grenades, ticking and about to explode, for me to jump on.

There was not much time for chitchat or visiting in the hallways or goofing off at work, because every six minutes has to be accounted for, and your billed hours are examined every day and month. It often made me anxious and frustrated at the end of the day if I could only account for seven hours of billable time when I had been at the office for ten hours.

Going to restaurants back then, I would carry a syringe in my pocket with a vial of Regular R (meal-time) insulin and inject it after my meal arrived. But I had to wait thirty minutes to start eating, staring at my food getting cold while everyone else was already finished eating. I could take the risk and inject before the food arrived and risk being surprised that it did not have as much carbohydrate as I had expected. In those cases I would have to stuff bread or sweet tea or anything else with carbohydrate in my mouth to keep my blood sugar from dropping and me dropping out of the conversation or onto the floor.

I also had to inject a long-acting basal insulin twice a day called NPH, at morning and bedtime, to keep a constant basal does of insulin circulating in my body. A healthy pancreas will secrete a small dose of insulin constantly throughout the day to help your body process glucose in your bloodstream to fuel your bodily functions—keep your heart beating, your lungs expanding, your brain thinking, your body walking around. Muscles and cells all need glucose to function. But that NPH basal insulin in the 1990s was a witch's brew. It was unpredictable when it would peak, and it would sneak up on me with dangerous low blood sugar if I did not have enough carbohydrate in my bloodstream to match it. *Will the NPH insulin peak in two hours or four hours today?*

It was like a guy following me around all day, hiding in the shadows and crowd, waiting for when I least expected it, and then suddenly jumping out of nowhere and hitting me in the face with the hypoglycemia boxing glove, leaving me dazed, wobbling, and stumbling. Then he would disappear into the shadows and not appear again for days. I remember days finding myself in the stairwell of my law firm, dazed and confused. I may have entered the stairwell with some degree of cognitive function, realizing that I had low blood sugar, going to the basement to get a sugary drink from the break room soda machine, but getting confused and lost on the way. *Where am I going? Why did I go into the stairwell? How do I get out?* Meanwhile my blood sugar kept dropping.

I soon started keeping fruit juice and snacks in my office, checking my blood sugar as often as possible with a meter that I kept in my desk drawer. I also did not want to get a reputation for always having to tell people that I needed to get something for my blood sugar. I could be seen as a risk. Partners may not select me to work on a new case or in a trial in court if they thought I always had to take breaks or would lapse into confusion. I would not blame them. I had to keep diabetes from affecting my performance or reputation.

My strategy was to make diabetes a nonevent—control it so well, and so discretely, that most people did not know I was dealing with it. I did not want to be known for my diabetes. I wanted to be known for me and some other accomplishment I earned. But controlling it is not easy, and it was even harder back in the 1990s when the insulin was so unpredictable.

I also lived alone. One morning I was getting ready for work in my apartment and woke up several hours later on the kitchen floor, sweating in my dress shirt and pants. I don't know what I did or did not do to cause that low blood sugar that morning. I no doubt gave myself insulin and forgot to eat breakfast soon enough. That diabetes guy got in my apartment that morning and clocked me so hard in the face in my kitchen it knocked me out. Fortunately I woke up and was somehow able to get myself some sugar to recover. But it scared the crap out of me. My endocrinologist later told me it was not a good idea for me to live alone or sleep alone. I asked if he could write me a prescription for that. Being a single guy in my twenties, I could use that. "Hey, my doctor says I'm not supposed to sleep alone. See, I have a doctor's note."

I was angry at my diabetes, resentful that it had invaded my body. I was determined to prove that I could be just like everyone else, even better. Diabetes became my motivation to get even with it.

But after a few years of living with this disease, I was sick of it. I wanted to prove that I was stronger than my diabetes. I was frustrated. I wanted a challenge—something hard. I wanted to prove myself. I was angry at my diabetes, resentful that it had invaded my body. I was determined to prove that I could be just like everyone else, even better. Diabetes became my motivation to get even with it.

I exercised, ran a little, and lifted weights, but I did not swim, bike, or run competitively. I didn't even own a bike or have a membership at a pool.

Diabetes was the worst thing that ever happened to me, but it ignited motivation in me. And because of that, it would soon become the best thing, too.

CHAPTER 5

MAKE THE BAD THING THE BEST THING

Topic: Strength from Difficulty

I was frustrated.

By the time I approached thirty years old in 1997, I had been living with diabetes for six years and I was sick of it. I knew by then it was not going anywhere. I had been hiding it from everyone but those who needed to know. I didn't want to appear sick or weak, and I didn't want people to feel sorry for me. Part of that was my pride, and part was my insecurity.

Diabetes requires such constant, daily, even hourly management that it is hard to keep hidden. It was even harder to conceal before insulin pumps became available in the early 2000s that could be tucked discretely in your pocket or under your clothes. I toted around syringes and vials of insulin in my pocket, having to take shots at the table every time I ate a meal or a snack. I either had to keep it hidden and sneak off to the bathroom to inject myself or do it right there at the table for all to see and wonder. "What's that? A syringe? Ooh, ouch! I can't watch."

I would have thought that same thing if someone had whipped out a syringe and done that at the table before I was diagnosed. Syringes and shots make people uneasy; most people dread just one flu shot a year. I was doing it right in front of you at the table, in the meeting, in the airplane seat, in the locker room, and I was doing it multiple times a day. Type 1 diabetes is not a condition where you go to a doctor's office for a treatment, have therapy in private, or take pills or medication at home in the morning. You have to manage it in the open, in front of people, all day, everyday, and the symptoms of low blood sugar are hard to conceal when your brain and muscles are malfunctioning.

I did not want to be known as the "diabetic" guy with a scarlet "D" on my chest, like Hester Prynne in Nathaniel Hawthorne's classic *The Scarlet Letter* who was required to wear a scarlet "A" for "adulterer" on her dress. I did not want diabetes to be my label, my identity.

Ironically, only a few years later it would become my identity in a positive way when I would be profiled in newspapers and magazines and speak about racing Ironman triathlons with diabetes. Like many people, my attitude and approach to diabetes and many other things went through a necessary evolution over the years. Your journey to overcome obstacles is necessary. It solidifies your determination once you find your solution. Where are you in your journey?

It wasn't until a few years later that I developed the determination to achieve something *because of* my diabetes and even be proud to be *known for* my diabetes. But at this point in my life in the late 1990s, approaching thirty years old, seven years after my diagnosis, I kept it hidden. I was not living in denial; I was living in determination. I was determined to control diabetes so well that people did not know I had it.

But I was still intimidated by it and wondered what limits it placed

> **Your journey to overcome obstacles is necessary. It solidifies your determination once you find your solution.**

> **I was not living in denial; I was living in determination. I was determined to control diabetes so well that people did not know I had it.**

on me. I wanted to test it. I respected my diabetes, but I would not surrender to it.

In 1997 I was working on a large commercial fraud class action lawsuit, traveling all over the United States and taking depositions with and against lawyers twenty years older than me from other law firms from other states. I was just a twenty-nine-year-old fourth-year associate, and it was a great opportunity for my career.

I respected my diabetes, but I would not surrender to it.

I had pursued it with the partner in charge of the case at my firm to prove to the partners that I was capable of handling big complex cases. Besides, it was better than spending all my time handling automobile wreck cases and slip and falls at the grocery store. I got to travel and observe some of the best lawyers in the country. The case involved bribery and kickbacks certain crooked Honda dealers paid to officials at Honda Motor Company during the 1980s and 1990s in order to receive new dealerships and the best allocation of top-selling cars. We represented a class of hundreds of "clean" Honda dealers who had not participated in the bribery and were suing Honda for allowing it to happen, discriminating against them, and damaging their businesses. The case lasted five years and ultimately settled for over $330 million dollars. That was one of the reasons I made partner two years early at my law firm, in just five years, when the normal partnership track was seven.

Of course, I was not yet a partner when the case settled, so when the door to the conference room closed, leaving me outside in the hall while the partners divided up the fee, I learned a hard lesson about how associates don't get to share in the spoils of war. It was great to make partner early and I appreciated that honor. But it would prove difficult for me given that I had achieved it largely by working on one giant successful plaintiff case, not by building up a large base of my own clients to continue working for after I made partner. Partners are not supposed to need help getting work. They are supposed to have their own clients. That's why they make partner. I didn't have a lot of clients, just a lot of experience. But many at my firm did not recognize the unique situation I was in—a thirty-year-old partner only five years out of law school. I still needed others at the firm to include me in work from their long-established clients. Indeed, struggling to find work as a young partner would ultimately create a problem for me.

One of the outside lawyers I worked with on that Honda case was from Sacramento, California, named Bill Kershaw. His hobby was rock climbing—a very California, West Coast thing—not many rock climbers in Greenville, South Carolina. I liked his attitude about life and work. A lot of working men in South Carolina spent their spare time hunting, fishing, or playing golf. None of that seemed difficult enough to challenge my diabetes, and sitting in a deer stand to ambush a defenseless deer with a high-powered rifle did not seem like a fair fight. I liked playing golf, but it is not known as an achievement of physical fitness.

CLIMBING MOUNT WHITNEY, CALIFORNIA

In August 1998 Bill allowed me to join him on a climbing trip with a small group of five people to climb the highest mountain in the lower forty-eight states—Mount Whitney, California, 14,505 feet. I had summited Half Dome in Yosemite Valley the year before by making the eight-hour amateur hike up the trail and climbing the cables to the top. I loved that challenge and the adventure, so climbing was starting to interest me. I had also heard the reports and read the book *Into Thin Air* by Jon Krakauer about several groups climbing Mount Everest in 1996, a gripping tale of perseverance and ultimately disaster and death portrayed in a movie twenty years later. Mount Whitney was nothing compared to Mount Everest, but I was captivated by the challenge.

Climbing Whitney would be a climb, not just a hike. It would take several days, a much more serious adventure than a day trip hiking a public trail to the top of Yosemite's Half Dome. It would be high altitude camping at over twelve thousand feet and strenuous climbing for several days. I trained for several months that summer, hiking and running hills to prepare. It takes over a year to get a permit to climb Mount Whitney and camp on the mountain a few thousand feet below the summit. Being the experienced climber, Bill handled all the permits and planning.

We hiked and traversed thousands of feet to tent camp overnight by Iceberg Lake at 12,621 feet. Bill and his climbing buddy would do a technical rock climb with ropes up a sheer rock face for the remaining two thousand feet to the summit. The other three of us would take a more amateurish but still very steep route called the Mountaineer's Route that did not require technical climbing experience. Some would call it bouldering because you crawl, climb, and pull yourself up rocks and boulders, still hanging on for dear life in some sections near the summit. The slope for this Mountaineer's Route is about 35 percent.

We started our summit climb before sunrise the second morning, needing enough time to summit and return to camp before dark. At fourteen thousand feet I could see aircraft *below* me heading for an airport in the distance. After a few hours of climbing I was just below the summit when I saw dark clouds approaching in the valley below.

I watched these clouds closely, hoping the wind would carry them away from this peak. But gradually they moved up the mountain and the wind increased. Soon they enveloped me and I could not see more than a few feet in front of me, like a whiteout in a snowstorm. The storm cloud began pelting me with an icy mix of hail, rain, wind, and sleet. I found a gap in the rocks to wedge myself, with lightning popping all around. If one of those strikes hit anywhere around me, I was gone, fried on the side of a big rock like a sausage on a stone grill. I had never been *inside* a storm cloud. Usually I look *up* at them thousands of feet above as the rain and lightning thunders down. It is truly a frightening and powerful experience to be inside the engine of one. It felt like I was inside a microwave oven with things roaring, buzzing, and popping. I could feel the electricity in the air, in my body, and in my hair. It was like standing next to a power station on the ground, humming and buzzing while millions of volts of electricity travel through the high-voltage wires and transformers around you. I was shivering. The temperature dropped to near freezing. Thirty minutes before that the temperature had been about sixty degrees in the middle of August.

I huddled against that rock wedge and thought about the mistakes those climbers had made on Mount Everest in 1996, pushing for the summit despite being behind schedule with a storm approaching. Nine people died. I thought about climbers I read about dying on Mount Whitney in 1990 in a lightning storm.

After about thirty minutes the storm let up, but the cloud was still covering me. I could not see more than twenty feet around me. *Is there another storm cloud nearby?* There was no way I had time to summit and get back before dark, and I didn't want to get caught in another storm. I spent the next four hours slowly climbing down the wet, rocky face of the route back to Iceberg Lake. I was not going to be a story about dying or getting rescued on the summit of Mount Whitney.

Those three days I spent climbing and hiking up and down that mountain, I was amazed at the fitness and leg strength of Bill's climbing partner. We were each carrying heavy packs with all of our food, cooking gear, tents, water, and clothes—forty to fifty pounds on our backs. He bounded up the rocks like a monkey climbing trees in the forest. I also noticed that his legs were smoothly shaved, which I had never seen before on a guy. I thought that was kind of odd, but it made it easy to see how fit his legs were. Over the course of the trip I found out he was a road cyclist. I had never met a cyclist. In 1998 cycling was not a popular or well-known sport in the United States, and it still is not. But before Nike and the US media publicized Lance Armstrong winning his first of seven consecutive Tour de France titles starting in 1999, nobody in the US was a cyclist. At least I was not, and nobody I knew in South Carolina was.

I was amazed that this guy could ride his bike for a hundred miles. *Ride a bike a hundred miles? Are you kidding me? That is insane!* But cyclist-rock-climber-shaved-legs-California-guy just smiled as he bounded up the mountain while I struggled to keep up.

Hmm, cycling. Sounds kinda hard, but I'm not sure that's my thing. But I made a mental note. I liked the outdoor purity of it and the fitness that it required. But I did not think much more about it. I didn't own a road bike or know anybody who did. The last bike I had was a red Schwinn when I was eleven years old. I knew that doing anything like that with diabetes would be even more difficult.

So cycling didn't catch my interest … yet.

Now that I had climbed (or came real close) to the summit of the tallest mountain in the lower forty-eight states, I was confident that I could do other things with diabetes. But what other things? I was proud of my accomplishment climbing Mount Whitney, and I loved the challenge of it, but I needed something else now.

I had more confidence, and I was becoming more resentful of my diabetes—a battle against myself. I wanted to prove that I was stronger than it was. Fear and frustration became determination and resentment, just to send a message to this disease in me.

I was also still insecure about how people would perceive me with diabetes. I did not realize how much that combination—insecurity and revenge—is a powerful motivator. In their book *The Triple Package*, Chua and Rubenfeld found certain immigrant groups succeed in America because they faced disrespect and scorn, which led to resentment and a constant determination that they need to prove themselves, an "I'll show everyone" mentality.

That is exactly how I felt about my diabetes. I was insecure about it. And I resented it. I wanted to prove to it and anyone else that I was not sick, that I was not weak. *I'll show you that I can do anything you can do and even things you cannot do.* I wanted to crush diabetes in my body by pushing myself to do something hard. I wanted to teach diabetes a lesson. It picked on the wrong guy. It was that "angry resolve" repeatedly trying to make my high school basketball team.

Obstacles and adversity are often what make champion athletes. Psychologists conducted interviews of ten gold medalists in different sports at the 2012 Summer Olympics to determine if adversity had a beneficial effect. The researchers published their findings in a report entitled "What Doesn't Kill Me ... : Adversity related experiences are vital in the development of superior Olympic performance" in the July 2015 edition of *Journal of Science Sport and Medicine*. They found that these champions "encountered a range of sport- and non-sport adversities that they considered were essential for winning their gold medals, including repeated non-selection, significant sporting failure, serious injury, political unrest, and the death of a family member."

Malcolm Gladwell calls these a "desirable difficulty" in his 2013 bestseller book *David and Goliath*. Gladwell researched how obstacles and disadvantages can lead to success. He noted how an extraordinary number of successful entrepreneurs are dyslexic. Some of those include Richard Branson of Virgin Industries; discount brokerage firm developer Charles Schwab; cell phone pioneer Craig McCaw; David Neeleman, founder of JetBlue; John Chambers, the CEO of technology giant Cisco; and Paul Orfalea, the founder of Kinko's. Gladwell found that "they succeeded, in part, *because* of their disorder—they learned something in their struggle that proved to be of enormous advantage."

One of America's most prominent lawyers, David Boies, handled cases involving Microsoft antitrust violations and the Supreme Court battle *Bush v. Gore* involving the disputed result of the 2000 presidential election. He has dyslexia. He learned at an early age to be a good listener to compensate for his inability to read well. That helped him be a better lawyer, a different lawyer, capable of listening and asking questions and boiling complex subjects down to their basics for judges and juries to grasp quickly. His dyslexia became his advantage and no doubt fueled his determination to succeed.

Gladwell also notes a study in the 1960s of over seven hundred successful innovators, political leaders, artists, and entrepreneurs in history—from Homer to President John F. Kennedy—finding almost half of them lost a parent before they were twenty. Sixty-seven percent of British prime ministers before World War II lost a parent before the age of sixteen. Twelve of the first forty-four American presidents, over 25 percent, including George Washington and Barack Obama, lost their fathers while they were young.

This is not to say that losing a parent as a child is a good thing and prepares you for success. Indeed, prisoners are between two and three times more likely to have lost a parent in childhood than the rest of the population. It is a difficult trauma emotionally and often leads to a difficult life of emotional and financial deprivation.

But as Daniel Coyle notes in his book *The Talent Code*, in which he traveled the world to research talent hotbeds in sports, arts, music, math, and many other areas, it can create a motivational trigger. "Losing a parent is a primal cue: *you are not safe.*" It creates a massive outpouring of energy created by that lack of safety and redefines the child's identity and affects how he or she faces the dangers and possibilities of life. It can flip a self-preserving switch at an early age to overcome obstacles and frustrations standing in the path of achievement. It can make a child work harder than others and rise to greatness in many aspects of life and persevere when things get difficult.

In her 2016 autobiography *Settle For More*, former Fox News and current NBC television anchor and commentator Megyn Kelly expressed how her father's sudden death when she was in high school affected her life. "It took many years for me to see my father's death as anything but a burden. ... But I realized that his death had given me a gift: the clear awareness that I couldn't afford to waste a second." That realization gave her the courage at age thirty-two to quit the practice of law after eight years and pursue her dream of becoming a television news anchor.

While diabetes is not near the devastation of the death of a parent, it awoke that primal cue in me. It made me feel like I was not safe because it invaded my life one day without warning and demanded every day that I deal with it after that. It said, "You have to work harder to overcome and achieve."

Gladwell calls this a desirable difficulty. I call it making the bad thing the best thing. When you're dealing with it, the difficulty does not feel desirable, and the bad thing does not feel like the best thing. It hurts. It sucks. That's to be expected, and it's necessary to feel that way. It's your struggle to overcome difficulty that creates your success.

> **It's your struggle to overcome difficulty that creates your success.**

Psychologists have labeled this process "adversarial growth," or "post-traumatic growth." In his book *The Happiness Advantage*, author Shawn Achor calls this "falling up." Something difficult knocks you down, and you come back stronger or better than before. After the tragic 2004 train bombings in Madrid, Spain, that killed 192 people and injured over two thousand, psychologists found some residents experienced positive psychological growth. Researchers in a 2002 study published in the *Journal of Psychosocial Oncology* found that some women diagnosed with breast cancer experience positive emotional growth. Following trauma and adversity many people experienced positive changes in spirituality, compassion, self-confidence, and a heightened appreciation of social relationships, according to a 2004 study published in the *Journal of Traumatic Stress*. "The people who can most successfully get themselves up off the mat are those who define themselves not by what has happened to them but by what they can make out of what has happened. These are the people who actually use adversity to find the path forward. They speak not just of 'bouncing back' but of 'bouncing forward.'"

You may not be responsible for what happened to you, but you are responsible for how you respond to it.

You may not be responsible for what happened to you, but you are responsible for how your respond to it.

So what is the difference between the person who gets knocked down and comes back stronger and those who don't? The difference is mind-set. How do you perceive the setback? As an opportunity? A wake-up call? A rebirth? Or is it the worst thing that ever happened to you? It takes time to process it. But soon you can view it as an opportunity to go a different direction rather than an obstacle in your path. Sometimes we need those obstacles forced on us because otherwise we would not make those changes ourselves. It's like the old saying, "The only good thing about hitting rock bottom is there is nowhere to go but up." Now change is necessary, we have no choice, and its easier to make changes when the old path is now blocked or unavailable.

A BAD THING CAN BE THE BEST THING FOR ... YOUR CAREER

Steve Jobs, the founder and CEO of Apple, got fired by the company's board of directors in 1985. Speaking at the commencement ceremony at Stanford University in June 2005, Jobs said, "How can you get fired from a company you started? What had been the focus of my entire adult life was gone, and it was devastating."

"I didn't see it then, but it turned out that getting fired from Apple was the best thing that ever happened to me. The heaviness of being successful was replaced by the lightness of being a beginner again, less sure about everything. It freed me to enter one of the most creative periods of my life." He started the company Pixar, which created the world's first computer-animated feature film, *Toy Story*, and is now the most successful animation studio in the world. He started another company called NeXT, which was eventually bought by Apple and became part of Apple's success when he returned.

Jobs concludes that "I'm pretty sure none of this would have happened if I hadn't been fired from Apple. It was awful tasting medicine, but I guess the patient needed it. Sometimes life hits you in the head with a brick. Don't lose faith. I'm convinced that the only thing that kept me going was that I loved what I did. You've got to find what you love."

How do you recover from a career setback like getting fired? Not everyone is the CEO of a billion-dollar company like Steve Jobs, with many contacts and connections to kindle a new start. What if you are a mid-level manager, just one employee among hundreds, even thousands at the company? We've all heard of the "golden handcuffs." You are trapped in your career path, in your job, because you've invested years in it, you and your family depend on the income now, and starting over would mean the loss of income and security of a paycheck.

This career devastation is vividly portrayed in a scene from the movie *Up in the Air*, in which George Clooney plays Ryan Bingham, a downsizer for hire. Bosses avoid the messy and difficult task of telling their own employees "you're fired" and outsource it to Bingham to do. He flies around the country terminating people, leaving them adrift and jobless, hence the double entendre title for both of them with their lives *Up in the Air*.

But his character is amusing and witty and develops insight and perspective. In one scene he breaks from his usual well-practiced termination script to offer some sound advice to a man he is firing named Bob. Bob appears to be a mid-level manager with many years at this company. He is understandably distraught and angry when Bingham's young, inexperienced colleague picks the wrong time to tell him that there can be "positive effects" from being laid off.

Bob: I make about ninety grand a year now. Unemployment is what, 250 bucks a week? Is that one of your *positive effects*? Well, we'll get to be cozier because I'm not going to be able to pay my mortgage on my house. So maybe we can move into a nice, fucking one-bedroom apartment somewhere! And I guess without benefits, I'll get to hold my daughter as she suffers from her asthma that I won't be able to afford the medication for.

Ryan Bingham: Your children's admiration is important to you?

Bob: Yeah. It was.

Ryan Bingham: Well, I doubt they ever admired you, Bob.

Bob: Hey asshole, aren't you supposed to be consoling me?

Ryan Bingham: I'm not a shrink, Bob. I'm a wake-up call. You know why kids love athletes?

Bob: I dunno. Because they screw lingerie models.

Ryan Bingham: No, that's why *we* love athletes. Kids love athletes because they follow their dreams.

Bob: Well, I can't dunk.

Ryan Bingham: No, but you can cook. Your resume says you minored in French culinary arts. Most students work at a fryer at KFC, but you bussed tables at El Pique A'tore to support yourself. Then you get out of college, and you come to work here. How much did they first pay you to give up on your dreams?

Bob: Twenty-seven grand a year.

Ryan Bingham: And when were you going to stop and come back and do what makes you happy?

Bob: Good question.

Ryan Bingham: I see guys who work at the same company for their entire lives. Guys exactly like you. They clock in. They clock out. And they never have a moment of happiness. You have an opportunity here, Bob. This is a rebirth. Now if not for you, do it for your children.

That sounds nice in the movies, but it is hard to do when you have a mortgage, spouse, and kids depending on you in real life. It feels like a devastating setback rather than a wonderful opportunity. You don't think, *Yippee, I've got diabetes!* or, *Yippee, I've been fired!* That's how I viewed diabetes for many years—as a setback. It's that difficulty and hardship, the emotional toll and struggle to recover, that makes it ultimately become the best thing that happened to you. It's the fear and difficulty that triggers the primal cue "you are not safe." You better work hard to recover and succeed because you just learned that bad things can happen at any moment. Nothing is guaranteed. Your parents, your employer, your government, and your god cannot shield you from bad things and misfortune. It is up to you to respond to them.

A BAD THING CAN BE THE BEST THING FOR ... YOUR BUSINESS

Wendell August Company is America's oldest and largest forge, founded in 1932. It is a family-owned company where craftsmen create custom commemorative pieces and gifts by heating and shaping metal. Its original factory in western Pennsylvania is on the National Registry of Historic Places. The recession of 2008 and 2009 was devastating to the company. It had to lay off almost half of its employees. Analysts told the CEO and board of directors that they should consider closing the company and selling off the assets.

CEO Will Knecht admits, "We had been in the same building for eighty years and settled into a kind of business rhythm, a 'this is how we've always done it' syndrome. We had become comfortable with the fact that we would just be a local regional lifestyle business, so that's how we operated." Their factory, headquarters, and retail store were all located on a dead-end street of a residential neighborhood. As a family-owned business investment capital was not available to relocate or build a new factory.

But in March 2010, just when things seemed the worst, the company received an order to create over twenty thousand commemorative pieces for the Pittsburgh Penguins NHL hockey team to give to fans for the final game in the team's arena. It was the largest order in the company's history and had to be completed in record time—just four weeks—in its factory located in Pennsylvania, the only factory it had. This order would save the company.

Two days later that factory burned to the ground.

The fire could not have happened at a worse time. A few days after the fire Knecht received a call from the president of the Pittsburgh Penguins on his cell phone. His corporate office was burned and had no working telephone. He had been expecting this call and dreading it. The Penguins were going to cancel the contract and find another supplier to fill their order. They needed a rush order. He would understand.

But that's not what happened. The Penguins had seen and heard about the fire. They were sure the company would be in for difficult times, unable to fill orders or make sales, and cash flow would be gone. So the Penguins offered to pay the entire balance of their contract up front if Wendell August could still fill their order. The Penguins president said, "we still need those twenty thousand pieces in four weeks. Can you do it?"

CEO Knecht says he pulled himself up off the ground and stammered, "Yes! We can do it!" Then he turned to his employees and said, "How are we going to do that?" But salvaging some of the equipment and renting space in a temporary workshop they were able to deliver the company's largest order just four weeks after the fire.

Knecht says, "We were forced to, given the opportunity to, think differently. The thought change was most important. We literally had a foundation of eighty-seven years of history to build on, but the canvas was now blank, ready to be painted on. We received a tremendous amount of national and international publicity, which began to open doors for us." Three years after the fire the company moved into a new state-of-the-art facility twice the size of their original factory with a retail store near a major interstate and outlet mall. Sales have increased significantly, and the company now has a strategy for long-term growth it never had before the fire.

It was not easy, but the company made the fire the best thing that ever happened to them.

In the movie *Apollo 13*, the spacecraft bound for the moon, orbiting thousands of miles above the earth, is crippled by an explosion, stranding three astronauts with time running out and problems mounting, such as the lack of oxygen, food, water, and battery power. NASA officials and scientists work around the clock to invent solutions for problems for which they never planned to keep the astronauts alive and bring the damaged craft back to earth without burning up on reentry. One NASA official laments that "this will be the worst disaster that NASA has ever experienced." But mission control director Gene Kranz, played by actor Ed Harris, responds, "With all due respect sir, I believe this is going to be our finest hour."

If you are feeling hopeless or helpless—about some setback in your career, a change or loss in your job, a difficulty in your personal life or business—remember that you have two choices. You can let it crush you and block you, or you can use it to go a different direction and try a new path upward. Success is not about never falling down or even falling down and getting up once. Success comes from perseverance—getting up again and again. It takes angry resolve, using that setback to propel yourself in a new direction with relentless determination fueled by that failure. It is capturing the negative energy of that setback and rechanneling it into productive drive to become even happier, to find your purpose and go after it. You've been given a blank slate. You've hit bottom, so everything now will be an improvement. Where do you want to go?

Success is not about never falling down or even falling down and getting up once. Success comes from perseverance—getting up again and again.

For many years, as I was trying to understand diabetes, I perceived it as a handicap, a disaster. It kept knocking me down, punching me in the face, and I did not know if I would ever be able to prevent low blood sugar seizures or high blood sugar nausea or the long-term complications of blindness, amputation, and kidney dialysis. Diabetes was an intimidating curse that followed me, rising up at inopportune moments to say, "I'm still here, and I'm going to make this difficult for you—this deposition, this conversation, this night of sleep, this relationship, this car ride, this pickup basketball game. You'll never get rid of me."

It was not until I had some experience with the disease and some success controlling it that I started looking at diabetes not as an obstacle but as an opportunity—an opportunity to prove how strong I am, that I am stronger than it is, to get revenge on it. That's when I started conquering it.

That's how diabetes, the worst thing that ever happened to me, would eventually become the best thing that ever happened to me. I was determined. I was looking for something. I just did not know what it was.

I was about to find it.

CHAPTER 6

SET GOALS WITH FAILURE POTENTIAL

Topic: Setting Goals

In 1999 a postcard appeared in my mailbox from the American Diabetes Association (ADA). It said, "Run a marathon, raise money for the ADA."

That sounded like a ridiculous idea. *Who runs marathons? A bunch of endurance freaks. Skinny runner people in dorky looking Bill Clinton short-shorts.* The ADA would provide you a coach and people to train with and coordinate all the travel to one of five marathons around the world. All you had to do was raise them some cash, as in three or four thousand dollars. One marathon was in Hawaii in June the following year. *Well, that sounds like a nice place to be when you finish.*

But I had never run a marathon. I had never even run a 10k (6.2 miles). I did not run track or cross country in high school or college. Running a marathon seemed like the hardest thing to do in the world, and that's for people who don't have diabetes. *Run 26.2 miles? Those people are fit. Really fit. I've never done anything like that. I don't know if I can do that.*

Scott Jurek is one of the world's best ultramarathon runners, winning the sport's most prestigious races multiple times, including Badwater Ultramarathon twice (2005, 2006) and the Western States Endurance Run seven times (1999–2005). In July 2015, he broke the

Appalachian Trail through-hike speed record, hiking the 2,200-mile trail from Georgia to Maine in forty-six days, eight hours, and seven minutes, breaking the record by just three hours. Jurek said, "Every single one of us possesses the strength to attempt something he isn't sure he can accomplish."

The risk of failure and fear limits us all. Nerves and fear are a part of everyone's life no matter how old you are or what you do, whether you are a beginner or a seasoned professional. Don't be afraid to fail, because if you've never failed, you're not very successful. You have to overcome the fear of failure as an artist before a performance, an athlete before a competition, a lawyer before trial, a businessperson before an important sales presentation, or a boy asking a pretty girl out for a date. Even if you have done it many times before, it is normal to be nervous, fearful that you might fail, that you might not make it.

> **Don't be afraid to fail, because if you've never failed, you're not very successful.**

In his book *The Talent Code*, Daniel Coyle studied the secrets of talent searching for tools that anyone can use to maximize potential in themselves and others they lead. Drawing on neurology and researching talent hotbeds from the baseball fields of a tiny Caribbean island to a classical music academy in upstate New York, Coyle identified three key elements necessary to develop and optimize performance in sports, art, music, math, and anything else.

One of those elements he called "deep practice." Deep practice is built on a paradox: struggling in certain targeted ways and operating on the edge of your ability, where making mistakes and failing makes you better. From a neurological standpoint, deep practice builds myelin, a microscopic neural substance that adds vast amounts of speed and accuracy to your movements and thoughts. Neurologists believe that myelin in the brain forms the foundation of greatness, whether its painting like Leonardo da Vinci or playing basketball like LeBron James.

The good news is that myelin grows and can be cultivated, which means talent can be grown and cultivated. You are not limited by what you are born with. You are limited only by how hard you are willing to work and how much you're willing to fail. Find and use your strengths and work on your weaknesses. Adapt and improvise to overcome your limitations. You can't make yourself taller or shorter, but you can make yourself faster or stronger. You can't change your voice, but you can make yourself the best dancer or musician.

> **You are not limited by what you are born with. You are limited only by how hard you are willing to work and how much you're willing to fail.**

Set goals with failure potential that you might not reach, and even be glad when you don't, because it gives you something to learn from and try for the next time. You have to be willing to be bad in order to one day be good.

According to Coyle, we all confronted fear and failure first as a "staggering baby" learning to walk, but only a select few people continue this practice as a child and an adult because falling (i.e., failing) hurts. We don't like failing, and we try to avoid it. "It's the feeling … of being a staggering baby, of intently, clumsily lurching toward a goal and toppling over. It's a wobbly, discomforting sensation that any sensible person would instinctively seek to avoid. Yet the longer the babies remain in that state, the more willing they are to endure it, and to permit themselves to fail, the more myelin they build, and the more skill they earn. The staggering babies embody the deepest truth about deep practice: to get good, it's helpful to be willing, or even enthusiastic, about being bad. Baby steps are the royal road to skill."

Set goals just out of your reach but not out of sight—goals that cause you some fear and intimidate you or goals that have failure potential but are not foolish fantasies. Will Rogers said, "It's a fine line between courage and foolishness. Too bad it's not a fence." You have to decide what is courageous and what is foolish and target your effort.

Be willing to fail but unwilling to quit. I learned that getting cut from that high school basketball team twice before I finally made it. Besides, it makes for a much better feeling when you succeed to admit how bad you used to be, how many times you got your butt kicked. Everybody loves to hear that story.

> **Be willing to fail but unwilling to quit.**

The ADA's card about running a marathon sat on my kitchen counter for a few days and then a week, mocking me. It was really starting to get on my nerves. I could have thrown it away. *Stupid little postcard. Shut it up.* But soon I thought, *I wonder if I could do that?* I was nervous, but I signed up. I might not make it, but it was the perfect situation to give it a try. At least I would fail while daring greatly. I could raise money for a diabetes charity. They'd give me a coach and training plan and other people to train with and handle all the entry and travel details. And I'd get a trip to Hawaii. All I had to do was raise $3,500.

Oh yeah, and run 26.2 miles.

I trained for six months. I had to learn the basics of endurance training like every person attempting their first marathon: running form, proper socks and shoes, nutrition, pacing, hydration, recovery. Who knew there was so much to running a marathon? I thought you just put on running shoes and whatever basketball socks you had and start jogging as far as you could go and eventually you'd make it 26.2 miles.

As a diabetic, I also had to learn how to manage blood sugar levels and insulin dosing. It's one thing to manage your blood sugar for a short five-mile run. It is an entirely different challenge to manage it for training runs of fifteen or twenty miles. What do I eat or drink before, during, and after these runs? How much will running make my blood sugar go down? Does it start falling in the first thirty minutes? A lot depends on what I've eaten in the two hours before I start running and what I eat or drink during the run. Do I run with a blood sugar meter? Insulin? How do I bring food and drinks with me while I run?

I was a baby staggering through a marathon. I probably even looked like that when I ran. After about two months of training I was getting used to the miles. Some runs were just five miles and some were ten, building up to long runs of eighteen and twenty. As the weather started warming in May and June, temperatures in South Carolina reached the eighties and nineties, so it was good preparation for the hot Hawaii marathon. On my first twenty-mile run I learned a painful lesson about hydration. After about fifteen miles of running I could not go any further. I sat down in the driveway of a random home because I was too exhausted and dehydrated to even walk. My stomach was queasy and in deep pain, which I now know is common when you are dehydrated. *Don't mind me. Nothing to see here. I'm just dying in your driveway.*

Fortunately, I was running that day with a training partner. She was a good runner and in great shape, an aerobics instructor at a local gym. It was a challenge to keep up with her some days. On some early training runs I tried not to let her know that she was killing me, but you tend to lose your pride after a lot of miles of pain. On this day I had no choice but to finally stop. She kindly ran the last five miles alone back to where our cars were parked and drove back and gave me a ride back to my car. I learned a lot about hydration that day.

COMING OUT OF THE DIABETES CLOSET

As I started fund-raising, I realized that raising $3,500 would not be easy—maybe even harder than running twenty-six miles. So I kept putting it off (avoiding it) and just focused on my training. I had to get my body in shape and figure out this whole endurance running thing.

The ADA gave us a sample fund-raising letter to mail out. It sounds archaic now, but we were actually supposed to sign and mail paper letters with real envelopes and stamps. Paper! I know, crazy! In 1999 the Internet was still a sputtering, slow, dial-up, pay-by-the-minute clunky new thing, and many people did not have email yet. Fund-raising websites were nonexistent.

With only about eight weeks until the marathon, the ADA asked for fund-raising dollars to be submitted. I was running a little behind—okay, really behind. I had not even sent out a fund-raising letter. The ADA needed to make flight and hotel reservations. They wanted me to turn in some money fast or I would not be allowed to go.

I was at a pivotal crossroads with my diabetes. Do I send out a letter to dozens of family, friends, business associates, coworkers, friends of friends, and anybody else I could think of—most I knew but some I did not—and tell them that I have diabetes? Or do I follow the sample letter and just say I'm doing it as a fund-raiser for the millions of people that have diabetes?

My plan had been to do the marathon first and then let people find out I did it with diabetes. But the ticking fund-raising deadline looming over me was forcing my decision. Do I come out of the diabetes closet?

I guess I have to put it in the letter. I didn't really want to, but I was kind of desperate to raise a lot of money fast. I had a feeling that would make them more likely to contribute money if they knew I was battling it myself. I know it would influence me if I received a fund-raising letter. I labored over that letter more than a brief to the Supreme Court. I didn't want to sound whiny or like I was pressuring anyone to contribute.

I told them that I was taking on the challenge to run a marathon to raise money to help people with diabetes, that it was a struggle to run a marathon, and that it was a struggle to live with diabetes. And I would know because I was trying to do both. I didn't want people to contribute unless I was willing to run the marathon myself. I included a stamped self-addressed envelope like an RSVP for a wedding. I wanted to make it easy. All they had to do was write a check to the ADA and drop it in my envelope and in the mail. It was a short letter and I mailed it to about seventy-five people.

A week went by and no money came in. I was nervous—nervous that I had just disclosed my little secret that I had diabetes. And I was nervous that I needed some fund-raising dollars fast or the ADA would not let me go. I would be all trained up and have nowhere to run. A few more days went by.

Then one day one of my self-addressed envelopes appeared in my mailbox with a check and a note encouraging me and saying how glad they were to contribute. The next day was another check with a note. Then another and another. With each day more and more envelopes appeared in my mailbox. The outpouring of support was overwhelming. Some wrote me long sincere notes about how proud they were of me trying to run a marathon with diabetes or how they knew someone who had diabetes and thanked me for helping them. Others just stuck a check to a post-it note that said "good luck," "pulling for you," or "happy to contribute."

Their support gave me daily shots of encouragement at the mailbox. In less than six weeks I raised over $7,000, more than double what was required. I was the top fund-raiser from my group and one of the top fund-raisers in the country for that marathon.

And it was all because I finally admitted that I had diabetes and was willing to do something about it. This marathon fund-raiser was the right time and the right way for me to do that. I had been searching for this method since I was diagnosed nine years earlier. *Don't feel sorry for me, or think I am weak and sick because I have diabetes. Diabetes picked on the wrong guy. To prove that, I am taking on this challenge to run a marathon and help some other people while I do it.*

The training became easier now because I was doing it for a purpose greater than myself. I could not let these people down. The pain of running was now easier to endure.

In his book *I'm Here to Win*, two-time Ironman Triathlon World Champion Chris McCormack said he was a young accountant in an office cubicle in Australia when he started racing triathlons to honor his mother, who had recently died of breast cancer. He improved rapidly after several years, but when he was not selected for the Australian national team, he went on his self-described "rampage of racing." He wanted to suffer.

Chris said, "In 2000 I went to the [United] States with a chip on my shoulder the size of the Sydney Harbor Bridge, out to show the Australian Olympic officials that they'd made a terrible mistake. I wanted to humble them and make fools of them, and I would do it by winning every race that I could run. Whether it's raw talent, your ability to train like an animal, or something else: if you want a long career, to be a champion and transcend your sport, you need to understand what makes you good. It can't just be because your coach tells you you're good. You need to get in your head and break it down: 'I'm good because …' What makes you tick, mentally as well as physically? Once you understand that, your purpose becomes clear. You might be good because you're trying to prove something to someone."

I had that purpose—a desire to suffer to prove a point, to prove that diabetes had picked on the wrong guy. I wanted to prove it to myself, to my diabetes, and to anyone who might think I was sick, weak, or unable to do something because of diabetes. *I'll show you!*

I got to Kona, Hawaii, for that first marathon in June 2000. I had no idea that the Ironman triathlon was staged on this same course in October every year. I had never even heard of the Ironman triathlon. I was just trying to run a marathon, which seemed hard enough to me.

That marathon was 26.2 of the most painful, miserable … wonderful miles of my life. Kona in June is very hot, so they start this marathon at 5 a.m. *Who runs a marathon in June in Hawaii?* You run for two hours in the dark before the sun even comes up, just to avoid the Hawaii summer heat. Years later, looking back, I find this attempt to avoid the heat amusing when I would start all of my Ironman marathons at midday in the most intense heat, after first swimming 2.4 miles and biking 112 miles.

I was just trying to break four hours, a very pedestrian nine-minute, ten-second per mile pace. I thought this was a reasonable goal for my first marathon and in such hot conditions. I kept close to my goal pace for the first eighteen miles but started having trouble once the heat and my blood sugar started hurting me. I checked my blood sugar at mile eighteen—over 300 mg/dl. *Wow. Not good.* Way too high, three times the normal level. I had not taken enough insulin, worrying about getting low blood sugar, and drank too much carbohydrate-loaded sports drinks. My stomach was queasy from the high blood sugar, the dehydration from running eighteen miles, and the heat now above ninety-five degrees radiating off the asphalt and lava fields on both sides of the road. I struggled those last eight miles, jogging slowly.

I finished that race in four hours and fifteen minutes. I was slower than my target time but very happy I ran my first marathon. I finished 35th out of 134 in my age group, so I was happy to know I could run a marathon and finish in the top 25 percent, even though this was not a world-class field. There were only 958 people in the race. Most marathons in the United States usually have five thousand to ten thousand runners, up to the New York and Chicago marathons with forty-five thousand runners. But Kona is not an easy marathon. For much of the race, you are running alone in the quiet, listening to nothing but your breathing and feet hitting the ground, in the dark until the sun (and heat) rises, looking out at the lava fields and the Pacific Ocean in the distance. There are no bands playing or crowds lining the route cheering and encouraging you. It is just you and the road and your determination to get you to the finish line.

ANOTHER GOAL—THE IRONMAN TRIATHLON

I sat in the grass under a tree at the finish line feeling absolutely miserable … and ecstatic. I was nauseous and exhausted, dehydrated and over-heated, and very proud of myself. I had just run a marathon with type 1 diabetes. I had proven to myself, and anyone else, that I could pass what I thought was the most difficult test of fitness in the world. I did it with diabetes. Diabetes would not hold me back. I beat it today.

A guy was sitting next to me at the finish line. We had some initial conversation about the race, how his was, how mine was, how hard it was, how hot it was, blah blah. But I was so exhausted and felt so queasy, I really did not feel like talking.

Then he said, "You know, this is where they race the Ironman triathlon. Those guys, they swim 2.4 miles out there in the Pacific Ocean. Then they bike 112 miles up the coast of Hawaii and back." He pointed to the finish line. "*Then* they run this marathon."

I was exhausted and dehydrated, with a churning stomachache that had been building in me, sweating in the midday heat, sitting in the grass near the finish line. I had been forcing Gatorade down my throat to rehydrate myself, but it had only made me more uncomfortable, sloshing in my queasy stomach.

I thought about the absurdity of what this guy said, the absurdity of the Ironman triathlon. My nausea rose. I leaned over … and I threw up on him.

> I thought about the absurdity of what this guy said, the absurdity of the Ironman triathlon. My nausea rose. I leaned over … and I threw up on him.

What kind of freak of fitness can do that? Swim 2.4 miles, bike 112 miles, and then run a marathon? And who could do that with type 1 diabetes? I just ran a marathon with diabetes. Wasn't that good enough for you?

I spent a few days in Hawaii soaking the soreness out of my legs. Every time I walked down steps I had to hold the handrail. I had to push and pull myself up with my arms every time I stood up. I liked that sore feeling. It was a constant reminder that I had pushed myself farther than I ever had. I wanted the marathon to be hard, and it was. I loved it.

But on the long nine-hour flight from Hawaii to Atlanta, watching the Pacific Ocean pass underneath me, I thought about what that guy said. I felt another goal building in me—a goal with a lot more failure potential than just running a marathon. *If I can run a marathon with diabetes … maybe I can do the Ironman.*

Improvement comes from trying something, succeeding, and then thinking, *Maybe I can do more.*

Improvement comes from trying something, succeeding, and then thinking, *Maybe I can do more.* Teachers and parents, coaches and bosses do that for us. They congratulate you on your success and then set an even higher goal for you. Has anyone ever done that for you? Do you do that for someone? Your children? Your team members? Your students? Your employees? Sometimes it is annoying and frustrating to hear that, and you want to say, "Wasn't that good enough for you?" But that's how you improve. "If I just did this, maybe I could do that!"

I did not know how to race a triathlon, much less the longest of all triathlons—the Ironman. The Ironman is the longest, most grueling one-day athletic competition in the world. It intimidated me. It was so far beyond anything I had ever thought about doing. I did not know if I could do it. I did not know if diabetes had a ceiling for me, if there was a limit, and if the Ironman was beyond that limit.

I knew that I would have to prepare meticulously, do all the training possible, and dedicate myself to it completely. It would take me a long time to even get to the starting line, and then I might not even make it to the finish line. I might fail.

And that's why I wanted to try.

DO NOT BE AFRAID TO FAIL

Jack Canfield is the cocreator of the *Chicken Soup for the Soul* book series. He is a successful speaker and wrote a book called *The Success Principles: How to Get from Where You Are to Where You Want to Be.* Canfield talks about the need to risk failure in order to improve, how high achievers "fail forward."

"Many people fail to take action because they're afraid to fail. Successful people, on the other hand, realize that failure is an important part of the learning process. They know that failure is just a way we learn by trial and error. Not only do we need to stop being so afraid of failure but we also need to be willing to fail—even eager to fail. I call this kind of instructive failure 'failing forward.' Simply get started, make mistakes, listen to the feedback, correct, and keep moving forward toward the goal. Every experience will yield useful information that can be applied the next time."

The poet T.S. Elliot, winner of the Nobel Prize for Literature in 1948, said, "Only those who risk going too far can possibly find out how far one can go."

In January 2015, climbers Tommy Caldwell and Kevin Jorgeson completed what is arguably the most difficult ascent in the history of rock climbing—the El Capitan Dawn Wall in California's Yosemite National Park. The duo remained on the wall for nineteen days, climbing three thousand vertical feet along widely spaced, razor-thin granite holds, sleeping in tents suspended thousands of feet in the air and attached to the wall by ropes. After they finished Caldwell said, "If we allow ourselves to be exposed to challenge, then that challenge can energize us and show us who we are."

LEADERS SET GOALS WITH FAILURE POTENTIAL

Leaders inspire us to follow them because they have the courage to set that goal. A leader has the courage to call others to action and say, "We can do this."

Leaders inspire us to follow them because they have the courage to set that goal. A leader has the courage to call others to action and say, "We can do this."

President John F. Kennedy provided one of the most memorable calls to action in a speech at Rice University on September 12, 1962, setting a goal with failure potential. Kennedy said, "We choose to go to the moon. We choose to go to the moon in this decade … not because [it] is easy but because [it] is hard, because that goal will serve to organize and measure the best of our energies and skills, because that challenge is one we are willing to accept, one we are unwilling to postpone, and one we intend to win."

Many things happened in the 1960s that could, and should, have made that goal fail and cause people to question it. Just one month after that speech Soviet nuclear missiles were discovered just ninety miles off US soil. Those thirteen days of the Cuban Missile Crisis in October 1962 were the closest we ever came to full-scale nuclear war. The leader who set the goal, President Kennedy, was assassinated just over one year later in November 1963. The scourge of racial segregation plagued the country leading to two hundred thousand people marching on Washington to hear Martin Luther King Jr.'s famous "I Have a Dream" speech in April 1963. King was murdered in 1968, leading to riots and more racial tension. The Vietnam War escalated throughout the 1960s, causing protests around the country. The Soviet Union appeared to be winning the space race with the first satellite to orbit the earth and the first human spaceflight. Meanwhile, the United States suffered a tragedy in 1967 when the Apollo 1 spacecraft caught fire on the launch pad, killing all three astronauts.

All of these failures, challenges, and obstacles could have caused this goal to put a man on the moon before the decade ended to fail. Ironically, those obstacles may have in fact strengthened the nation's resolve to succeed. The country needed something to be proud of, to unify us, to inspire us.

How much pride did we feel, and do we still feel, when we watch the grainy black-and-white video and hear the faint words of Neil Armstrong as he stepped off onto the surface of the moon on July 20, 1969, just six months before the end of the decade, saying, "That's one small step for man. One giant leap for mankind."

We are inspired because we knew how hard it was, and we succeeded.

RISKING FAILURE IN BUSINESS

It is not only athletics and life that you have to risk failing. You have to do the same to succeed in business. Richard Branson is the billionaire owner of Virgin Group. He started by owning a small record store in London, England, and eventually started the Virgin Records label in 1972 by installing a recording studio at his house and leasing studio time to fledgling bands and artists. By the 1980s and 90s he opened over a hundred Virgin Megastores in the UK and around the world, including New York City's Times Square, selling music and books. In the 1980s, after years of being a music industry executive, Branson announced that he wanted to get into the commercial aviation business.

It was a risky business move to be sure, in an industry in which he had no experience. As Branson stated in his book, *The Virgin Way*, his partners and colleagues at Virgin Records "were convinced I had totally lost my marbles. Not unjustifiably, they were terrified by the immensity of the financial risks involved in such a capital-intensive industry, and believe me they used a lot of choice words to let me know just how they felt about such a lunatic venture. Not least they quite correctly observed that, other than as an (economy class) paying-passenger, my knowledge of commercial airlines hovered right around the zero mark."

Virgin Airways struggled at first to compete against the powerful large airlines like British Airways but eventually succeeded through savvy marketing and self-promotion, mostly by Branson himself pulling stunts and adventures to get media attention and free exposure. Virgin Airlines eventually became Virgin America, Virgin Atlantic, and Virgin Australia. It is fortunate that he took that risk to venture out of the music industry because the Internet and Apple's iTunes online music downloading soon made the traditional brick-and-mortar music store obsolete. Every Virgin Megastore is now closed, and he is out of the music business.

Branson has tried many diverse industries that succeeded such as Virgin Mobile (cell service), Virgin Money (banking), Virgin Hotels, and Virgin Vacations (hospitality). But he also tried many things that failed such as Virgin Cola, Virgin Vodka, and the ideally named Virgin Brides (bridal wear). He even considered selling Virgin Condoms but was talked out of that inherently contradictory name by his wife.

Branson admits that risking failure, and enduring it, is necessary in business. "There's often a very thin dividing line between success and failure. My daughter Holly reminded me how I sat her down when very young and told her I would likely have to take her out of school. We were struggling to make ends meet and my wife Joan offered to sell our old car to help. Fortunately we were able to make it through and Virgin has gone from strength to strength. But for every success story there are hundreds of near misses. Every entrepreneur fails several times before succeeding, and the important thing is to get up and keep trying again."

A leader displays courage that inspires others to keep trying and working even when failure has occurred and could occur again. Growing up I watched my father use this product with an odd name called WD-40 to lubricate everything in our house that squeaked, rattled, or got stuck. It has been said that you only need two things in life: duct tape and WD-40. If it moves and shouldn't, use duct tape. If it doesn't move and should, use WD-40. But where did they get that name?

It comes from the number of times they failed before they got it right.

WD-40 was developed in 1953 by chemist Norm Larsen. It was originally designed to repel water and prevent corrosion on the Atlas space rocket and nuclear missiles. It took him forty tries to find the right formula. WD-40 is the abbreviation for "Water Displacement, 40th formula," the name and sequential numbers he etched in the lab book with each attempt. In 1973 the company went public and is now traded on the NASDAQ stock exchange. A study in the 1990s found that WD-40 was in four out of five households in America and selling over one million cans per week.

A leader displays courage that inspires others to keep trying and working even when failure has occurred and could occur again.

How many people or companies would try and fail at something thirty-nine times before they got it right? The name of this product proves that Larsen did.

HOW DO YOU RACE A TRIATHLON?

After I ran the Kona Marathon in 2000, I made a plan to race an Ironman triathlon. I did not know how long it would take me, but I had to start somewhere. I had a lot to work on—swimming, biking, and running. I borrowed a road bike that belonged to a staff member at my law firm. I had not ridden a bike in almost twenty years and that was just casual neighborhood cruising for a couple of miles. I had no idea what real cyclists did to ride and race forty, sixty, or a hundred miles. In 2000 the Internet was barely functioning, thus I could not just Google a YouTube video or find people to teach and inspire me. I visited local cycling shops and tried to tap into any local cycling groups and rides, but I did not feel qualified to join any until I was ready. So I just road miles alone, trying to build up endurance and cycling strength.

I planned to race my first triathlon in September 2001. It was just an Olympic-distance event at Kiawah Island, South Carolina, only a few hours from my home. The swim would be 1,500 meters, about nine tenths of a mile, in the surf of the Atlantic Ocean, then bike for 24 miles, and then run 6.2 miles. Easy. Piece of cake.

In 2001 I trained for that race like it was the Ironman. I had almost a year to train, and I felt like I needed it.

WHEN IN ROME ... RUN A MARATHON

To help prepare in March 2001 I ran my second marathon as another fund-raiser for the ADA. This one was in Rome, Italy. Like the marathon in Hawaii the previous year, Rome was a nice place to be when you finish and also raise money for a diabetes charity.

It was also a good way to tour the ancient city. The race started at the base of the most awe-inspiring symbol of the Roman Empire—the ancient Colosseum. I felt like I was a gladiator running for my life with fifteen thousand loud Italians running with me. In Italy people shouting at each other is called a conversation. I ran by St. Peter's Basilica at the Vatican, the Spanish Steps, the Trevi Fountain, the Pantheon, the Circus Maximus of *Ben Hur* fame, and finally back to the Colosseum. I finished that marathon over twenty minutes faster than my first one in Hawaii just eight months before. I was happy with my improvement, but I still wondered if I could do my larger goal one day—the Ironman triathlon.

A few weeks after the Rome marathon I rode a charity bike ride of about seventy-five miles for the ADA, another diabetes fund-raiser. I had never ridden that far in my life. Hundreds of people, some real cyclists and some just beginners like me, were on this charity ride. After about fifty miles I was following two guys on a flat stretch of road. We were not in the lead, but we were going pretty fast up toward the front. I was happy to hitch my wagon to these guys and see how long I could hang with them. I noticed that they had fancy cycling shoes with cleats that clipped into their pedals and snazzy matching uniforms (called kits) from their local cycling club or team. They rode shiny, cool, expensive road bikes. They looked like they knew what they were doing.

I, on the other hand, was impressively clad in my only pair of plain black cycling shorts that I had bought off the rack at a local bike shop. I wore the cycling jersey they gave me at the start for signing up. I was riding the fifteen-year-old road bike that I had borrowed several months ago, with gear shifters on the down tube of the frame rather than on the handlebars like current designs. The orange paint was faded and accented with touches of rust and road grime.

But by far the best parts of my cycling getup were my running shoes. My bike had the old-school leather straps on the pedals, like I was riding in the 1956 Tour de France. I did not have cycling shoes that clipped into real official cycling pedals like these roadies that I was tailing. And lest anyone overlook all those glaring signs of rookie-dom, the most obvious sign was my unshaven hairy legs. I did not look the part. But I was making it work.

As we pedaled I noticed that they would chat with each other in front of me and occasionally glance at me behind them. *Hi guys. Just me here. In my running shoes. Nothing to see back here. Carry on. Happy to be tagging along for the ride. Nice weather, isn't it?*

They would occasionally rotate and ride behind me, but as soon as they did, I would immediately rotate behind them. It was much easier to ride behind them rather than face the wind, called "pulling"—as in pulling the train—in the front. After each of these guys would ride a few minutes in front of me while I was tucked in behind them, my front wheel about twelve inches from their back wheel, I noticed that they would look over their shoulder at me. Sometimes they would flick their elbow or head forward.

I had no idea why they were doing that. With the wind blowing, whistling through my cycling helmet, riding over twenty miles per hour with cars driving by occasionally, you can't really hear much, so nonverbal communication is required in cycling. That arm and head movement meant something, but I didn't know what it was. Our little dance drifted down the road. I never lead more than about fifteen seconds.

After about twenty minutes of this, the two of them got in front of me, had some conversation, and accelerated suddenly. I gunned it hard to try to stay with them. *Hey guys! Wait up! Slow down! I can't keep up!* But they were hammering up the road and soon were fifty yards, and then a hundred yards, in front of me. They had dropped me.

It was some time later that I realized what had happened. I was such a rookie about cycling. I did not realize that when riding in a group of three or more, called a pace line, it is expected that each rider will take a turn "pulling" at the front, blocking the wind for the others, so the pace stays high and the others can rest and recover by drafting behind until their turn at the front again. But I had just sat in the back the whole time, drafting and never taking my turn at the front. It's called "sitting in"—not cool.

I'm sure I made it worse with my running shoes, hairy legs, and a beginner outfit on a dingy, old borrowed bike, when I should have been several miles behind them with the rest of the cycling newbies. But these guys didn't talk to me and seemed a bit standoffish and snooty cruising down the road with their fancy bikes and outfits. When they left me, I slowed and soon got absorbed by a larger group from behind and made my way to the finish with them. Another sport, another lesson learned.

In addition to running and riding, that summer I swam laps at a local outdoor pool after working all day at my law office. I had no lessons on proper swim form and stroke technique. I found a book on triathlon training for beginners that offered suggested workouts. My first attempts to swim just a few laps, only a hundred yards, ended with me hanging onto the wall at the end of the pool out of breath. *How am I going to swim almost a mile in the ocean? How do Ironman triathletes swim 2.4 miles?*

KEEP YOUR DAY JOB AS AN ATTORNEY

While all of this triathlon training was going on, the summer of 2001 was also a busy and important one for my professional career as an attorney. I was thirty-four years old and only seven years out of law school, still relatively young in the legal profession even though I had made partner early. That year I was working with several senior attorneys in my firm for our client, Unisys Computer Corporation, a large multinational computer company, in a lawsuit involving hundreds of millions of dollars. After many years of litigation, the case was now on appeal before the Supreme Court of South Carolina. The client asked me to present the oral argument before the Supreme Court rather than my two more experienced partners who each had been practicing law for over thirty years. I was honored and flattered by the opportunity. Most lawyers go their entire career without ever having the opportunity to make an oral argument to the highest court in the state.

On June 6, 2001, I stood below five Supreme Court justices staring down at me in black robes from the bench, peppering me with legal questions about constitutional law and statutory interpretation of the state procurement code. But I loved the challenge and relished the honor of this opportunity. I had to keep my day job as a lawyer.

In addition to all of the training to improve in the three sports, I had to carefully practice ways to manage my blood sugar during each of them. I had recently started using an insulin pump. It was a device about the size of a pager holding a cartridge of insulin with a flexible rubber tube about two feet long that was attached to an infusion set in my skin. I would have to change the infusion set every three days, a painful procedure jamming that big needle in my belly, but it eliminated the multiple daily injections of insulin. The insulin now just flowed through the rubber tube planted in my skin. It was a cumbersome device, with the rubber tube dangling off of me, and I often got it snagged on a passing door knob and jerked myself around or ripped the infusion set out of my skin.

Workouts with the pump required some planning. It was not waterproof, so I could not wear it swimming (or in the shower). I just had to hope the infusion set did not come off during the swim so I could reconnect the pump in the transition before the bike. I practiced this many times during training. I experimented with various tacky, sticky products and tapes trying to keep the adhesive patch of the infusion set attached to my skin in the water.

Where was I going to put the pump during the bike and run? When not racing, I would keep the pump in my pants pocket. But my triathlon outfit had no pockets, and I couldn't hold it for several hours while also holding the bike handlebars and running 6.2 miles. I would have to come up with a solution.

By the end of the summer, the triathlon was a few days away. I was nervous. I was excited. I was a triathlon rookie. And I was ready.

My journey to the Ironman was about to begin.

CHAPTER 7

GET TO THE STARTING LINE

Topic: Achieving Goals

I stood on the beach in the predawn darkness at the start of my first triathlon in September 2001, staring out at the Atlantic Ocean as the sun came up on the horizon. The race was on Kiawah Island, about twenty-five miles south of Charleston, SC. The wind blew and the waves crashed on the beach. It was just an Olympic-distance race, only a 1,500-meter swim, 24-mile bike, and 6.2-mile run, but I was nervous. It felt like an Ironman to me staring out at the ocean.

I could see the first turn buoy, a large inflated orange triangle, bobbing and swaying in the swells of the ocean just past the breakers about 250 meters out from the beach. We would swim out to that buoy, turn right, swim about a thousand meters parallel to the beach, turn right at another buoy, and swim about 250 meters back to shore. It was just 1,500 meters, about nine tenths of a mile, but it looked a lot longer in the ocean than it had in the pool.

Where are the lane ropes to stop all the waves? And the little black line at the bottom to keep me going in the right direction?

As the sun rose I finally got a look at the other four hundred or so athletes standing around me. The first thing I noticed was that they all wore wetsuits. I wasn't wearing a wetsuit. I didn't have a wetsuit. I didn't know you were supposed to wear a wetsuit or why you would want to.

It was September in South Carolina. The air and ocean were still pretty warm from the summer.

You wear wetsuits in cool-water triathlons to keep yourself warm. But the neoprene rubber also provides some buoyancy, making it easier and faster to swim. So triathletes generally always want to wear wetsuits if the water temperature is cool enough to be "wetsuit legal," usually around seventy-two degrees or below. If it's warmer than that, wetsuits are not allowed.

You can't just borrow a water skiing wetsuit from your friend or rent one from a dive shop. Swimming wetsuits are thinner to allow proper flexibility for a swim stroke. They are also very expensive at several hundred dollars. I was learning that the right gear makes you faster, but I was not ready to drop that kind of cash in my first race. I'd be swimming the old-fashioned way, *au naturel*, nothing but skin. I guess I wasn't completely au naturel. I did have on shorts.

Another thing I had noticed in the transition area prior to the race was that most of the male competitors had shaved legs—and very fit legs at that, not a whisk of hair in sight. Some of them could have thrown on a pair of heels and looked like a chorus line from the Rockettes. *What's with these cyclists and triathletes always shaving their legs?*

I had not shaved my legs. I felt like a caveman.

So here I was: wetsuitless, with hairy gorilla legs, standing among hundreds of black-rubber-wetsuit-wearing triathletes, like a bunch of seals standing on the beach, staring at the pounding surf before my first triathlon. I felt like I stuck out, and I probably did. I looked like such a beginner—kinda nervous. And I needed to pee.

Maybe I should have started with a shorter triathlon. Maybe my first one should have been a pool swim or a nice calm lake, rather than the ocean.

But I had made it to the starting line.

In all of my years of racing Ironman triathlons after that, the most difficult time was always the nerves before the start. Water is intimidating. Open water, roaring oceans and large lakes, can be scary. Many people tell me that they wish that they could do a triathlon, but they cannot swim. Actually they can swim, but they are just afraid of the long swim in open water.

DO IT SCARED

It's okay to be scared. It's the fear of the unknown. And that fear is what makes it great when you reach the finish line. As Tom Hanks's character said in the movie *A League of Their Own*, "It's *supposed* to be hard. If it wasn't hard, everyone would do it. The hard is what makes it great!"

Do it scared. You can't be courageous unless first you are scared.

How many times have you been afraid to start something because you were scared? How many times have you been afraid to do something because you might look like a beginner, look stupid, or feel stupid? It happens to all of us. Even after I was on the US national team for long-distance triathlon, I was nervous, maybe even a bit scared, before every triathlon, just like I was before my very first one. There was always someone better than me. Both the beginners and the pros are nervous and scared. It's okay to be scared. It's okay to be nervous. It's okay to be intimidated. Just know that you are not the only one who feels that way. That's the attitude that makes successful people and high achievers overcome fears and reach their finish lines.

Do it scared. You can't be courageous unless first you are scared.

The late Zig Ziglar, an iconic motivational speaker, once said, "You don't have to be great to start, but you have to start to be great."

Once you start, you're halfway done. Like many things in life, not just a triathlon, getting to the starting line is the hardest part. Most of the hard work happens before you start.

You don't have to be great to start, but you have to start to be great.

You have to overcome the doubts, fears, and obstacles for months to make it to the starting line of the first day of school, of a new job, or to the gym. It's easier to quit before you start because you have not made a commitment and no one will know you never tried. It can feel safer not to start, because at least we know that we won't fail.

Whether it's a race, the start of school, or a new career, just get to the starting line. Do not worry that you don't have a wetsuit and everyone else does. Do not worry that you have diabetes and no one else does. Do not worry that you are not the smartest and don't have all the latest gear and equipment yet. That will come. And it makes a more interesting story when you're a champion one day and can say at your press conference, "I may look like I know what I'm doing now, but you should have seen me when I started."

Getting to the starting line starts with your "ignition moment." That's the moment I discuss in this book regarding finish line vision. As Daniel Coyle describes in his book, *The Talent Code*, the ignition moment is "a mysterious burst, an awakening … lightning flashes of image and emotion, evolution-built neural programs that tap into the mind's vast reserves of energy and attention. Ignition is the set of signals and subconscious forces that create our identity; the moments that lead us to say *that is who I want to be.*"

This ignition is generated by the outside world, not from within. You see something or someone and say, "If she can do it, why can't I?" Something ignites the fire in you. You link your identity to a high-performing person, and that motivation starts burning in you: "I want to be like that."

My triathlon ignition moment was sparked when that runner at the finish line of the Kona Marathon told me about the Ironman triathlon. I say it sparked because it did not ignite like a rocket in a roaring blaze of motivation … yet. But the flame was lit. Later, that smoldering ember was stoked the first time I saw highlights of the Ironman on television. That gave it emotion. Now I could feel it burn inside me. *I want to be like them.* It burned hotter and hotter. No way it was going to go out now.

That is motivation overtaking you. That is your finish line vision taking hold of you. That will keep you motivated. You know where you want to be. See the end first. All you have to do now is start.

The starting line is harder to cross than the finish line. It's not as scary after you start.

Will Rogers said, "Even if you're on the right track, you'll get run over if you just sit there."

If you are trying to start a good habit or working for a goal, you need to get over that initial effort to just get

> **The starting line is harder to cross than the finish line. It's not as scary after you start.**

started. In chemistry that is called "activation energy." It is the initial spark required to create a reaction. Humans need activation energy too. It is the physical and mental energy to overcome inertia and indecision, to kick-start a good habit and get off the path of least resistance, the one where you continue to just sit there.

Get that bike out of the garage. Get the guitar and put it in your living room so it is easy for you to practice. Put on your workout clothes and go to the gym for the first time. Then reduce the activation energy required to keep doing it: keep your bike cleaned, tires pumped, and easy to access each day, not trapped and cluttered behind boxes. Pack your gym bag of workout clothes and supplies every night and keep it in your car every day, even if you think you will not have time to work out. Many times I thought my day would be too busy to work out, and a meeting got cancelled and I was cursing myself for not having my workout clothes with me.

After several times you realize you can do it. Sometimes you need inspiration to start a creative project, and sometimes you have to just force it. I had to force myself to start writing this book. I had pages and pages of notes and an outline that I carried around with me for years.

Audiences attending my speaking engagements constantly asked me to write a book. My outline became so cluttered and full of quotes and citations, examples and sources, that I almost could not read it. I did not start, because I kept finding something else I wanted to say. I wanted to start, but I did not know how to start. Finally, I decided that I was just going to write a short digital book, an e-book, that would in essence be a summary. That broke the barrier. Soon I was writing and on my way, and here we are.

Start small and work your way up. Focus on the short-term goal, but keep thinking about your bigger finish line vision. It was just like first doing that shorter Olympic-distance triathlon, when my real goal was the much longer Ironman.

_____

The biggest nation in the world is procrastination.

The biggest nation in the world is procrastination. Do not let time pass you by, because it will if you do not start. Consider the somewhat-woeful lyrics from the song "Time" by Hootie and the Blowfish.

Time, why you punish me?
Like a wave bashing into the shore
You wash away my dreams.
Time, why you walk away,
Like a friend with somewhere to go,
You left me crying...

Don't let time punish you, wash away your dream, or leave you like a friend with somewhere else to go. Get to the starting line.

Force yourself to start by creating a deadline. You would not have studied in school if you did not have a test coming up. Enter a competition. Sign up for a class. Whatever your dream is, make a commitment to do something related to it that will make you start working on it. If you have a fitness goal, sign up for a race, a walk, or anything to put a deadline on your calendar. Every race in my career was a looming deadline in the distance. It gave me motivation to train every day because I wanted to be ready and do well on race day, but I also did not want to suffer and hurt on race day being out of shape. Desire and fear both motivated me to keep me working. I would not have trained if I did not have a race in the future.

> **Force yourself to start by creating a deadline. You would not have studied in school if you did not have a test coming up. Enter a competition. Sign up for a class.**

THE KIAWAH TRIATHLON— WHO IS THAT GUY?

I came out of the ocean in my first triathlon at Kiawah Island in 2001, thrilled that I had just completed the swim. I ran into the transition and checked my blood sugar beside my bike. I had rigged up a homemade contraption to wear my insulin pump during the race. I found a pouch about the size of a beeper (I needed a beeper pouch because cell phones were the size of bricks in 2001) that was a perfect fit for my insulin pump. It had a Velcro closure flap so it would not fly open during the bike and run. Imagine trying to ride a bike and run with your cell phone in a pouch on a belt with a rubber tube from the phone attached to your stomach. This was 2001, before Apple had introduced the iPhone or iPod, so personal small electronic sport straps and holders did not exist. That was my look.

I had sewn that pouch onto an elastic strap and then stitched patches of Velcro onto that strap to keep it secured tightly around my waist during the bike and run. I'd spent some time at fabric stores and seamstress shops creating this one-of-a-kind insulin pump belt-thingy. I clicked the two-foot-long tube into the infusion set that was attached to my stomach with adhesive and its rubber tube lodged underneath my skin to deliver the insulin subcutaneously. Later in my racing career companies like Fuel Belt created snazzy belts with secure pouches and pockets for endurance athletes to carry sport bars, gels, keys, cell phones, children, kitchen sinks, and pianos on long training runs. But those products were not available in 2001. I may have missed my chance to make a gazillion dollars with my insulin pump belt gizmo.

This was all a big experiment to see how the logistics worked doing a triathlon with an insulin pump. Would the infusion set stay attached to my stomach? Would I be able to ride and run with the pump and its two-foot rubber tube around me? I had done plenty of test swims, rides, and runs in training so I felt confident everything would work. You have to figure things out yourself sometimes or just make it up and see what works. Necessity is the mother of invention.

One thing I noticed during the bike was that many of the athletes were riding triathlon bikes. These slick, fast, aerodynamic bikes had time-trial aerobars (handlebars) that placed their hands out in front of them in a streamlined aerodynamic tuck position like a downhill ski racer. I was riding a standard road bike, sitting up with my hands spread wide. I looked like I was carrying a laundry basket. My body caught the wind like one of those parachutes that pop out of the back of a dragster racing car to slow it down. Like the wetsuit, a triathlon bike would be another piece of equipment I would eventually have to buy to get faster.

There were many benefits from racing my first triathlon: getting over the beginner nerves, experiencing the pain and difficulty of the event for the first time, seeing some of the equipment to go faster, and testing my blood sugar for an event like this.

But the most significant benefit happened after I had finished the bike and was just starting to run the 10k (6.2-mile) run. I was tired from the swim and bike but thought I'd be okay for the run.

Leaving the bike-to-run transition (T2), in my first five hundred yards of running, I saw an athlete running toward me. The run course was an out-and-back route—leave the transition area to run 3.1 miles out and turn around and head back 3.1 miles to finish right by the transition. The first and last half mile was a straightaway on the beach so athletes would pass each other like cars going in opposite directions on a two-lane road. Running in sand is always tough.

I was just starting my run, and this guy coming at me was almost finished. He had already run 6.2 miles. He raced by me, heading the other way for the finish line. He looked like he was flying, just gliding across the sand like he was Luke Skywalker riding a hovercraft in *Star Wars Return of the Jedi*. His feet barely touched the ground, skipping lightly in a blur of speed. He had short, spiked blonde hair. He looked like a cross between rock singer Billy Idol and Ivan Drago from *Rocky IV*. There was no one in sight of him. He could have sat in a beach chair and had a cold drink enjoying the ocean breeze. He was so far out front it was almost ten minutes before I saw the guy in second place coming up behind him.

Who is that guy? Holy &%+@! He is fast! How did he do that? He looked like he was just cruising effortlessly, and he was destroying the field.

I learned another lesson during that run. Don't let you pride or your ego get wounded. In the first couple miles of running, a few athletes came up behind me and passed me. One of them was a female. Of course, my male ego kicked in. *No way I'm going to let this girl beat me.* So as she passed me I kicked it up a notch and tried to run with her. As I ran right behind her for about half a mile, trying to hold her faster pace, I noticed a couple benefits. First, she made me run faster, which helped my time. And second, she had really nice calves. I couldn't keep up with her and had to let her and her nice calves go, but it was worth the effort. I made a mental note to look for nice calves in a wife one day (among other qualities), and I'm pleased that I eventually found some good ones. Among the many lessons I learned in that first triathlon were don't let your ego get bruised, women might pass you, and maybe you'll see some nice calves when they do.

That day I finished my first Olympic-distance triathlon in two hours and forty-four minutes. It was not an impressive time by any means, only in the top half of the race, but I was happy. I was learning the sport and how to do it with diabetes. It took less time than running my first two marathons, but the pain and difficulty was greater. I loved it. It was three sports, not one, and three different challenges. I was now a triathlete, not just an aspiring triathlete. I was hooked, and I knew that I wanted to race the Ironman now. I also knew that an Ironman would take a lot more work and pain. This Olympic-distance race was only thirty miles. The Ironman race is 140.6 miles, almost five times longer. I would have to do this Olympic-distance race four times and still have another twenty miles to go.

That winner who cruised by me did it in exactly two hours. I'm sure he could have done it faster, but no one challenged him. He could have done the run twice and still beat me. I saw his name in the results after the race—Peter Kotland, from Travelers Rest, SC. *What? Travelers Rest?* That is a sleepy little country town just outside of my home in Greenville at the base of the Blue Ridge Mountains. *Who knew somebody that good lived just a few miles from me?* He looked like he should have just flown in from the Czech Republic, and that's what he sounded like. I heard him talking at the finish area after the race with a thick Eastern European accent. I could not tell where he was from, but he definitely did not grow up in upstate South Carolina in Travelers Rest. He not only looked but *sounded* like the intimidating Russian Ivan Drago. He seemed like he loved the sport for the pain it required and inflicted.

I wanted that feeling.

Peter Kotland. I'll remember that name.

I had no idea how important he would soon be to my success in Ironman racing.

CHAPTER 8

CREATE YOUR FINISH LINE VISION

Topics: Motivation, Leadership

A few months after racing my first short triathlon in 2001 I watched the NBC television highlight show of the Hawaii Ironman from Kona, the same location I had just run the Kona Marathon in June the year before—the one where I had vomited on the guy at the finish when he told me about the Ironman. An Ironman is too long to televise live, so NBC films portions of the Hawaii race and creates a ninety-minute highlight show every year. Even though there are dozens of Ironman triathlons raced around the world every year, the Hawaii race is the only one televised in the United States, and it's more of a feel-good story of the participants and the difficulty of the race. By the time it airs a month later everybody already knows who won.

The emotion and drama of the NBC broadcast is well produced. I watched that broadcast and felt the fire building inside me. I saw the videos of people running toward the finish line, exhausted and ecstatic, crying with tears of joy and pain for what they had accomplished and what they had overcome to reach that finish line.

I watched that mesmerized, thinking, *I want to feel that ... I will race the Ironman ... I will do that ... I will make it to the finish line.*

Watching that broadcast was my ignition moment. It created a vision in my mind of what it would be like—a finish line vision.

In the next ten years of my racing career I would ultimately race fourteen Ironman triathlons and spend three years on the US national team for long-distance triathlon at the ITU World Championships in Europe and Australia. I raced over twenty half Ironman triathlons; eight marathons, including three times at the Boston Marathon; and a bike race of over three thousand miles across the United States with my team to win the Race Across America. The Ironman is the longest, most grueling athletic competition in the world—a 2.4-mile swim, followed immediately by a 112-mile bike race, followed immediately by a full 26.2-mile marathon run, all in one day. It is a brutal, grueling test of strength, fitness, discipline, and endurance, but it is so much more than a physical test. It requires something to drive you to the finish line, something to draw you there, something deep in your soul that powers you long after you think your strength and fitness are gone. It tests your body and your mind.

What motivated me?

MY FINISH LINE VISION—THE LAST ONE HUNDRED METERS

I was motivated for each race by my finish line vision—the last one hundred meters. What I see and feel running down those last one hundred meters to the finish line is magic. Before I experienced it I imagined it, and when I experienced it the first time it was even better. All of the pain and difficulty it took to get there made it more powerful. It had taken every bit of strength that I had

> I was motivated for each race by my finish line vision—the last one hundred meters.

to reach that first Ironman finish line. I had joy and emotion unlike anything I had ever felt as I ran down those last meters to that line.

That first time was so vivid and real, and I wanted to do it again. I wanted more of it, to do it faster and better. It was a drug for my soul. I wanted that high again. I began to see it, feel it, and imagine it every day as I drove my car or trained in the months leading up the next race. With every stroke I made in the pool, training alone at 6:00 a.m., I imagined that feeling of the Ironman race eight or ten months in the future. I visualized my finish line moment, sweating in ninety-five-degree heat in July as I rode my bike a hundred miles up the Appalachian Mountains of South and North Carolina, alone with nothing but my thoughts and the pain in my legs pushing me higher and higher up the mountain, my lungs burning as I panted and gasped for oxygen. I thought about it as I ran fifteen miles at sunrise in the sleet and rain of winter, hearing nothing but the *tap tap tap* of my feet on the asphalt and the panting of my lungs. With each breath, I could hear the crowd and music blaring at the finish and the race announcer calling my name, taste the salty sweat on my lips, and feel the pain in my legs, as if I were at that race right now.

WHAT IS YOUR FINISH LINE VISION?

Do you have a moment that you want in your life?

Goals don't inspire us. Dreams do. Moments do. You can feel your dream deep down in your soul. A goal is just a number, an object, a benchmark to reach your dream. We cannot visualize a number, a weight, an income, or a title. Those are goals. You don't think about goals; you think about what it will be like when you reach them. You can visualize how you look at that weight and what you

> **Goals don't inspire us. Dreams do. Moments do. You can feel your dream deep down in your soul. A goal is just a number, an object, a benchmark to reach your dream.**

will be wearing at the party when everyone says, "Wow, look at her! She looks great!" You can visualize the new home for your family or the vacations with them when you have that job or income. You can visualize your small business open, with customers inside or orders coming in. You can visualize yourself hitting that shot, holding that trophy, crossing that finish line, or fishing with your son on a quiet lake one day.

We are inspired by these moments because they carry emotion and feeling that stimulate our senses and our heart. When you feel and see something, you want it more. You will work for that moment.

Your moment is your finish line vision.

When you feel and see something, you want it more. You will work for that moment. Your moment is your finish line vision.

When you plan a vacation, you visualize and imagine you and your family at the beach, on the amusement rides, touring the sites, on a hike, swimming in the water, or shopping. You will do the work—save money, research locations and activities, make travel reservations, work late and early, schedule time off work, find someone to feed your pets, stop the mail, and dozens of other tasks—to make it there and to live those moments.

You can visualize your wedding day: the people there, the venue, the music, your wedding dress or groom's attire, the wedding party, and the look of the reception. You will work for that vision for months, dieting and exercising to look your best; reserving the caterer, florist, and the venue; sending the invitations; and all of the other details to make your vision happen. You are working for that moment.

The same is true for career goals. Your goal may be to make a certain income or achieve a certain title in your company. But what motivates you are the moments you can imagine—the things you will spend your income on, the security you and your family will feel, and the respect and pride of being a leader and influencer in your new position. Those moments are your why, your purpose, your finish line vision.

Turn your goals into moments—something unique to you that you can visualize, feel, hear, and replay in your mind like a cherished memory from the past. That's what it means to have finish line vision. See the end first; visualize your moment when you are working to achieve it or when you need motivation to do that work. You become what you think about all day long. It will draw you like a magnet, and magnets never run out of power.

> **Turn your goals into moments—something unique to you that you can visualize, feel, hear, and replay in your mind like a cherished memory from the past. That's what it means to have finish line vision.**

Finish line vision is the same as the second habit in the bestseller book *The 7 Habits of Highly Effective People* by Stephen Covey: Begin with the end in mind. "To begin with the end in mind means to start with a clear understanding of your destination. It means to know where you're going so that you better understand where you are now and so that the steps you take are always in the right direction."

> **You become what you think about all day long. It will draw you like a magnet, and magnets never run out of power.**

Covey cites the work of Dr. Charles Garfield, who holds a PhD in psychology and a doctorate in mathematics and did extensive research on peak performers, both in athletics and business. He worked with NASA, watching astronauts simulate everything on earth before they went into space. Covey noted that "one of the main things Garfield's research showed was that almost all world-class athletes and other peak performers are visualizers. They see it; they feel it; they experience it before they actually do it. They begin with the end in mind."

This concept of finish line vision is not just a motivational platitude or self-help slogan. It's rooted in science and biology. It's how our brains work. We can relive experiences through memory by recalling people, color, sounds, feelings, and surroundings in surreal clarity. Just like memories from the past, our brains can also create images for events we want to occur in the future. Our brain creates and stores those visions like files on our cerebral hard drive.

But how do some people achieve those dreams—high achievers who work diligently and overcome obstacles, staying motivated and focused when others never get started or quit before achieving them?

Neurosurgeons and psychologists have studied this. Dr. Karl Pribram was a neurosurgeon and professor of psychology and psychiatry at Stanford University. He passed away in 2015 at the age of ninety-five. He consulted on a program called *The Neuropsychology of Achievement* that asserts that high achievers have "sensory goal vision"—visualizing what they want to achieve and using that vision to stay motivated and disciplined, overcoming obstacles along the way. It is a practice of translating a goal into a moment with sound, touch, taste, smell, and emotion, pre-living the achievement of that goal in rich sensory detail. You want that moment because you created it, it is important and unique to you, and you can see it and feel it.

In his excellent book, *The Happiness Advantage*, Harvard professor Shawn Achor researched how we can reprogram our brains to visualize. The concept is called neuroplasticity. Our brain is malleable and can change throughout our lives. For example, before modern GPS automobile navigation systems, researchers proved that London cab drivers developed more cerebral hippocampi, the brain structure devoted to spatial memory, than the average person. Why? Because the streets of London are not a grid of parallel and perpendicular streets like Manhattan or Washington, DC. London is a byzantine maze of disjointed small streets that require a cab driver to have a vast internal special memory. These cab drivers weren't born that way; they just developed that brain function later in life to perform their jobs. They learned to visualize the streets like a map, drop a pin on a location, and find a route like Google Maps does when you input an address. They became visualizers.

Now that is some deep neuropsychology. I can hear some of you saying, "I'm just not a visual person. My brain doesn't work that way. This is all psychobabble nonsense." I would have thought that too until I realized I was doing it.

I was curious. *How do I stay motivated to hurt myself in so many hours of painful and exhausting workouts? And why do I love it and want to do it again tomorrow?* When I told people I was motivated by my finish line vision, I could not explain why or how it worked, just that it did. So I went looking for science and research that explained why my finish line vision was so powerful for me.

But as Christopher McDougall writes in his bestseller *Born to Run*, "You can spout any theory you want about human performance, but in the end, you can't make the shift from appealing notion to empirical fact if you don't come up with the goods."

Whether it is a proven medical fact or just an interesting theory, I know it is real because I have felt that attraction force of my finish line vision. I've felt it in different ways that you will see in this book—to race Ironman triathlons, to make my high school basketball team, and to become a professional speaker on a main stage in front of thousands.

What this means for you is that you will work for your dreams, for your moment. You will work your finish line vision.

Even though your dream is what you want, you must have goals to achieve that dream. Two-time Ironman triathlon world champion Chris McCormack said, "A goal is a dream with a plan." Until you have a plan to achieve it, a dream is just a

Until you have a plan to achieve it, a dream is just a fantasy.

fantasy. Psychologists call a dream without a plan "positive fantasizing." Angela Duckworth, PhD and professor of psychology at the University of Pennsylvania, states in her book *Grit: The Power of Passion and Perseverance*, "Indulging in visions of positive future without figuring out how to get there, chiefly by considering what obstacles stand in the way, has short-term payoff but long-term costs. In the short-term, you feel pretty great about your aspiration … in the long-term you live with disappointment of not having achieved your goal."

Success comes from a combination of why, what, and when. Your finish line vision is your *why*. It is your mission and purpose. It gives you motivation and meaning.

Goals are the *what* and the *when*. Goals like "I want to lose weight" or "We will improve our sales" give little tangible direction. There is no way to chart progress or achieve incremental satisfaction. Specific goals provide clarity, starting with where an individual or organization is currently (*x*), where they want to be (*y*), and a target date for when that goal will be achieved. These are called "*x* to *y* by when" goals. For example, in my plan to race the Ironman I set goals like, "I will race an Olympic-distance triathlon and two half Ironman-distance triathlons the year leading up to the Ironman."

This concept is taught to students and educators in the book *The Leader in Me,* by Sean Covey, Stephen Covey, Muriel Summers, and David Hatch. The book offers a program for improving performance in students and teachers in schools based on Stephen Covey's seven principles. I encourage my kids to improve their performance in school with "*x* to *y* by when" goals like, "I will move up two reading levels by the end of this grade period." To improve diabetes management a person may set goals like, "I will test my blood sugar at least five times a day, eat healthy meals every day, and exercise five days a week to have an A1C reading of 7.0 in six months."

Vision without execution is just hallucination or delusion. I had a dream to race the Ironman, but within that I had a specific plan to finish under a certain time and even more specific goals to finish the swim in a certain time, bike a certain speed, maintain an average heart rate, and keep a certain run pace and run time.

I had a plan to finish certain shorter races before the Ironman. But those intermediate goals did not inspire me. My dream did. My finish line vision did.

Vision without execution is just hallucination or delusion.

Now when you think about your finish line, you are not overlooking your next opponent or already planning your victory party. You still have day-to-day tasks that get your full attention, like the twice-daily workouts I had with specific targets for each. Sometimes I hit those workout targets and sometimes I missed them and was disappointed, but I attacked them with vengeance because they were steps to my finish line vision. Similarly, an athlete or team can, and must, give complete attention to the next opponent or workout but always have that burning fire inside of a long-term championship dream motivating them. A student studies for each test, every class, every year, while visualizing that graduation ceremony in the future. A business owner must work each day on essential tasks while visualizing the new location or other moments of success.

EXPECT TO SUCCEED

The beauty, and power, of finish line vision is that it is success thinking. It is positive. You expect to succeed. You are not thinking about (or over-whelmed by) the difficult tasks ahead of you—the years of difficult school, miles of painful running, months of workouts and diets, years of career building, and months of practice. You

The beauty, and power, of finish line vision is that it is success thinking. It is positive. You expect to succeed.

are thinking about the joy you will feel when you achieve your dream. That creates happiness in you before you even achieve it. Happiness and positive thinking will *create* success, so keep thinking about *why* you are doing it rather than how hard it is (or will be) to do it.

Your finish line vision may come from watching others achieve something you want in life, business, or art. Daniel Coyle calls this "windshield phenomenon"—igniting and refueling your motivation by filling your windshield with vivid images of your future self. It may come from a movie, video, photograph, or live event. It sparks an intense, nearly unconscious response in you that burns. *I want to be like them. I want to be that.* Bookmark and save those videos and photos and look at them before you work out, go to bed, or practice your instrument. They are your finish line visions.

Muhammad Ali is regarded by many as the greatest boxer in history. He was loved for his personality, entertaining showmanship boxing style, social activism, and bravado, shouting "I am the greatest!" when he won the heavyweight championship multiple times. But his most profound admission was when he said, "I am the greatest. I said that even before I knew I was." He expected to succeed.

Our *expectation* of what will happen can actually affect what *does* happen. Psychologists call this "expectancy theory." According to Dr. Marcel Kinsbourne, a neuroscientist at the New School for Social Research in New York, our expectations create brain patterns that are just as real as those created by real events. In one interesting study, Yale researchers told half of the cleaning staff of different hotels how much exercise they were getting every day at work and the calories burned by vacuuming and other daily activities. The other half of the cleaning staff at the same hotel, doing the same work—the control group—was not given this good news. Several weeks later, researchers found that those who had been told how much exercise they were getting had actually lost weight and even had drops in their cholesterol, even though they had done the same work as the control group. The only difference was how their brains perceived the work they were doing. Their mind changed their bodies. Of course, the optimistic belief that they were losing weight and becoming healthier also may have had the positive effect of influencing them to eat healthier and make healthier choices daily in their lives.

This doesn't mean that all you have to do is sit back and expect good things to happen and do nothing to make them happen. It just changes your attitude about the work you must do. Dreams don't work unless you do.

Endurance training is great for developing and nurturing visions of your success because it often involves solitary workouts of several hours—long runs, bike rides, swims, walks,

Dreams don't work unless you do.

rowing, whatever you enjoy—even if you are not an endurance athlete. It helps you cut out the distractions of everything else in your life and just focus and visualize, shutting off the brain and listening to your breath going in and out. It is essentially meditating while you exercise. Later in this book I'll talk about how one of the keys to work–life balance is maximizing your time, doing two complimentary things at once. We are busy people, so don't just visualize—visualize and exercise at the same time.

You don't have to be a marathon runner or Ironman triathlete. Dr. George Sheehan is considered by many to be the father of the recreational running movement. He was a cardiologist who started running in his midforties in the 1970s. He wrote a weekly column in his local newspaper about running and eventually became medical editor and writer for *Runner's World* magazine until he died in 1993 at the age of seventy-four. He said, "For every runner who tours the world running marathons, there are thousands who run to hear the leaves and listen to the rain, and look to the day when it is suddenly as easy as a bird in flight. For them, the sport is not a test but a therapy, not a trial but a reward, not a question but an answer."

Alex Honnold is one of the world's best free climbers, climbing the world's tallest cliffs free solo (i.e., without a rope), holding on with nothing but his hands and feet and climbing three thousand feet straight up walls like Yosemite's Half Dome, El Capitan, and Mexico's El Sendero Luminoso. In 2015 he told *Sports Illustrated* that even though his sport requires strength training, he does long-distance endurance runs just to prepare his mind. "I spend all of the time [running] thinking and visualizing and fantasizing about my objective," he says. "It's a long, slow process, but eventually something that's a crazy fantasy goes to being inevitable."

Visualize your dream while you exercise, while you practice, while you work for it.

Visualize your dream while you exercise, while you practice, while you work for it.

Many young athletes visualize themselves playing tennis on center court at Flushing Meadow in the US Open, walking up to the eighteenth hole at Augusta National in the Masters, or making a game-winning catch in the Super Bowl. Performing artists visualize themselves playing a violin solo with the New York Philharmonic Orchestra or singing on stage before thousands of people. While those may be the pinnacle of world-class achievement and may not be your dream, your finish line vision is unique to you. It is just as powerful if you can visualize yourself running out onto the floor of your high school gymnasium in front of packed bleachers, wearing the uniform of your state champion high school varsity basketball team; delivering a motivational speech to thousands of enthusiastic people listening intently with energy and a drive to achieve; crossing the finish line of the Ironman triathlon; or racing for the US national team with "USA" across your chest in a foreign country. Those have been some of my finish line visions. And I have achieved all of them.

Can you visualize yourself in six months wearing a swimsuit at the beach or pool, with a new body, wearing a new outfit, and with all eyes noticing the new you? That finish line vision will get you off the couch and exercising in the cold of January or the heat of July and will help you turn down that dessert or unhealthy meal and replace it with a healthy serving of fruit and vegetables.

Individuals don't just create success for themselves; good leaders create a finish line vision for others. Coaches can do it for players, corporate executives for employees, teachers for students, and parents for their family.

FINISH LINE VISION FOR COACHES

Coaches must be both managers and leaders. Yes, coaches are managers by teaching techniques, workouts, drills, and game-day strategies and plays. But the great coaches are great leaders when they give their athletes a finish line vision—something to play for, to work for.

The late Jim Valvano was the coach of the North Carolina State men's basketball team from 1980 to 1990. His team won the NCAA National Championship in 1983 in what is considered to be the greatest upset in college basketball history against the University of Houston, the tournament's number-one seed riding a twenty-six-game win streak with two future Hall of Famers. This championship game upset was preceded by an even more dramatic and improbable run of victories by Valvano's team to even get into the tournament as a lowly number-nine seed and then to make it all the way to the championship game.

NC State was not considered a very good team, having lost ten regular season games and barely finishing above .500 in the Atlantic Coast Conference (ACC). They had to win three straight games in the ACC conference tournament to even qualify for the NCAA tournament, including beating the defending national champion North Carolina Tar Heels, led by future Hall of Famers Michael Jordan, James Worthy, and Sam Perkins. They also had to beat the University of Virginia, led by 7'4" Ralph Sampson, the two-time college national player of the year. To win the national championship, Valvano's mediocre team won nine straight games in the ACC and NCAA tournaments against the country's best teams—six games by three points or less, two games in overtime, and the national championship game on a last-second miracle shot at the buzzer.

How did Valvano lead his team to do it? How did he do that in the face of such overwhelming odds when nothing would indicate his average team had the ability to do it? How did he light that fire, get them to keep believing each game, sustain that determination, and repeat it over and over again until they reached their dream?

He had created a finish line vision before the season had even started.

Valvano had a dream of winning the national championship. He wanted his players to see his dream, to feel it, and to want it like he did. In the ESPN Films documentary *Survive and Advance* about the NC State 1983 tournament run, Derrick Whittenburg, a guard on that team said, "Coach Valvano was a big dreamer. From day one, he sat us all in a circle, telling us his goal was to win the national championship." Forward Thurl Bailey said "He starts telling us this dream he has. 'I know I'm going to win a national championship.' Who says that on day one? But the more he spoke, the more we sat up, the more we listened. He painted a picture for us. He said, 'If I can get you to see what I'm seeing, to dream what I'm dreaming, we can get there.'"

Valvano did more than just *tell* his players his vision. He took another step by allowing them to experience it, to feel it, and imprinting that finish line vision in their minds. In basketball it's a tradition for the winning team to cut down the nets after the championship game, with each player and coach climbing a ladder to cut a strand in a prolonged victory celebration for fans, media, and television. In that documentary, Valvano says, "We have one practice every year, where all they do is come up on the court. There's no balls, no drills. All we do is practice cutting the net down. We have gold scissors. All we do is cut the nets down. ... That's my dream, cutting the nets down. And I am going to dream my dream."

Coach Valvano got his players to feel his dream, his finish line vision, and want it like he did. He led them to it in 1983.

Over thirty years later another coach did the same thing. Doc Rivers became the coach of the Los Angeles Clippers NBA basketball team in 2013. Before his first meeting with his team, he mapped out a parade route through Los Angeles and told his team to visualize themselves taking that ride as NBA champions. The crosstown mighty Los Angeles Lakers have won the NBA championship sixteen times. The Clippers? Never. Before the next season Coach Rivers gathered them in a suite in the Staples Center, the arena where the Clippers play their games, to watch the Los Angeles Kings NHL professional hockey team raise their Stanley Cup championship banner. He told them to take in that moment and visualize themselves raising their own banner. Since Coach Rivers took over, the Clippers have been title contenders, among the league leaders in wins with packed arenas, and have reached much more success than their once-mighty counterpart Lakers who have sunk to one of the worst-performing teams in the league.

Are you the leader of an upstart company with a mighty competitor in the market whose product has dominated your industry for years? Is your competitor so big and successful that it barely notices you because it does not need to and could crush you with its market power or just let you starve yourself into obscurity out of business?

It takes patience and perseverance to reach a finish line. It takes failure and disappointment, pain and

If you are a leader, create a finish line vision for your team, your employees, your family. Give them a vision, a moment to think about, a dream to work for.

frustration, and hard work. That's what makes achieving it so much more fulfilling.

If you are a leader, create a finish line vision for your team, your employees, your family. Give them a vision, a moment to think about, a dream to work for.

FINISH LINE VISION FOR BUSINESS LEADERS

In business, your company may be facing difficult competition entering a new market with several big players already dominating with established products. Create a finish line vision for your employees where you are the market leader with the best or new products. Create a culture that is based on company core values and customer service.

For example, in 1999 Tony Hsieh was asked to invest in a new company with the plan to sell shoes online. He initially rejected the idea but eventually joined the start-up company Zappos as CEO in 2000. By 2009 Zappos's revenues reached $1 billion and Amazon.com acquired the company for approximately $1.2 billion. In his 2010 book *Delivering Happiness*, about his life and building Zappos, he counseled business leaders that your company's culture is your brand. Build your company's workplace culture and you build your company's brand. He had a vision for Zappos, and he advises business leaders to "chase the vision, not the money."

In her book *Broadcasting Happiness*, author Michelle Gielan researched how happiness and company culture improve performance in the workplace. Gielan's research shows when employees are passionate, happy, and engaged about a company's goal, sales and productivity increase and stress decreases. Happiness leads to sales, not the other way around.

LEADERSHIP VERSUS MANAGEMENT

There is a difference between leadership and management. Organizations need both, and often the same person must fill both roles, particularly in small organizations where staff and personnel are limited. But many organizations are overmanaged and underled.

A leader looks at the destination and creates the long-term finish line vision: "This is where we will go." A manager must look at the day-to-day tasks to get there (e.g. "Are we on budget?"). Leadership is about inspiring people; management is about optimizing people, like plant and equipment resources, shipping resources, and accounting and payroll resources. The leader makes connections and goals; the manager makes schedules and deadlines. A leader builds relationships and complimentary teams; the manager builds complimentary systems.

Even simple nomenclature and titles can create a leadership mind-set. It frustrated me that my large law firm used the terms "management committee" and "managing partner" for the group and person who made decisions about the firm. Use terms like "leadership committee" and titles such as "regional leader" and "department leader" rather than "manager." Every time people are referred to or introduce themselves as leaders they realize and remind themselves, "I'm supposed to be leading, not just managing. … I'm supposed to be taking my team somewhere, not just maintaining the status quo. … I'm supposed to be leading my team to new heights, not just making sure things don't fall apart."

Leaders also inspire others to become leaders, not just keep themselves in power. It has been said, "A sign of a good leader is not how many followers you have but how many leaders you create."

A sign of a good leader is not how many followers you have but how many leaders you create.

FINISH LINE VISION FOR TEACHERS

Teachers can create a finish line vision for students. Take them to a graduation ceremony. Let them visualize themselves walking across that stage to receive their diploma, dressed in a cap and gown with a sash for graduating with honors, in front of thousands of classmates, family, and friends smiling and proud of them. I saw a quote recently in the teachers' lounge of a school: "In years to come, students may forget what you taught them, but they will always remember how you made them feel." Make them feel what it is to succeed. Give them a finish line vision.

> **In years to come, students may forget what you taught them, but they will always remember how you made them feel.**

FINISH LINE VISION FOR PARENTS

Give your family a finish line vision. Take them to a local running race or athletic event to see other healthy people in your community enjoying and celebrating crossing the finish line so that your kids and spouse will say, "We can be like that." Take them to a neighborhood and say, "This is why we are saving as a family, so we can live here one day." Show them athletes, dancers, musicians, or singers, and tell them that playing video games, texting, and watching television will not improve their grades, their skills as an athlete or artist, or their life. Lead them by example in the way you live your life. Go to sleep reading books with them rather than watching television. Exercise and eat healthy. Kids will remember what they see you do more than what you say.

Think about your finish line moment—how it will feel and the pride, joy, and satisfaction that will envelope you. That is your finish line vision. Hold onto it and think about it every day when you struggle to keep working, studying, exercising, dieting, or practicing. Your finish line vision is calling you.

Now let's talk about how you will get there.

CHAPTER 9

FIND A COACH

Topic: Keep Improving

After completing the short Kiawah Olympic-distance triathlon in September 2001, I was pumped up and motivated to do an Ironman. But I had to find one. The closest one was Ironman Florida in Panama City Beach in November. That looked promising. It was close enough to drive from my home in South Carolina. Hopping on a plane with your running shoes for a marathon is pretty easy, but packing a bike and gear for an Ironman takes some experience. I didn't need the stress and pressure of air travel for my first one. In 2001 there were only five official Ironman races in North America: Ironman Florida, Ironman Lake Placid New York, Ironman Canada, Ironman Utah (now defunct), and Ironman Wisconsin. I say "official" because these races were all licensed and sanctioned by the World Triathlon Corporation (WTC), owners of the Ironman trademark brand, the same brand name licensed to Timex for the watches. Only these races could call themselves an "Ironman" triathlon. I wanted to hear the classic announcement from the race announcer at the finish line, after years of training and hours of suffering: "Jay Hewitt! You are an Ironman!" I expected I might cry. Then I would pass out or die. But I would die happy.

Ironman triathlons were not very well known or popular in 2001, but they have become a lot more popular with the endurance racing now. The Ironman brand was purchased by a venture capital company in 2007 that injected millions of dollars into it, marketing and recruiting more people to try them, so they could make more money. It must have worked because in 2015 WTC was sold again to a Chinese investor for $900 million. The entry fee for most Ironman races around the world is over $500. Staging a 140-mile race is incredibly expensive and the logistics are enormous to staff a 2.4-mile swim course, a 112-mile bike course, and a marathon, all on open water and public roads. The permits, volunteers, race nutrition, local law enforcement support, and transitions areas all require a lot of logistics, much more than just staging a marathon.

There are other triathlons of the same Ironman distance in the US put on by local race organizers, but there aren't many, because of the expense and manpower required, and they are not allowed to use the official "Ironman" logo and name. These local races of the same distance hurt just as much and use various descriptions such as "iron distance" and "ultra distance"—anything to keep the WTC trademark lawyers from sending nasty letters. I know what those lawyers are like. They can be quite determined. Many of these unsanctioned races are run very well, and I eventually would do some of them, but in 2001 there were not many of them. For my first one I wanted to do one of the "official" ones just to see if I could call myself an "Ironman." At this point I didn't know if it would be my only one.

So in September 2001 I got online and looked at the registration process for Ironman Florida. No way was I ready to enter the November 2001 race coming up in just two months. Besides, that race was already full. You have to register a year in advance, and registration is capped at about 2,500 entrants and fills up in one day with athletes from all over the world. So I had my eyes set on the race the following year, in November 2002. That would give me over a year to train. Scanning the results of the race the previous year, one name jumped out at me: "Peter Kotland, professional, 4th overall, 8 hours, 55 minutes."

What? You mean that guy from right outside my hometown? The one who had destroyed the field in the short Kiawah Island Olympic-distance race I just did? This guy is a professional Ironman triathlete? And finished fourth overall at Ironman Florida?

Now I was really impressed. That little Kiawah victory was just a local race. He was not just some guy beating up on the amateurs at the local triathlon. This guy was for real.

If I was going to race Ironman Florida next year, I needed to find other races leading up to it to get ready. I needed a half Ironman first. That is just what it sounds like—half the Ironman distance—a 1.2-mile swim, a 56-mile bike, and a 13.1-mile half marathon run for a total of 70.3 miles. Years later in 2008, for reasons I don't really understand, the WTC changed the name of these races from "Half Ironman" to "Ironman 70.3." Have you ever heard someone say they ran a "marathon 13.1" rather than a "half marathon"? I haven't either. Maybe WTC didn't like "half" sounding like it was not as great of an accomplishment as a full Ironman, which technically it isn't, but a half Ironman is still a huge accomplishment and worth celebrating. I certainly planned to celebrate my first one.

I found a half Ironman in Panama City Beach, Florida, set for May 2002—the Gulf Coast triathlon. It was conveniently the same location and much of the same course as the Ironman Florida course in November. Perfect. It would be a great training race. Scanning the results from previous years, I saw that name again: Peter Kotland, fifth overall one year and seventh overall the next year out of several thousand. *This guy is everywhere. Looks like I'll eventually run into him again if I do these races, but he'll be finished and showered and driving out of town before I come stumbling across the line. I wonder what his story is? How is he so good?* I assumed he must train with the triathlon gods in the clouds while I'm schlepping along here on the ground.

In the winter and spring of 2002 I swam, biked, and ran training for that first half Ironman coming up in May. I did not have a triathlon coach to give me customized workouts, and I was also still trying to figure out how to manage blood sugar and insulin injections as the difficulty and distances increased. I read sample workouts in magazines and experimented with sport nutrition, checking my blood sugar before, during, and after workouts. There was no manual or website for racing marathons or triathlons, much less an Ironman triathlon, with type 1 diabetes. I would have to figure it out myself through trial and error and calculated and cautious experimenting.

In March 2002 I ran a local 10k running race. There I met a local female triathlete, Katie Malone, who was also planning to race the same Gulf Coast half Ironman in May. She was a great runner, better than me, and had done several triathlons before. I asked if I could train some with her and pick up some pointers. I could tell she was very good and experienced. My perception was well placed because several years later she raced as a professional and now has a successful triathlon coaching business. She was also really nice and always helpful to newbies.

On one of our training bike rides she mentioned the workouts that her coach had given her.

"Your coach? Who is your coach?" I asked, struggling to keep up with her pedaling down the road.

"Peter Kotland. He's a pro. Lives in the area."

"Really? Peter Kotland is your coach? He coaches people?" The wheels started spinning in my head like my feet on the pedals. "Do you think he would coach others? Like ... me?"

"I don't know," she said. "He's kind of particular. He only coaches about five people. He races full time himself. Peter is an interesting guy. He's from Czechoslovakia."

When the learner is ready, the teacher appears.

When the learner is ready, the teacher appears.

WILL YOU COACH ME?

She gave his number and I sat on it for about a week, not wanting to bother him, a little nervous to call. Finally, in April, I called.

"Allo?" this odd voice answered the phone with a thick Eastern European accent.

"Uh, hi, is this Peter Kotland?" I was more nervous than asking a girl out for a date. Cold calling has never been my thing, but I was determined. *What if this dude tells me to get lost? I'm sure he gets calls all the time, people asking him for things. He's probably wondering how I got his number.*

"Ya," came the response. Awkward silence.

"Uh, Katie Malone gave me your number." *That's good, quick, drop a name he knows, establish a connection.* "I'm training for a triathlon and she said you do some coaching?"

More awkward silence. Crickets.

"I was wondering if I could find out more? Maybe if you could coach me?"

More awkward silence. *Is he still there? Did he hang up?*

"Vell, I dunt coach miny peeples. I race." I could barely understand him through his thick Czech accent. He sounded like one of the athletes racing for the Eastern European countries interviewed at the Olympics. Katie had prepared me to show him that I was serious, not just looking to do a local race and waste his time.

"Yeah, I know. I saw you at Kiawah last September. You won. I'm racing Gulf Coast in May. The same race Katie is doing. Then I'm going to race Ironman Florida in November." *There, show him I've got big plans. Half Ironman. Ironman. I'm serious.* I felt like I was rambling. I found myself speaking slowly and carefully, not sure if he was having as much trouble understanding me as I was him.

"Vell, I unly coach a few peeple. Dunt haff time to do shedules for evybody."

This guy was playing hard to get—no chitchat or warm conversation. And I could barely understand him anyway. Now I know how hard it was for the US to get information out of Eastern Bloc spies during the Cold War.

Then he said, "Maybe we meet? Talk?" He wanted to size me up before he agreed to anything.

I pounced. *Yes, meet! That would be great!* But I tried to act cool.

"Sure, yeah, that would be good. When do you want to meet? Any time is good for me."

Now I really felt like a teenager getting excited that a girl agreed that she *might* go out with me. This was pathetic, but I wanted his help. I needed his help. This guy was obviously good, but at this point I still did not realize just how incredibly good he was. And he lived in my backyard. If he would coach me, I felt pretty sure he could get me to my Ironman finish line.

Success leaves clues. If you want to get better at anything, find a mentor, a coach, a veteran. Find

Success leaves clues.

someone better than you, who's been there before and knows how to do it. Whether it's athletics, art, your career, or school—find a teacher. Look for those who have been successful and ask for their help. If you can't find someone to teach you, study people who are good. Study their form, their technique, their preparation, then copy them.

Steal it. Daniel Coyle authored a how-to manual called *The Little Book of Talent: 52 Tips for Improving Your Skills.* Coyle said, "We are often told that talented people acquire their skill by following their 'natural instincts.' That sounds nice, but in fact it is baloney. All improvement is about absorbing and applying new information, and the best source of information is top performers. So steal it.

"Stealing has a long tradition in art, sports and design, where it often goes by the name of 'influence.' Steve Jobs stole the idea for the computer mouse and drop-down menus from Xerox Palo Alto Research

Center. The Beatles stole the high 'woooo' sounds in 'She Loves You,' 'From Me to You,' and 'Twist and Shout' from their idol Little Richard. The young Babe Ruth based his swing on the mighty uppercut of his hero, Shoeless Joe Jackson."

If you copy from one it's called plagiarism. If you copy from many it is called research.

Early in my legal career a wise older lawyer told me that if you copy from one it's called plagiarism. If you copy from many it is called research. So do your "research," find your "influence"—copy and steal it from many.

While I was self-reliant and prided myself on being able to do things myself, I realized quickly with something like an Ironman triathlon that I needed some coaching just to be able to do it at all. With Peter, I might actually be able to do it well.

I met him the next week at a local pizza restaurant. He asked me questions like it was an interview to be accepted into his training program: my race results, what races I planned to do, what bike I had, my goals, how much time I had to train. He wouldn't agree to coach you if you just paid him. You had to prove yourself to him. He wanted to know if you were willing to work. Otherwise, you were wasting his time. I felt so inadequate telling him about my piddling little races so far—two marathons and some 10k runs, a few bike charity rides of seventy-five or a hundred miles, one Olympic-distance triathlon—and my road bike off the rack from a local bike shop.

He gave me blank gazes that at times felt like disgust. The more I talked, the more inadequate I felt. *You're right. I'm not worthy. I can't believe I'm even considering this. You'll never coach me. Sorry I wasted your time.*

But beneath that somewhat stern demeanor, I detected a deep sense of character in him that said, "I will help you get better but only if you are willing to work hard, not like some whiny American crybaby looking for something easy." I respected his toughness, and I did not even know his story yet. You had to earn his respect. I liked him immediately.

I had to ask him to repeat a few things, still struggling with his thick accent, and I was worried that I was irritating him so I began to just smile and nod like I understood what he was saying. I either agreed that it is "very hard to race an Ironman" or that "cherry is hard to taste in a pan." I don't know. I didn't care. He seemed like he was going to accept me and agree to coach me. He asked me how much time I had to train and I told him about my job as a lawyer but that I could train before and after work and weekends.

I also told him a little about my diabetes, but he did not seem to understand much or have any experience with that. So I quickly changed the subject. I did not want to get sidetracked on that. There would be time for that later. I did not want him to decline coaching me, thinking I was going to be a problem because of some medical condition. I would figure out the diabetes stuff myself. He'd be my triathlon coach, not my diabetes coach.

After about an hour of talking and eating, he agreed that he would coach me. He only coached six athletes. The other four lived out of state and Katie and I were local. He would send everybody weekly workout "shedules" by email on Sunday night and check in with us, helping us pick races and progress. He would also help with equipment and nutrition, recommendations, and suggestions. He was a one-man triathlon Google that would answer everything and customize it for me. I was elated. This is what I needed. I had a coach.

I joke that it was like I was asking a girl on a date, and this first dinner meeting was our first date, even more so because I paid for his meal. But little did I know that this would be the first of dozens of meals that I would pay for Peter over the next four years. And I was glad to do it this time because of the amazing story he told me of his life. He didn't tell me much that first meeting, but I got all the details in thousands of hours I spent with him in the coming years.

His story is the best I have ever heard of overcoming obstacles, discipline, and hard work to succeed. It inspires me.

COMMUNISM AND MILKY WAY CANDY BARS

Peter was born in 1972 in communist Czechoslovakia, now known as the Czech Republic. While I grew up in the freedom and luxury of America in the 1970s and 1980s, watching *Batman* and *Star Wars* and whatever I wanted on TV and movies, going to Disney World, Peter grew up under communist government rule. His father was a journalist, so he had permission occasionally to travel out of the country and would bring Peter magazines and treats from the Western world. One treat was Milky Way bite-size candy bars. As a child Peter was so appreciative he would save the bag and eat just one bar a week. How many kids in America appreciate a bite-size candy bar that much?

At an early age he displayed promise as a cross-country skier, so he was placed in the government athletic training program, which kept him away from home sometimes two hundred days a year. Without his parents there to pamper him or fight his battles or argue with the coach about playing time, he developed toughness and learned how to work hard on his own. When the Berlin Wall and the Soviet Union fell in 1989, he left Czechoslovakia at the age of eighteen to look for a better life in the Western world. He made it to Canada and began selling flowers door to door to make ends meet. He came to America and worked in a textile plant in South Carolina while he studied English at night. Because of his endurance background he asked the cross-country running coach of a local small college, Wofford, for a tryout. The coach sent him on a practice run with several members of the team. None of them could keep up with him. He was accepted on a small scholarship but had to work in the school cafeteria to pay tuition and expenses. How many American college students would be willing to work in a factory and the school cafeteria in order to go to college?

His senior year in college he convinced a professor to let him write a research paper about running a marathon. He had never run a marathon. He entered the 1994 New Orleans marathon and won it in a time of two hours and thirty-three minutes. And he got college credit for it.

After graduating, he started racing triathlons and eventually raced the Hawaii Ironman from 1995 to 1997, finishing each time in under ten hours. The average Ironman finish time for most amateurs is over twelve or thirteen hours. Any athlete finishing under ten hours is considered elite. In 1997 he won the ultimate masochist sufferfest of endurance competitions: The Hawaii Ultraman World Championship, a three-day competition of swimming, biking, and running. The first day is a six-kilometer swim in the Pacific Ocean, followed immediately by a ninety-mile bike race to the other side of the big island. The second day is a 160-mile bike race, climbing the mountains and volcanic peaks of Hawaii. The third day he ran the double marathon 52.4-mile run in a world record time of five hours, thirty-three minutes, and fifty-seven seconds, averaging an amazing 6:22 per mile. *Rolling Stone* magazine featured him on the cover and pronounced him "the fittest man in the world." He was racing as a professional Ironman triathlete when I met him.

He had overcome incredible obstacles to make it to this country and pursue his dream. My obstacle to overcome diabetes suddenly seemed less difficult.

I was in good hands, if I could just survive the training.

OVERCOME YOUR OBSTACLE

Do you feel like you have obstacles in your life? Do you find it difficult to overcome your past? Do you feel like life, fate, or someone has dealt you a raw deal?

I remember seeing a quote in college that stuck with me: "Ninety percent of success in life is determined not by what happens to you but by how you *react* to what happens to you."

Do not waste your time or energy being bitter or looking for someone to blame. Dwight Eisenhower said, "The search for a scapegoat is the easiest of all hunting expeditions." Channel that energy, that anger, that resentment, toward proving that your obstacle will not hold you back.

Have you ever noticed how a child with an older brother or sister becomes the fastest or most successful in athletics, arts, or other fields? In the *Talent Code*, author Daniel Coyle discovered that an abnormal number of the world's fastest male runners in Olympic and international competitions are the youngest or almost the youngest child in their families. Here are the last ten world record holders in the hundred-meter sprint and their birth-order ranks in their family:

1. Usain Bolt (second of three children)
2. Asafa Powell (sixth of six)
3. Justin Gatlin (fourth of four)
4. Maurice Greene (fourth of four)
5. Donovan Bailey (third of three)
6. Leroy Burrell (fourth of five)
7. Carl Lewis (third of four)
8. Burrell (fourth of five)
9. Lewis (third of four)
10. Calvin Smith (sixth of eight)

Notice a pattern here? It suggests that speed may not always be a genetic gift but rather an ability that grows by overcoming an obstacle that says, *You're behind—keep up!* The younger boy learns from an early age that his older brothers and sisters are bigger, stronger, and faster than he is. That struggle to keep up with their older, faster siblings and their friends soon made them the fastest runners in the world. The obstacle and disadvantage created their strength.

Sometimes there is nothing you can do to change what, or what you perceive, is holding your back—your height, your race, your parents, where you grew up, your divorce, or your chronic health condition. You can't make it go away or go back in time. You may not be responsible for your obstacle, but you are responsible for how you respond to it.

Some obstacles are not there at birth. Rather they are changes that happen to you in life. Change is inevitable, but growth is optional. It can make you bitter, or it can make you better. Channel that bitterness into drive to prove that you will be better

You may not be responsible for your obstacle, but you are responsible for how you respond to it.

because of it. Remember the lessons of the previous chapter about making the bad thing that happens to you the best thing that ever happened to you. Get even with that guy, that no-good ex-spouse, by getting yourself fit, healthy, and better looking than you've ever been, just to spite them and show you're better off. Use your anger as fuel to improve yourself. Show that boss that passed you over for a promotion or that coach that cut you that you will make them regret it. One day, you will sing "How Do You Like Me Now?" by Toby Keith.

I saw this quote attributed to Captain Jack Sparrow, played by Johnny Depp in the *Pirates of the Caribbean* movies: "The problem is not the problem. The problem is your attitude about the problem." I can picture Sparrow, the often-inebriated pirate, spouting profound pearls of wisdom as he finds himself mired in problem after problem on the high seas, clutching his bottle of rum as island natives attack his ship or a giant sea monster is about to swallow his vessel in a violent storm. But he emerges each time, ready to toast his success with another shot of rum. I researched the quote, like every other source I cite in this book, but I could not confirm that he actually said this in any of his movies, but it sounds like something he would say, and the wisdom is still valid.

In April 2002, I finally had a triathlon coach. There was not enough time for him to do much for me before my first half Ironman race coming up in less than a month. But Peter did offer some pre-race advice and insight on what to do and what to expect. That gave me great peace of mind. He was also participating in the race, as he had many times. I was ready to watch and learn from the best.

ARE YOU WILLING TO … SHAVE YOUR LEGS?

Four weeks later I was in Panama City Beach at the Gulf Coast half Ironman-distance triathlon. There were about two thousand people in the race—a much fitter, experienced field of triathletes than I had seen at the short Olympic-distance race eight months before. I was stepping up the ladder now.

I was a lot fitter, if not a lot more experienced. I had also done something significant, something that was a lot bigger deal than racing a half Ironman.

I shaved my legs.

That may be the most serious commitment I've ever made to anything. If I was going to be a real triathlete, I had to look like one, and I could see now why the male triathletes did it. Most elite swimmers shave their arms and legs. I felt sleeker and more streamlined swimming. The first time I dropped into the pool after shaving my legs, I felt like a greased vegetable. I slithered through the water like an eel. It was an odd feeling. I guess women know what that feels like, but then again, maybe they don't. Most women don't let their leg hair grow for thirty years before they shave it and go swimming. I don't know if it made me swim faster, but it sure made me feel that way. Confidence is important.

Ever since I saw that cyclist hiking and climbing Mount Whitney with me in California, I had wondered why male cyclists and triathletes shaved their legs. There are many explanations. Cyclists say it's easier to prevent road rash if you fall on your bike. Legs hairs grab the pavement and rip your flesh when you slide down the road. It's a painful thought, but I did find it to be true several times in the coming years when I had a few nasty bike wrecks.

Other cyclists say that not having leg hairs catching wind as you ride helps with aerodynamics. I'm not sure many amateur cyclists could actually notice a measurable difference in drag caused by leg hairs, but I definitely could tell that it felt sleeker gliding through the air with no leg hair. Again, confidence and positive vibes are important. You need to *feel* fast.

While the cycling benefits may be debatable, I could definitely notice benefits for triathlon. No leg hair makes it a lot easier to pull a wetsuit off your wet legs as you try to make a fast transition to the bike. I still did not have a wetsuit yet, but I would confirm that when I got my first one for cold water races later in the year. I never found, or heard, a benefit for running, but two out of the three events in triathlon were enough for me to do it.

So, yes, there are performance reasons for why male cyclists and tri-athletes shave their legs. But the real reason is probably that every other male in the race is doing it and you look like a hairy-legged caveman if you do not. And many triathletes probably just like to show off their fit, sculpted legs from hours of cycling, running, and swimming. After several weeks of doing it, I felt shaggy and unkempt if I did not.

MY FIRST HALF IRONMAN TRIATHLON

The Gulf Coast half Ironman was a painful but glorious experience. I made it through the 1.2-mile swim in the Gulf of Mexico with no problem and rode the fifty-six-mile bike course as hard as I could, trying to pace myself and save some energy for the half marathon. I was still riding my standard road bike. I had clip-on temporary aerobars attached to the road cycling bars to give me a little better aerodynamics. I was still getting dusted by the guys riding fancy triathlon time trial racing bikes. I would have to get one of those expensive machines one day.

The half marathon was a hot, humid 13.1-mile run on a sizzling asphalt road crammed with beach houses that turned around in a beachside state park. I made a mistake with my blood sugar and ate too many sport bars and drank too much carbohydrate sport drink during the bike race. This race was as much a test for blood sugar management as it was learning to race a long-distance triathlon.

I had to walk part of the run, feeling nauseous and weak, and finished the race in five hours and fifty minutes. It was a disappointing time, slower than I had hoped for, primarily due to my blood sugar problems and dehydration and heat on the run. It gave me a lot to work on and learn from. Peter finished in four hours and twenty-three minutes, fourth place among the professionals. He beat me by over an hour and a half. He had enough time to shower, take a nap, and have lunch before I came across the line. He was in a different league, and I was excited to see how I could improve with him. But right now I was exhausted.

The rest of 2002 was a busy year of racing and training, all focused on getting ready for Ironman Florida in November. Peter gave me weekly "shedules" and I followed them diligently. By day I was a lawyer, wearing a suit to the office, taking depositions, and going to court for motions and trials. But my life and mind away from the office was focused on one thing—becoming an Ironman triathlete. I swam in the mornings at 6 a.m. before work and ran or cycled at lunch or after work with long summer daylight. On weekends I did long bike rides of three or four hours and long runs of ten to twenty miles. The month after Gulf Coast I ran the Kona Marathon a second time in June 2002, again as a fund-raiser for the American Diabetes Association. This year I improved my marathon time over twenty minutes from 2000, even though I was running it more to help pace a few first-time marathoners. I guess I was now a veteran in my third marathon.

I also did cycling events. A triathlon is three sports, and it helps to train and race each separately to improve them independently and then combine them all on race day. A triathlon is like having three children. You need to give each child individual attention to develop and some days combine them in a joint family activity. Each child (sport) has its own unique needs and characteristics that you must work on and develop. Race day is the family vacation when you pack all three kids up together for a great big (painful?) good time. At the end you may say, "Oh my god, that was exhausting … I'm never doing that again." But a few days later you remember the good feelings and you've forgotten the bad, the expense, and how exhausted you were or how much work it took to do it, you start planning the next family vacation … I mean triathlon. The next one will be even better.

> **A triathlon is like having three children. You need to give each child individual attention to develop and some days combine them in a joint family activity.**

DIABETES DISASTER

I was gaining fitness and learning to train well but also learning to manage my blood sugar with this intense workout load. I made some mistakes with insulin and blood sugar that were pretty scary.

One week after I ran the 2002 Kona Marathon in Hawaii I was back home and rode in a long bike ride on July 4th in the mountains of North Carolina. They call it the Fabulous 4th Bike Tour, but for the hardcore local roadies it's a *race* of several hundred cyclists starting in Tryon, NC. The race features sixty-five miles of cycling all up and down mountain roads, about 6,500 feet of climbing. I did it in about three and a half hours. Immediately after the ride I ran a short "brick" run of four miles. A brick workout stacks cycling and running back-to-back to train your body to recover from cycling while you begin your run. It also trains you to hold some energy in reserve cycling in order to have energy left to run. Many beginner triathletes push too hard swimming and cycling and then run out of gas running.

On this hot July 4th day after a combined seventy miles of hard mountain cycling and running, I drove one hour home, stopping to pick up a pasta meal with salad and some bread. I was hungry and knew I needed a lot of carbohydrates in that meal to recover from the workout and keep myself from having low blood sugar later. I tried to be cautious and calculate the correct amount of insulin for the carbohydrates, but that is always somewhat of a guess when you factor in the exercise I had just done. I was supposed to drive three hours to the beach in Charleston, SC, later that afternoon. I ate the meal, injected some R mealtime (fast-acting) insulin, and packed a bag at home, getting ready to drive to the coast.

After a few hours I was so exhausted I laid down on my sofa for what I thought would be a quick nap. I thought I must just be tired from the cycling. The July temperature outside was almost a hundred degrees, and my house was sweltering even with the AC running. I did not know it then, but I was not just tired and hot from the workout. I was having very low blood sugar, and it was dropping. I fell asleep on my sofa and dropped into a dangerous hypoglycemic state. I essentially lost consciousness.

I woke up several hours later, covered in sweat, shaking and trembling, unable to stand or communicate. Extreme low blood sugar causes the body to sweat, and a hundred-degree July day in the South does too.

My body was twitching and jerking, muscle spasms causing my legs and arms to flail. I could kind of detect this, but my brain was incoherent. I have been told what it looks like when someone is in hypoglycemic shock. Somehow I managed to have a few flashes of coherent thought to realize I was in trouble. These thoughts are like lightning in a dark, violent storm, allowing you to see for just a second before plunging you back into confusing blackness and noise. My hands and fingers were jerking and jumping uncontrollably. My legs were immobile. I could not stand and had no muscle control. My flailing arm knocked the lamp off the table. I could not think to look for the phone and would not be able to punch 911 or any number even if I could find it.

I rolled off the sofa onto the floor, gasping, jerking, and convulsing. I struggled to crawl and drag myself about thirty feet to my kitchen in the next room. I assume that took me some time, probably thirty minutes, but I don't know. I was delirious and in a seizure. I collapsed in the pantry underneath a low shelf where I always kept some Sprite sodas to correct low blood sugar. I don't know how I knew to do that.

The confusion and helplessness of hypoglycemia is difficult to describe to someone who does not have type 1 diabetes and does not inject fast-acting mealtime bolus insulin. In fact, 95 percent of the people in the world who have diabetes have type 2 diabetes. Most people with type 2 do not inject fast-acting mealtime insulin but rather control it with an oral medication or a once-a-day slow-acting basal insulin. They don't experience the violent, overwhelming low blood sugar that can overtake your body and brain.

The closest simulation I can describe to the most severe episodes of hypoglycemia is to imagine that you have consumed ten shots of vodka or tequila in one hour on an empty stomach, and you are not a heavy drinker. Within an hour your fingers are hooked to an electrical charge that makes your hands and arms jerk and flail uncontrollably. Your brain is plunged into a pit of confusion and clumsiness, disoriented and hallucinating. You cannot control your thoughts or your body. You cannot speak or stand, and you do not know how to help yourself and may not even realize that you need help.

That day I managed to pull my body into my pantry and flail my hand at those cans of Sprite, pulling them down crashing on my chest. I don't know how long it took me to pry open one of those cans as I lay on the floor twitching and convulsing, but eventually I must have gotten one to my mouth and poured it on my face, sucking some in. Then I laid there and slowly, gradually, regained some consciousness.

That's where I found myself later when I woke up. I was covered in sweat and Sprite. The path from my sofa to the kitchen was wrecked. I had dragged myself across the rug and hardwood floors and between furniture from one room to the next. I was able to retrace my path and see what I had done and how I ended up in the pantry.

That was a scary valuable lesson. After that I ate large carbohydrate meals of pasta and lowered my insulin dosage after long, hard workouts and races.

BE CAREFUL WHAT YOU AGREE TO

Something else happened in July 2002, but like most things, I did not know how significant it was at the time. I was trying to keep this one quiet. In June I was flying home from Washington, DC, after meeting at the office of a computer software company that I was representing in a large lawsuit in South Carolina. Sitting on the plane to Greenville next to me was a girl that I did not know—Kelly McCorkle. As we talked she said that she recognized me from some connection in Greenville. In a weak moment a few years earlier, I had agreed to do some modeling for a local agency in Greenville. Trust me, I did not quit my day job for that. Kelly also did modeling for them. She was a pretty girl and had a nice personality. As we chatted, she said her boyfriend was in the military and could not attend some kind of event she had coming up that next month. She was in a bind and desperate. She just needed a sub, a stand-in. She asked me.

"All you have to do is stand with me for a minute or two," she said. *Stand? That's easy. I can do that.*

"Okay. I guess I can do that. Sure. No problem," I said.

"Oh, and dance with me a little just for a few minutes," she added. *Dance? Hm, now wait a minute. That's a little different. But I'm an excellent dancer. At least I claimed I was.*

Since I had already just agreed, I felt like it was rude to back out now. I still had not asked what the event was. It was clear that I was just an empty suit filling in for her boyfriend.

"What is this event?" I asked, finally.

"It's the Miss South Carolina pageant," she replied.

I gulped. *The what? The Miss Who pageant?* I had never been to a pageant. I didn't know anything about pageants or dancing, really. I was planning on faking it for a nice girl just to help her out. Now I had just agreed to dance on stage and television in front of thousands of people in four weeks.

The pageant occurred the second week of July. Each day that week I was busy at my office and working out mornings and at lunch. Each night I would drive twenty-five miles to Spartanburg, SC, and practice dancing on stage with Kelly and the fifty or so other contestants and their boyfriends, brothers, or stand-ins like me. The final night was Saturday, July 13. That morning I did a long bike ride of about sixty miles in mountains. Near the end of the ride I was descending a very steep hill going very fast, over twenty miles per hour around a curve, when I suddenly came upon a stop sign. I tried to brake but could not stop fast enough. I was about to end up in a street with cross traffic. In a split second I made the decision to go down, sliding like a baseball player into second base. I slid on the asphalt and ripped open my back, legs, and arms. I tore my cycling jersey and shorts, shredding them on the asphalt. Blood was everywhere. Fortunately, I had no broken bones and was able to ride in. But the final night of the Miss South Carolina pageant was in a few hours.

Kelly had already won the swimsuit and talent preliminary competitions the previous nights. She was definitely the favorite to win the title that night. And her fill-in dance partner had just ripped open his back and arms sliding down a mountain road. I had no choice but to attend.

I took a painful shower and put bandages on my back and arms, trying to soak up the blood. It is hard putting bandages on your own back. I put on my white dress shirt, tie, and dark sport coat and went to the pageant. My legs, back, and shoulders burned and were so sensitive I could not sit down or lean back on anything. We were doing a spirited dance where at one point I would pick her up and sling her around on my back and shoulders to land on my other side. Fortunately, none of the thousands of people in the audience and TV that night could tell that my back was seeping blood as she and I danced on stage. I forced a fake smile as I shrieked pain inside with each movement. She also had no idea. I didn't want to tell her and mess up her focus for her event.

Kelly won the title of Miss South Carolina 2002 that night. I'm sure it was because of my dancing, but I don't think that counted toward her score. I had planned to beat a hasty retreat out of the concert hall, but now I felt obligated to say congratulations to the newly crowned titleholder. Hundreds of people crowded into the reception room back stage. When I shook someone's hand, I noticed blood covering the cuff of my white shirtsleeve sticking out from under my sport coat. I quickly retreated to the men's room, took off my coat, and saw my entire arm and shoulder was coated in blood. My white dress shirt looked like someone had stabbed me like a murder in the concert hall of *Phantom of the Opera*. I threw my coat back on and ducked out a backstage door.

The real significance of that night was not my bike crash, my bloody dancing before thousands of people, or that she won the title. The real significance was that my future wife, Anna Hanks, and her mother were in the audience. I did not meet them then, but I would a year later only because they remembered seeing me on stage that night, or at least

Anna's mother did. Anna claims she did not remember me, which does not surprise me. She is not easy to impress, as I would find out a year later when her mother told her I did the Ironman. She thought that was a strength competition on ESPN, with beefy guys flipping giant tractor tires and pulling a bus with a rope, and told her mother "that doesn't impress me."

So the lesson is, when you agree to dance on stage in the Miss South Carolina pageant, and you crash your bike the morning of the finals and are covered in blood, do your duty and show up and dance, no matter how painful and bloody you are, so your partner can win the title. Your future wife might be in the audience that night.

In mid-September I raced my second Olympic-distance triathlon in Tugaloo, Georgia, a much hillier and more difficult course than the flat race at Kiawah Beach a year prior, but I finished over ten minutes faster. Two weeks later I raced my second half Ironman of the year (and my life) in Raleigh, NC. Again, it was another much hillier, harder course than my first one in Florida four months prior, but I finished this one twenty minutes faster. Two weeks after that in October I raced my third half Ironman in Clermont, Florida, a surprisingly hilly course in north Florida. I was still having difficulty managing blood sugar and finding the right balance of insulin, carbohydrate, and calories, but my times kept improving. I was getting faster and more confident.

> So the lesson is, when you agree to dance on stage in the Miss South Carolina pageant, and you crash your bike the morning of the finals and are covered in blood, do your duty and show up and dance, no matter how painful and bloody you are, so your partner can win the title. Your future wife might be in the audience that night.

But all of that was going to be pushed to a whole different level at the Ironman. It is double the distance of a half Ironman but requires much more than double the effort and mental toughness. It means double the time and distance for mechanical problems, pains, cramps, and any number of difficulties. You just have to figure out how to get through them and keep going until you reach that finish line 140.6 miles away.

I felt like Sylvester Stallone as Rocky Balboa when he said he "just wanted to go the distance" fighting Apollo Creed. He didn't have to win. He just wanted to be standing at the end.

I wanted to go the 140-mile Ironman distance and be standing at the end.

I was nervous. I was scared. I was ready to reach my Ironman finish line.

CHAPTER 10

BETTER BODY, BETTER YOU

Topic: Health and Fitness

I arrived at Ironman Florida 2002 in Panama City Beach several days before the race, renting a condo on the beach just a few blocks from the race transition area and the finish line. I was familiar with the area, having just raced the Gulf Coast half Ironman there in May. Even though it was early November, it was Florida so the weather was sunny with highs in the eighties. Snowbirds, senior citizens from the Northeast and Midwest, had already moved down for the winter to soak up the warm weather. It was a stark contrast to see white-haired senior couples wearing sweaters in eighty degrees on the same sidewalks as Ironman triathletes in spandex and sleeveless jerseys. They stared at us perplexed, like we were crazy kids.

The Gulf of Mexico was beautiful with its clear blue water, waves rolling in gently on the wide, white, sandy beach. Seafood restaurants and beachside bars welcomed you to relax and vacation.

That was about the only comfort I felt before this race.

Walking through the prerace expo and registration area was like a pageant of perfect bodies. This being my first Ironman I immediately noticed another competition that occurs each day leading up to the race—the body off. Competitors, and their fit spouses, girlfriends, or boyfriends, walk around the registration area, the transition area, and the expo to see and be seen. Clearly some of these type A, competitive

Ironman triathletes were proud of their bodies and wanted me to be impressed with them too.

I was. Don't get me wrong. I usually don't mind that kind of thing. It was indeed an impressive lineup of human form. Normally I would have just observed and been impressed, as you would watching the bodies of fit athletes on television or any professional or international competition. But it is different when you realize that you're going to have to race 140 miles against these people, and your body doesn't look quite like that, at least not yet. I was fit but still such a rookie racing triathlons that I didn't have a veteran Ironman triathlete's body at this point. But I certainly noticed those who did, and there were a lot of them. You could see it in their faces, tan, toned, with their skin and flesh taught and firm around their cheekbones and neck, not skinny upper bodies like so many professional cyclists and marathon runners who often starve themselves to drop an extra pound and wither every ounce of muscle and fat off their shoulders and arms. Ironman triathletes have muscular upper bodies for swimming and powerful legs for cycling and running. It's a total body physique.

Just because you look fit doesn't mean you're going to be fast, but these people strutting around the expo had done the work to look that way, so I did not fault them for showing off. They earned it. I was impressed and a little intimidated. Maybe I would look like that one day. But right now, I was just trying to do my first one. I hoped my rookie body was up for it.

I had no idea what my body was in for.

THE PHYSIOLOGY OF AN IRONMAN

The physiology of racing an Ironman is unlike anything humans ever experience. It has been said that if God invented marathons to keep people from doing anything more insane, then triathlons must have taken him completely by surprise. And that was just short triathlons. Ironman triathlons are the ultimate test of fitness ... or insanity.

Completing an Ironman is like aging two decades in one day. The changes your body undergoes in a day of this kind of extreme exertion is similar to changes that occur in over twenty years of normal aging. And you feel that way the day after the race. Fortunately, those years of aging are restored in a few weeks of recovery.

If God let humans invent marathons to keep them from doing anything more insane, then triathlons must have taken him completely by surprise.

The internal roiling you experience in your gut begins the moment you walk into the prerace expo area and see the thousands of other competitors. The anticipation of the exertion increases blood flow and oxygen consumption to the soon-to-be-working muscles. You can already feel nerves in your cycling and running legs and swimming shoulders. Your body releases hormones like epinephrine (adrenaline), flooding the cells with nutrients in preparation for the event that is still several days away. Nerves rumble in your stomach for days.

Walking around before the race you feel weak and sluggish because you have been tapering for two weeks, reducing your workouts to let your body rest and recover from months and years of hard training.

Completing an Ironman is like aging two decades in one day.

For someone who works out twice a day for three to six hours a day, cutting your daily workout to just one hour of easy cycling makes you feel like a lazy slob right before the race.

When the swim begins, respiration increases dramatically. Your heart rate explodes, even though you are trying to stay calm. That is impossible. You are battling the ocean and people. The ocean waves and two thousand other competitors pound your face, as well as your head, body, and legs trying to swim over the top of you. You are trying to survive.

While swimming 2.4 miles may sound like just a warm-up compared to the entire 140.6-mile event, swimming takes four times more energy to complete than running that same distance. You expend energy maintaining buoyancy, overcoming the drag of choppy open water, and battling other competitors for position.

Your core body temperature rises in the swim even if you are in cold water wearing a wetsuit. According to Jonathan Dugas, PhD, an exercise physiologist at the University of Chicago, core body temperature might rise to 101 degrees in the first 10 to 20 percent of an Ironman race, which is roughly the time of the Ironman swim. The bike and the run are the remaining 80 to 90 percent of the race. Almost three quarters of the energy that your muscles release during cycling and running is in the form of heat waste. The maximum safe core body temperature is 104 degrees, which Ironman competitors seldom cross even on the hottest days at tropical venues. Fortunately the brain monitors core body temperature and generates perspiration, but that requires fluid that is also being demanded by the other organs of the body. Unfortunately, this sweat cooling mechanism is essentially self-sabotaging. The more you sweat the more your blood volume shrinks, and the more your blood volume shrinks, the less heat your circulation can carry away from your working muscles, leading to a simultaneous downward spiral of dehydration and gradual climb of overheating during the race.

In a hot Ironman triathlon I will lose approximately five to seven pounds on race day, mostly from fluid loss. I will consume almost four gallons of liquid (water and sport drink) during races where the temperature reaches ninety-five to a hundred degrees. Most competitors will sweat in excess of one liter of fluid per hour during the bike and marathon. That amounts to almost twenty pounds of fluid loss during the race, which is why it is so important to hydrate constantly and consistently throughout the race. I use an alternating drinking strategy practiced in thousands of hours of training I would do over the coming years of my racing career. I must drink some sport drink for the carbohydrates and electrolytes to keep my blood sugar up and some water to provide hydration with no calories or carbohydrates that spike my blood sugar.

Most of that drinking is done on the bike (aside from the ocean waves slamming into your open mouth). This first Ironman I had two bottles in cages on my bike for sport drink and water, replacing bottles at aid stations every ten or fifteen miles. In later races in my career on a different bike I would have three bottles: one water, one high-carbohydrate drink, and one normal-carbohydrate sport drink. *Keep pushing. Keep drinking. But drink the right one. Don't spike that blood sugar, but don't let it drop too low.*

Dehydration is always going to happen in the Ironman. The challenge is to try to slow it and reach the finish line before it overtakes you and generates feelings of discomfort and fatigue that force you to slow down—a final self-policing, restraining mechanism to prevent us from overheating the engine like a car out of radiator fluid on a hot day. But this self-protective mechanism can fail if and when the brain becomes too hot to function in sweltering environments, causing the central nervous system to malfunction. A dehydrated athlete becomes dizzy, disoriented, and uncoordinated and may collapse.

That would happen to me a few years later in a hot-weather Ironman in Coeur d'Alene, Idaho.

BURN CALORIES: "ENGINE TO BRIDGE: WE NEED MORE FUEL!"

Calorie consumption is the greatest challenge of an Ironman. According to the Cleveland Clinic Center for Consumer Health, a 130-pound runner will burn approximately 2,200 calories in a marathon, and a

185-pound runner will burn over three thousand calories. Run that marathon after you swim 2.4 miles and bike 112 miles and you can imagine the calories you burn that day.

In an Ironman I will burn approximately ten to twelve thousand calories. That's roughly the amount that most people will burn in an entire week of normal activity. But you can't eat twelve thousand calories in the race or even sitting around watching TV or a computer all day, although it seems some people try to do that. The gastrointestinal system cannot tolerate the same rates and volume of fuel during intense exercise as it can relaxing or walking comfortably. The digestive system requires energy and fluid, and that energy and fluid is also being demanded by your muscles as you swim, bike, and run and by your blood and perspiration to keep you from overheating in the sun. There is just not enough energy and fluid for everybody asking for it.

In an Ironman I will burn approximately ten to twelve thousand calories.

Thus, in a cruel paradox of racing Ironman, you need extreme amounts of calories and carbohydrates to do the race, but if you consume even a quarter of what you need, your body can't digest it, rejects it, and makes you puke. *Give it to me, I need more! ... Ew. Ugh. I can't handle all of that. Now I'm going to puke. But I still need more.*

I try to consume about 2,500 calories during the race, spaced out evenly of about 300 to 350 calories per hour. I did not know it in my first Ironman—I was still learning my nutrition needs by trial and error at this point—but given my 6'3" size and 180-pound race day weight, I would learn that I need to consume between sixty and eighty grams of carbohydrate per hour. Any less than sixty grams and I will get low blood sugar. Any more than eighty grams and I will get high blood sugar. These calories and carbohydrates come from sport drinks, sport bars, gels, and a few items from aid stations, like a banana.

I never forget in the Ironman that I have diabetes. I just forget that the other athletes don't. The other athletes in the race are all burning and consuming roughly the same amounts, depending on their body size, but they do not have to worry about the dangers of low or high blood sugar. Their working pancreas monitors that perfectly. I don't know what those other athletes are battling, and some may be battling things much more difficult than diabetes—physical or health conditions, emotions from events in their life, or injuries. Everyone has obstacles to overcome. That's why everyone raises their arms and cries at the finish line.

> **I never forget in the Ironman that I have diabetes. I just forget that the other athletes don't.**

In the Ironman you have to use your brain and your body. You can't do the race just on strength, determination, and fitness alone. The Ironman is so *physically* demanding, ironically it is the *smartest* athlete who wins or even completes the race. All of the athletes are fit. But not all pace or fuel themselves properly in the race. That takes experience and using your brain to be disciplined while using your body to be powerful. Life is the same way. It is not always the fastest, strongest, most talented, or most intelligent who wins or succeeds in school, work, and life. It is the one who can use their skill but is also smart at the right time about how to perform—when to speak up or when to keep their mouth shut, when to act fast or when to be patient, when to keep emotions and ego in check, when to work hard on critical things at critical times, and when to avoid wasting time on unproductive tasks. These are all things that can determine success or failure in anything in life.

> **The Ironman is so *physically* demanding, ironically it is the *smartest* athlete who wins or even completes the race.**

CARBOHYDRATE: MY FICKLE FRIEND

Carbohydrates are the rocket fuel for an endurance athlete. After you eat carbohydrate, the stomach, small intestine, and liver break it down into smaller units of sugar called glucose. If the body does not need all that glucose for energy, it stores it in the liver and the skeletal muscles called glycogen. When glycogen stores are full, glucose is stored as fat. Glycogen stores are the energy source your body taps into when it needs more glucose than is available floating around in the bloodstream, during extended exercise, for example. But the body has limited storage capacity for glycogen, about two thousand calories. Endurance training greatly increases the body's ability to store glycogen, but even the fittest triathlete cannot store enough glycogen to fuel an entire Ironman. How quickly glycogen stores are depleted depends on the duration and intensity of the exercise. For low intensity (i.e., low heart rate) endurance exercise like a marathon or the Ironman triathlon, glycogen stores can last about ninety minutes. Obviously the Ironman triathlon lasts a lot longer than that.

So here's the challenge on race day. If you are burning about 12,000 calories, consuming only about 2,500 calories, and depleting glycogen stores provides another 2,000 calories, where are those other 7,500 calories going to come from? How do you solve this nutrition conundrum?

Evolution has done that for us.

GIVE ME SOME FAT

Fat stores are a major fuel source in the Ironman, just like fat stores have been the fuel source for animals and homo sapiens for millions of years during times of food deprivation. But I can hear you saying it now. "But Ironman triathletes are lean and fit. They don't have any fat." I'm not talking about blubber fat hanging over the belly from a poor diet and sedentary lifestyle. Endurance athletes burn fat stored within adipose tissue and within muscle tissue. There is a lot of fat stored there that you can't see.

During the swim and the first portion of the bike leg, carbohydrates and fat provide roughly equal portions of the fuel for the muscles, with protein providing just a sliver. But that ratio shifts to consuming more fat and less carbohydrate as the race progresses and glycogen stores are depleted.

The problem is fat does not burn swiftly. It takes time to process. Think of fat like food in your freezer. When you are hungry, you don't have time to wait on that frozen dish to thaw for several hours on the counter, in the oven, or even in the microwave. Similarly, it takes time to metabolize fat stores in your body.

When your heart rate is elevated in high-intensity, vigorous exercise, your hungry muscles are saying the same thing you are when you're really hungry and in a hurry—give me food now! Your body grabs it out of the bloodstream first, just like you grab food out of the refrigerator and go. But there's a limited supply of glucose and calories in your blood, just like there's a limited supply of convenient, fresh food in your refrigerator.

But there are a lot of extra calories stored in fat, just like there's a lot of extra food stored in your freezer. You know those white, frosted mysterious things in storage bags and containers stuck in your freezer? Yeah, that stuff. It just takes time to thaw and cook it, like that fat stored in your body. That's why Ironman triathletes train for years to go as fast and long as possible at a low heart rate, training the body to be patient in its fuel demands. The resting heart rate of elite Ironman triathletes can be anywhere from forty-two to fifty beats per minute. According to the National Institute of Health, the average resting heart rate of adults is sixty to one hundred beats per minute. A well-trained endurance athlete develops this low heart rate through a lot of training. The heart becomes strong and efficient, purring and pulsing powerfully with little strain.

THE IRONMAN CARDIO ENGINE

But you don't race an Ironman slowly or at rest. You race it fast and for a long time. That's why training to race fast and long at a low heart rate is important. It's like building a powerful engine for an Indy racecar to go 225 mph for five hundred miles. It's not a drag strip racer for a quarter mile at that speed. Fuel efficiency and speed are important for Indy racecars and Ironman triathletes. Your car on the interstate does the same thing, switching from first to overdrive gears so you can cruise comfortably at seventy-five miles per hour for several hours and hundreds of miles.

Ironman triathletes have to build their internal cardiovascular engine, their lungs and heart, in addition to their external body—muscles in their legs, shoulders, back, and abdominal core. I trained most days wearing a heart rate monitor. Some workouts were based not on speed or distance but purely on heart rate. It might be to run eight miles, keeping my heart rate below a certain level, or multiple three-minute intervals at a higher rate, then two minutes recovery, then three miles at a steady heart rate.

BURN FAT—HAVE A LABORED CONVERSATION

I could have a conversation with you the entire time I am racing the Ironman. It is labored, but I can still have a conversation. That means I am keeping my heart rate below my anaerobic threshold, which for me is about 162 beats per minute. Crossing that anaerobic threshold is when you gasp for breath, can't or don't want to talk, and feel lactic acid burning in your muscles. That threshold is roughly 80 percent of your maximum heart rate. Your maximum heart rate can be generally calculated at 220 minus your age.

Exercising between 50 percent and 80 percent of your maximum heart rate (labored conversation pace) is often called your "fat-burning zone" or the aerobic zone. That's the zone an Ironman triathlete needs to be in for as much of the race as possible so that the body has time to break down fat as a fuel source. The best Ironman triathletes train for years to be able to go extremely fast, 140 miles in under ten hours, with a low heart rate while being able to have a conversation the whole time.

USE MUSCLE

Muscle tissue stress is probably the greatest challenge the body faces in an Ironman. Muscle tissue stress starts in the second half of the bike when your body starts burning more fat than carbohydrate because your glycogen stores are being depleted. Over the last sixty miles of the bike portion and while running the marathon, your body's fat oxidation increases and turns to the last source of fuel: amino acids and muscle protein. This process of breaking down muscle protein for energy is called catabolism, which sounds creepily similar to cannibalism because your body is basically consuming its own muscles. This creates muscle fatigue and a burning sensation. Running the last thirteen miles of the marathon feels like weights are attached to your legs. It takes every ounce of energy, focus, and drive you have to continue to pick up that leg and put it back down, one after the other, mile after mile. Doing it at a fast pace takes even more energy.

A biomarker in the bloodstream called creatine kinase (CK), also referred to as creatine phosphokinase (CPK), can be measured to evaluate muscle strain and damage. CK is an enzyme in your muscles. Injury and strain to the muscles allows CK to leak into the bloodstream. Measuring the CK level is one of the tests, along with other symptoms and a physical exam, that doctors perform to determine whether someone has had a heart attack. In a heart attack, enzymes and proteins leak out from the injured heart muscle cells, and their levels in the bloodstream rise.

For males over eighteen, normal blood CK levels are approximately 125 units per liter (U/L). Strenuous exercise causes CK levels to rise and peak twenty-four hours after a workout and stay elevated for several days. According to Bryan Berman, PhD, an exercise physiologist at Carmichael Training Systems, a training and coaching service for endurance athletes, twenty-four hours after running a half marathon, the CK level doubles. One recent study cited in an *Inside Triathlon* magazine article by Matt Fitzgerald entitled "A Physiological View of What the Human Body Goes Through in an Ironman," found that sixteen hours after completing an Ironman, triathletes have an average CK level of 1,500 U/L—more than ten times the normal level.

This elevated CK level feels like burning, aching, throbbing soreness in the muscles of the back and shoulders and in the legs in your quads, calves, and hamstrings. This soreness can last several days to a week. It is difficult to sit down or stand up without grabbing something for assistance. Walking down steps requires the same assistance, holding a railing like a person ninety years old rather than a thirty-year-old athlete capable of racing an Ironman triathlon.

ACTIVE RECOVERY

The best way to recover from an Ironman is light, no-impact exercise like cycling or swimming—active recovery. The day after the race I ride my bike at an easy pace for approximately twenty miles to circulate blood and flush toxins and spread nutrients to cells and muscles. During the week after the race I eat extra carbohydrates and protein to refuel muscle tissue and cells. I also consume amino acids during and after the race in sport drinks and other supplements and get plenty of sleep.

Recovery time from an Ironman will depend on your ability, fitness, and how fast you raced. Amateur athletes racing a fourteen-hour finish time may take three months to fully recover. The faster and fitter I got over the years, my recovery methods and nutrition improved, and my recovery time decreased. I will discuss later how, after I had been racing several years, I raced four Ironman triathlons in six months, including two in one week.

YOUR KEYS TO WELLNESS AND FITNESS

You do not have to race an Ironman triathlon to be fit or burn fat. I know it is hard to exercise when you are working all day and come home to a family and house that need you. I know it is hard to eat well when you are always rushing to and from work and doing errands, stuck in traffic, late to appointments, with no time to get to the grocery store. I know it is hard to exercise when you don't have much time or extra money to join a gym and need to spend your time and money to provide for your family, your career, and your future.

But don't ignore your body and your health while you go to work every day and raise your family. Too many people spend their health gaining wealth and then have to spend their wealth to regain their health. You will be a happier person, live longer, and be a better mom, dad, and worker if you get fit and feel fit.

Too many people spend their health gaining wealth and then have to spend their wealth to regain their health.

Here are a few ways to do that. You can change your body, lose weight, trim down, and feel great by following these principles.

Change your diet. You must *change* your diet, not just diet. You cannot just cut out food. Eat *better* food. Change or reduce consumption of foods loaded with fat, carbohydrate, and calories. You can still eat some of them, just not as much of it. If you want to lose weight, then cut down the amount of calories you eat and change the quality of those calories. You can still feel full by eating healthy calories of salad, vegetables, and fruits and some lean meats, chicken, and fish. You can still eat some pasta, potatoes, and rice, but just keep the quantities lower.

You can still eat that cheeseburger and fries every once and a while, just not every day or even every week. I love a cheeseburger, but I make sure I earn it by working out, and it tastes a lot better too. You will soon not want it as much, because you will recognize how sluggish you feel after you eat it, like a bad food hangover.

Exercise. You must exercise. You get no benefit if you just change your diet but do not exercise. The weight will come back when you give in to temptation. But if you exercise, you can still eat some of the foods you like, even unhealthy ones like sweets and fried foods, in moderation. Those foods become your guilt-free reward that you earned from a healthy lifestyle.

Eat good calories *before you workout* to fuel your exercise, whether you do strength training for your muscles or cardiovascular exercise for your heart and lungs, and to lose weight. You lose weight after exercise, not during, so fuel your body so you can have a good workout. Exercise will give you more energy, strengthen your heart and muscles, increase your metabolism, burn fat off your body overnight, and help you sleep better. You will look better and feel better. If a doctor wrote you a prescription for that, would you take it? Exercise is the best medicine.

> **Exercise will give you more energy, strengthen your heart and muscles, increase your metabolism, burn fat off your body overnight, and help you sleep better. You will look better and feel better. If a doctor wrote you a prescription for that, would you take it?**

Burn body fat. If you want to burn fat off your body, exercise at a labored conversation pace—the fat-burning zone—which is 50 to 80 percent of your maximum heart rate, and do it for as long as you can. Build up your endurance from thirty minutes, to forty-five minutes, to an hour or more. You don't have to exercise so hard you can't breathe or talk and your eyes are popping out of your head. A labored conversation pace takes some effort, but you can still have a conversation. Invite a friend for a vigorous walk, jog, or bike ride with you for an hour at a pace that allows you to talk with them the whole time. Do that every day along with changing your diet, and you will lose weight. And you will enjoy it. I guarantee it.

Fuel your body before and after working out. You see how important nutrition is to an Ironman triathlete. The same is true for you. If you want to lose weight, you need to eat a healthy diet daily but also eat good carbohydrates and calories *before* you exercise so that your body has the glucose in your bloodstream to fuel the exercise. Many people make the mistake of exercising on an empty stomach and then feel weak and sluggish exercising and thus lose motivation to do it again. They think they should not eat before exercising, because they want to lose weight. That is wrong. Eat a banana or fruit or nutrition bar about thirty minutes before exercising to give your body fuel to burn. Then exercise at your labored conversation pace as long as you can to burn excess fat off your body.

Immediately after you exercise, eat or drink another small serving of healthy carbohydrates and calories to give your working muscles fuel to recover and replenish, which will help tone, shape, and strengthen them and prevent soreness so that you are ready to exercise again tomorrow. That thirty-minute window right after exercise is important because it is the brief period of insulin sensitivity for a person without diabetes who has natural insulin coming from the pancreas. Your cells are asking to be replenished and your pancreas has insulin waiting for you to refuel them. But if you wait longer than thirty minutes to refuel them, that insulin sensitivity is gone and you've missed the critical window. It's like the door closing to get on the plane or the train leaving the station. You missed it. Now you have to watch it leave and be sore about it.

Exercise to sleep better. People often ask me how much sleep I get. They assume I do not get much or enough if I'm working as a lawyer, speaking or traveling around the country, working out twice every day, and doing the other things life requires of the day—running errands, house chores, laundry, family time, etc.

I'll talk more about time management in the chapter on work–life balance, but know that I usually get at least seven hours of sleep every night. Even when I don't, the five or six hours I get are deep and restful. Your sleep will be so much better after you have exercised that day, and you will fall asleep easily rather than tossing and turning. You will sleep soundly and deeply and wake up refreshed and revived. In 2016 *Time* magazine reported that Americans spent an estimated $41 billion on sleeping pills and sleep aids in 2015. Rather than pills, try exercising to sleep better. You will be great in bed—sleeping, that is. But once you are exercising and eating healthy you will be better at other things in bed too, but that is not covered in this book.

OVERCOMING YOUR OBSTACLES TO EXERCISE

Here are some suggestions to overcome obstacles preventing exercise and physical activity.

Make the time. You always have time for the things that are important to you. You make meals, showering, and watching your favorite TV show a part of your daily routine. You plan for them and make time for them. Give exercise the same status. Make physical activity, exercise, and working out a part of your daily routine.

> You always have time for the things that are important to you.

Exercise will be important to you once you start to feel how good it feels and notice how good it makes you look. It will be like that glass of wine in the evening or cup of good coffee in the morning that you look forward to. But to get started you have to make yourself do it. Identify available time slots by monitoring your activities for a week and identify three thirty-minute or one-hour time slots you can commit to exercise.

Walk or ride your bike to work or shopping, organize school activities around exercise, walk the dog, exercise while watching TV, park farther away from your destination, take the stairs rather than the elevator.

Exercise will soon be as important to you as your favorite TV show, your favorite meal or drink, sleep, sex, and anything else that you make time for because you enjoy it.

Make it social. Explain your interest in exercise to family and friends. Ask them to support your efforts. Invite them to exercise with you. Plan social activities involving exercise: bike rides, walks, jogging, basketball, tennis, softball, kickball, golf without riding in a cart, etc. Do you need some quality time to talk to a friend or family member? Ask them to meet you each week for a walk, a jog, or a bike ride. Develop new friendships with healthy, active people. You will enjoy their spirit and their attitude of feeling good and healthy, and it will rub off on you.

Show me your friends and I'll show you your future. What do your friends look like? How do they spend their time? Are they healthy and active? If not, look for new friends. They are out there. Their healthy vibe is positive peer pressure to imitate their healthy behaviors. You will not want to disappoint your workout buddy by missing your agreed workout time. They are depending on you, and you realize that you are doing it for them as well as for you. You know it has become a good habit when you feel guilty that you can't meet your friend for your workout or they ask you why you were not at spin class or yoga class. That's healthy peer pressure.

> **Show me your friends and I'll show you your future.**

Create energy. Some may say that they do not have the energy to exercise. Exercise *gives* you energy. It creates energy. You want to keep exercising because you feel better and have more energy. Overeating, alcoholism, smoking, and drug addiction are all destructive habits that start small and then build and feed on themselves to damage you in a downward spiral. Exercise works the same way but in a healthy upward ascent. Start small and it will build and feed and fuel itself, making you want to exercise more and giving you more energy and motivation as you start to notice the difference in your body and how you feel (and you notice others noticing *you* looking good). You start to eat better and dislike unhealthy foods that now do not taste good and make you feel worse. They become unsatisfying. You will soon rather spend time walking, running, riding a bike, or moving than sitting. But when you do sit, you are more relaxed and refreshed.

Start out by scheduling exercise for times in the day or week when you feel energetic. Set a finish line six months in the future that you want to cross—a hike to a mountaintop, a 5k or 10k run, a marathon— whatever is appropriate for your age and where you are starting. Create your finish line vision.

Avoid injury. Warm up and cool down properly. Stretch. Watch healthy people your age and mimic their activities on a smaller, slower scale starting out. Consult with your healthcare professional and trainers at a fitness center. Choose activities appropriate for your age, fitness level, skill level, and health status by watching others and asking at running stores and fitness centers.

Improve your skill by starting small. Start with activities that require no new skills, such as walking, climbing stairs, and jogging. Join spin classes to improve cycling skill, and then ask questions about cycling routes and bikes at a local bike shop. Start swimming by taking a few stroke technique lessons. You will waste a lot of time and energy swimming with poor stroke technique, just like you'll waste a lot of time trying to hit a golf ball with a hockey swing. Learn the technique to do it right. Watch videos online on proper swim technique like www. totalimmersion.net.

Start free and cheap. If money is tight, don't spend it on gym memberships and expensive equipment at first. Select activities that require minimal facilities or equipment, such as walking, hiking, jogging, jumping rope, and home video exercise programs that keep you motivated and progressing to the next level. The road, trails, and sidewalk are free; use them. Once your fitness improves you will be ready and anxious to invest in a health club membership or equipment like a bike, cross-country skis, surfboard, tennis racket, and lessons.

But do invest in good running shoes at the beginning. Comfortable new shoes will motivate you to get your money's worth out of them. Your shoes will talk to you if you let them sit unused and clean in your closet, taunting you, mocking you, telling you to get in them and out the door. You will also feel good in new, comfortable shoes and excited to use them. Invest in anything to get you excited and motivated to get out and get moving, and imagine the sexy workout clothes you'll soon be wearing after you start seeing changes in your body. Your new body is your finish line vision.

Engage in low-impact sports. You may not want to admit it, but I will tell you straight—you can't play basketball, soccer, football, or racquetball in your forties and fifties like you did in high school. The knees, ankles, and hips don't stop, turn, pivot, and take the impact like they used to. What might have been a knee sprain twenty years ago is more likely to be ruptured tendon or ligament today if you have been out of the game for a while, and you have a few extra pounds on the frame. Even sports like tennis and softball may require some buildup to get your joints ready for them.

But age doesn't mean you quit exercising or competing. As you get older, look for "straight-line sports"—cycling, swimming, running, cross-country skiing, rowing—that do not require pivoting and strain on knees and ankles. Check out the great ebook *You Can Do Something Great: The Road Map for Middle-Aged Beginners in Triathlon*, by Joe Towson. Cycling and swimming are no-impact sports. There are plenty ways to challenge yourself competing in these individually and even together in a triathlon. Running has impact, so consult with a local running store for proper shoes and running form to prevent injury. Every sport has potential for injury—you can crash cycling, strain shoulders swimming, and injure legs running—so consult with coaches and trainers for the right skills and technique. You will improve faster and enjoy it more!

Overcome weather conditions. Develop activities that are always available regardless of weather: indoor cycling and spin classes, aerobic and Zumba classes, indoor swimming at an aquatic center, indoor basketball, mall walking, and stair climbing. I spent hundreds of winter hours riding my bike in my basement mounted on my indoor trainer watching TV at night or with bad weather outside. I spent many hours "swimming" in my basement by using stretch cords to mimic the swimming stroke and strengthening my shoulders and upper back muscles because I could not get to the pool before it closed. Be creative and find a way. Be proud of yourself for your creativity to figure out how to get exercise when others would not.

Work out when you travel. I always pack workout clothes when I travel, even if I don't think I will have time to do it. It doesn't take much space to pack running shoes, socks, shorts, and a shirt. I have been amazed how often I don't expect that I will have time, and then suddenly I do when an appointment gets cancelled or delayed. I packed my swim stretch cords to swim in a hotel room rather than trying to find a pool or the time to do it. Every hotel chain has a fitness room, and seek those that have decent facilities. I have run the stairs in hotels many times. You'd be amazed what just thirty minutes of walking or running your hotel stairs will do for your legs and burn off calories while you listen to music alone without having to worry about traffic, security, or getting lost at night. Set goals to make a certain time with each climb to the top. That beer or glass of wine in the hotel bar will taste a lot better. Look for hotels that have parks and walking trails nearby.

Incorporate your family. Join a health club that has activities or day care for your kids while you exercise. Ride bikes with your older kids, and pull your toddler or infant in a trailer behind your bike. Walk or jog with your kids and push your infant in a stroller. Sign your family up for a local walk, 5k (3.1-mile), or 10k (6.2-mile) run, and make it a family event—a family finish line vision. My eight-year-old daughter got so excited to do a kids triathlon and felt as much pride doing it as I did completing my first Ironman. She beams with pride every time she wears the race shirt and tells everyone about it. She loved riding her bike, running, and swimming with me to train.

Exercise at home while your kids are sleeping. Use indoor stationary bikes while watching something on TV that motivates you, like healthy people that you want to look like. Early in my career I watched replays of an Ironman triathlon, imagining that I was there, lost in my finish line vision. Or make the commitment to ride your stationary bike the entire time you are watching your favorite TV show. Invest in home video exercise programs like P90x or Insanity or Beachbody.

Change it up to keep it interesting. Nothing changes if ... you don't make changes. I do strength training at my local health club several times a week. I often see the same people doing exactly the same machines, the same weights, every day. They look the same and never see any improvement and eventually get bored and lose motivation. Mix up your workouts with some cardio and some strength training. Do different machines at the gym. Ride your bike one day, run another, swim another, lift weights another. Take a different route on your walks, rides, and runs. Keep your body guessing. Cross training and cross fit workouts are great for variety and challenging you. Your body likes different foods. It will like different exercises too.

Don't quit before you see results. Be patient. It will not happen in thirty days. If you change your diet and start exercising daily, you should start to see results in thirty days, but the real change will take three months. It takes ninety days for an activity to become a habit, and then it becomes a way of life. That's why you need to make it enjoyable so you will want to do it every day. In a few months you will walk into a room of people, friends, or relatives that have not seen you since you started, and heads will turn to notice you. "Wow. Look at her. She looks great." You will be thrilled. That's your finish line vision moment. Think about that moment when you are exercising. You will get there. Don't quit.

Five years old. I wish I still had those pants.

My youth football team. I'm No. 45 on the top. I didn't need a helmet with that hair.

1985, my high school basketball team, senior year. I worked hard to make that team.

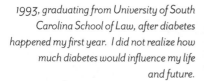

1990. Working on US Senator Thurmond's staff in Washington was a privilege and a learning experience.

1993, graduating from University of South Carolina School of Law, after diabetes happened my first year. I did not realize how much diabetes would influence my life and future.

At 14,505 feet, Mt. Whitney, California, is the highest summit in the contiguous United States. I climbed the mountaineer's route in 1998 hoping to throw my diabetes off the top. It didn't work.

2000, Kona, Hawaii, marathon. My first marathon and the hardest thing I thought I would ever do with diabetes. It was about a hundred degrees and I barely made it to the finish, then threw up on a guy who told me about the Ironman triathlon.

2001, Rome, Italy, marathon. It was great to have my mom and dad travel to Italy to watch me run my second marathon as a fund-raiser for the American Diabetes Association.

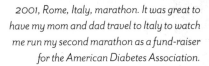

2002, Ironman Florida. My first Ironman. I was such a beginner, I did it on a road bike with removable clip-on aero bars.

A critical part of the early morning routine
before every race, checking blood sugar
multiple times. Controlling it is my triathlon's
fourth event.

Some races I ran part of the Ironman marathon
with my own bottle of high-carbohydrate drink
and gels to keep my blood sugar up. Nutrition
at the aid stations is not enough.

2004 Ironman Coeur d'Alene, Idaho. In the swim I always just tried to stay in contact with the faster swim leaders because I knew the bike was my best event coming up.

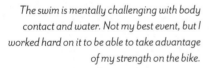

The swim is mentally challenging with body contact and water. Not my best event, but I worked hard on it to be able to take advantage of my strength on the bike.

Half Ironman St. Croix, Virgin Islands, known as Beauty and the Beast. Its vicious mile-long climb averaging 14 percent makes this one of the toughest bike courses.

Testing my VO2 max on the bike, a hard test leading to maximum effort with a mask on your face measuring your oxygen uptake capacity. I was doing anything to improve.

In the wind tunnel to improve my aerodynamic position at a facility for testing NASCAR and Indy racecars. My Omnipod insulin pump is attached to my right shoulder.

Triathlon is three sports so I tried to improve them all. Testing my max heart rate and lactate threshold training zones for the run. On this test you go as hard as you can as long as you can until you break. It hurts.

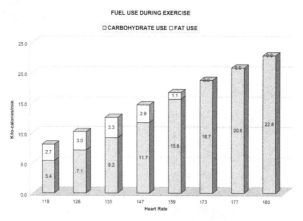

FUEL USE DURING EXERCISE

□ CARBOHYDRATE USE □ FAT USE

Testing confirmed that I burned the most fat in my heart rate zone 126–147 b/min, the labored conversation pace that I needed to race most of the Ironman.

After working hard and improving for several years, in 2004 I was honored to make USA Triathlon All-American and qualify for the US Long-Distance Triathlon team.

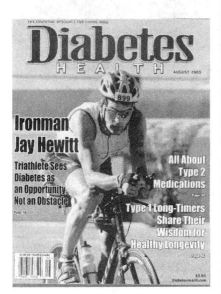

My results and making Team USA started catching the attention of the media. I was honored that I could be a positive influence and motivation for people with diabetes.

Ironman Louisville. I always looked forward to the bike, 112 miles of speed and fueling before the marathon.

Running the Ironman Lake Placid marathon in the shadow of the Winter Olympic ski jumps.

Stopping to test blood sugar at the special needs area halfway through the marathon. My special needs bag always had a blood sugar meter, insulin, and extra carbohydrates. Testing cost me time, but I had to do it.

2004, Ironman Florida. I had improved a lot since my first time at this race two years earlier: bike position, equipment, fitness, and results.

2004 Ironman Florida was a great race for me—painful and exhilarating. I beat half of the professional field as an amateur, but I really felt like I finally beat diabetes.

2005 ITU Long-Distance Triathlon World Championship for Team USA in Denmark. I don't know why I look so happy to battle these men and jellyfish for 4 km in the icy waters leading to the North Sea.

2005 ITU Long-Distance Triathlon World Championship, Denmark. It was always such an honor to race for Team USA overseas.

This reminder was on Team USA apparel. I never forgot it.

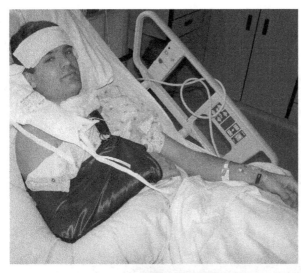

March 2006, after surgery to repair my broken collarbone from a crash in a bike race. I feel about as happy about it as I look.

Three days after surgery I was on my trainer with my arm propped on a stand. I couldn't ride outside but had to train for RAAM coming up in a few months.

June 2006, RAAM podium. It was great to cycle across America and be part of a team to inspire people with diabetes.

*October 2006, SC Half
Ironman, checking my
blood sugar in transi-
tion before the run. I
had a plan to propose
to Anna during the run
but crashed near the end
of the bike causing the
wounds on my shoulder,
hands, and knee.*

*Before I proposed to Anna, I tried to wash the
blood off my body holding the box with the
diamond ring in my left hand.*

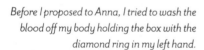

*I ran seven miles holding the bloody ring
box until I finally spotted Anna in the crowd.
She was shocked. I finished the race and we
celebrated our engagement at the ER to get
asphalt out of my back.*

November 2006, with
Anna before the ITU
Long-Distance Triathlon
World Championship
in Canberra, Australia.
The Aussies are great
triathletes and have an
amazing country.

2006 ITU Worlds Australia for Team USA.
Much of the bike was hard climbs in the barren
bush outback. I loved it.

It was great to travel
Australia with Anna after
the world championship
race. Excited to start
transitioning to new
events in life with my
family.

Some great kids after a swim-run biathlon I helped put on for several years at Camp Joslin for kids with diabetes.

I love inspiring any kid to overcome fears and obstacles to achieve a hard goal, like this one racing at Camp.

In 2008 I started my own company called Finish Line Vision to pursue career opportunities that arose from racing.

In 2009 I began motivational speaking to healthcare audiences and the public about managing diabetes and health.

I speak to corporate and business audiences about achieving goals and overcoming obstacles in life and work. I love motivating an audience.

Speaking and management consulting are a new passion that came from racing triathlons with diabetes. Diabetes has shaped my life and career.

I take more pride from my kids working to achieve hard goals like a youth triathlon than anything I accomplished on my own.

My family is my priority and love of my life.

CHAPTER 11

EARN YOUR FINISH LINE

Topic: Discipline and Hard Work

MY FIRST IRONMAN

Ironman Florida 2002 was everything I thought it would be and more. Since it was my first Ironman, I was not trying to race it too hard. I didn't even know what was too hard. I was just trying to finish it. Everything was a test: blood sugar, nutrition, insulin, swim pace, bike pace, and run pace. Unfortunately, I did not keep records of those things like I would in later races. For all I knew, this would be my only Ironman. There was no need to keep a record.

SWIM

One thing I was not prepared for was the intensity of the swim start. It was not really a start. It was more like a stampede. Over two thousand people crashed into the surf with me—or really on *top* of me. Half Ironman and shorter races are wave starts separating the field into smaller groups starting about every two to three minutes so there is less body contact. But in 2002 most Ironman races were all one mass start of the whole amateur field. It's hard to find thousands of people to prepare for that. Standing on the beach I felt like I was in that crowd of lunatics waiting to run from the bulls in Pamplona, Spain, or outside Wal-Mart at 5:00 a.m. on Black Friday. *Don't people die in soccer stampedes in Europe and religious pilgrimages in the Middle East? And we're getting ready to do this into the ocean?*

I positioned myself well off to the side of the field so I would not get crushed by better swimmers from behind or have to swim around (or over) slower ones. I wanted as much open water as possible. I generally knew my pace from racing three half Ironmans that year. When the cannon fired there was an explosion of humanity rushing to the ocean like a violent charge of savage, neoprene wetsuit warriors attacking a ship in the surf. It was a thunderous roar, and the ground seemed to shake either from the cannon blast, the cheering crowd, the pounding surf, the helicopters overhead, or the two thousand people running with me into the Gulf of Mexico.

Run! Jump! Dive! Swim! It was chaos—arms and legs and bodies everywhere. I got pushed underwater. I hit someone in the back and a foot hit me in the face. My heart was in my throat. I was close to hyperventilating. The thrashing of the water felt like I was in a giant pod of sea otters being attacked by great white sharks. I had been in enough half Ironman swims—one on this very beach just six months prior at Gulf Coast—that I knew I would eventually find some open water, calm down, and swim my pace. My body rose and descended with the rolling swells of surf as we cleared the breakers several hundred yards from the beach. Two laps around this 1.2-mile course and the swim was over before I knew it. I finished the 2.4 miles in one hour and ten minutes.

A study of over forty-one thousand Ironman athletes over several years in twenty-five different Ironman races and bodies of water (ocean, rivers, and lakes) reveals that the average swim time is one hour and sixteen minutes. The swim cutoff time is two hours and twenty minutes. So I was better than average but not great. I was happy with it for my first one, just trying to test this Ironman distance. I was not going to fret over a few minutes gained or lost in the swim. There was a lot more time to gain or lose in the next 138 miles. I was pleased that my blood sugar behaved during the swim when I checked it in transition before the bike. I did a lot of workouts in the pool swimming that same distance, so I didn't expect something dramatic to change in the race.

Swim done, onto the bike. Take it one stage at a time. The swim is the psychological test. The bike and run are the physical tests.

BIKE

Ironman Florida's bike is dead flat but with lots of wind, common for coastal races. Sometimes the wind is pushing you sideways, sometimes in your face grinding you into painful exhaustion, sometimes buffeting and swirling in different directions, but it seems like it is never at your back. I would much rather climb a long, steep mountain than fight the wind. On a mountain you can see the climb and pace your effort, and you know where the top is and can recover on the descent. The wind is constant and invisible. You don't know when it will relent and it usually doesn't.

A flat ocean course is not easier than a mountain course and is often harder, because you never get to coast downhill. You also can never draft behind competitors in the Ironman bike like you can in a cycling road race. You have to keep seven meters between you or make a pass. It's 112 miles of pedaling all on your own power. For this first one I was still racing my standard road bike with temporary clip-on aerobars. I watched with disgust (and envy) as guys cruised past me on their super-duper, aerodynamic, triathlon bikes with solid rear carbon fiber disc wheels. I knew my road bike with heavy spoked metal road cycling wheels was slowing me down. I felt like a rookie, and I was.

Triathlon bikes are very expensive—$3,000 to $4,000 just for the frame, and a carbon disk wheel and front wheel is another $2,000. Then you must purchase cranks arms, pedals, aerobars, cassette, shifters, chain, and brakes for another grand or two. I wasn't going to drop all that cash before I completed my first Ironman.

I felt like I was pushing an umbrella into the wind the way I was sitting up and sapping my energy. It's amazing to compare photos of me cycling in this race to later races when I would have a racing bike and better aero position. If I finished and liked it, I could invest in one of those.

I used an insulin pump for the race, attaching it to my body after the swim like I had in shorter races that year. I finished the bike in five hours and forty-three minutes. The average Ironman bike time is six hours and twenty-five minutes, so just like the swim, I was better than average—not great, but I was happy with it for my first one.

RUN

I checked my blood sugar in the transition and started the marathon. I had never ridden 112 miles and then run a marathon. You don't practice the whole event in training. In training several times I had cycled a hundred miles and run five just to get a feel for it. My legs were beat, but I tried to hold a pace and keep moving.

I was targeting a four-hour marathon—a conservative just-see-how-it-goes pace. But I had to walk a few times in the last thirteen miles from an upset stomach and cramping in my legs. The average marathon time in the Ironman is four hours and fifty-four minutes. I did 4:38—really slow. Just like the swim and the bike, I was just better than average but not great.

I got emotional running down the last hundred meters. Crowds lined the route screaming, cheering, and banging on the barriers, with music blaring over loudspeakers. The last fifty meters was carpeted, lights lining the route because the November sun had set. The race started at 7:00 a.m. and it was almost 7:00 p.m. now. My exhaustion enhanced the delirium, my emotions raw and unrestrained. I had no strength in my body to resist the emotion. As the race announcer shouted, "Jay Hewitt, you are an Ironman!" I raised my arms crossing the line. I knew how far I had come and what I had to overcome to cross that line. It was the most powerful moment of my life up to that point. While I had been proud of racing multiple marathons and half Ironmans, finishing this first Ironman I felt real victory over diabetes.

While my memory of much of the race is fuzzy and clouded by fatigue and pain, the last hundred meters are crystal clear, branded on my brain. That was my first finish line moment. I would relive it many times as my finish line vision, drawing me to the next one.

A NEW GOAL

Another significant moment happened after the race. The next day thousands of people gathered for the awards banquet at a convention hall near the race site. The average finish time for an Ironman is twelve hours and thirty-five minutes. Like my individual split times, I had just barely beaten that with my eleven hours and forty-eight minutes, so I wasn't scaring any awards. Better than average but not great. But I was still pretty proud for my first one.

I was an Ironman—an Ironman with type 1 diabetes. I wanted to find that guy from the finish line of my first marathon in Hawaii over two years ago—the one I threw up on when he told me about the Ironman—and say, "How do you like me now?!"

Then I watched the top finishers called up on to the stage to receive their awards. These guys did the race in under ten hours. The guy who did it in nine hours and forty-five minutes beat me by two hours and finished fiftieth overall out of two thousand. *Two hours?! These guys had time to cross the finish line, shower, go to a movie, stop by Starbucks for a latte, and return a few emails and then come back to watch me stumble and wobble across the finish line! I about lost a lung and puked a kidney to do it in the time I did and these guys did it two hours faster? How did they do that?*

I was in awe. Before the race I did not know who the best were. Now I could see them. I studied them. They looked fit and powerful, strong and fast, their bodies and faces tight with low body fat and solid muscle just beneath the skin. I could almost see the cardiovascular engine of their lungs and heart purring that had powered them 140.6 miles in less than ten hours. Their legs were tight and ripped, and their calves looked like tight balls of rubber. Health and fitness radiated out of their bodies like beams of light.

That's what an elite Ironman triathlete looks like. That's what the fittest guys in the world look like. They were on the US national long-distance triathlon team and the German and Australian national teams and from other countries around the world.

A fire started burning in me—another dream. I now had a goal with a lot more failure potential. *I don't want to just do an Ironman. I want to be one of the best. Cut two hours off my time. Break ten hours. Make the US national team. And I'm going to do it with diabetes.*

But how am I going to do that?

GET BETTER EQUIPMENT

I used my road bike in that first Ironman and it was like bringing a wooden racket to a tennis tournament. It worked, just not very well. The day after the race Peter took me to the expo tent for Elite Bicycles, a small company in Pennsylvania that made custom bikes for triathletes. They measured my body, legs, arms, reach, torso, and every possible dimension. They would build me a custom-made frame from light-weight but stiff aluminum. I needed a stiffer, more rigid frame than most triathletes because my body was larger and heavier at 6'3" and over 180 pounds. Most triathletes are under 5'10" and 150 pounds. I generate more torque and power with my pedal stroke, and the bike frame needed to be able to handle that power without flexing or wobbling while descending or cornering at high speeds.

That was only the frame. I also ordered carbon fiber aerobars and brake shifters and gear components with several cassettes of different gear ratios to ride on flat courses, rolling hill courses, and steep mountainous courses.

We also visited the booth for Zipp wheels, and I ordered a carbon fiber solid disc rear wheel that would be used in most races and wheels with deep, four-inch rims. These carbon wheels would be much lighter and faster than the standard road cycling wheels with metal rims that I had been racing on.

I basically built a triathlon racing bike piece by piece. The new bike would be much more aerodynamic and about five pounds lighter than my road bike. My bike and my wallet lost a lot of weight that day.

I did not deserve this racing bike until I had been racing triathlons for a year, had completed my first Ironman, knew what the demands were, and was committed to continuing and getting better. Is there better equipment that can help you reach your goals in your career, athletics, passions, or life? Have you earned it yet?

Before you invest money, prove to yourself (and others who may control your money: parents, spouse, your boss) that you are committed to your goal by doing it cheap first. Show your dedication and test your resolve. You do not want a brand-new expensive bike (guitar, racket, computer, etc.) sitting in a room, unused, wasting money. You will use it more and appreciate it when you know what it was like not to have it. You worked hard to get better without it, and now you are committed to getting better with it. Earn your gear first.

KEEP RACING, KEEP IMPROVING

Whatever your goal is, to get better you have to keep doing your sport, art, exercise, writing, or work. Keep testing yourself and doing what you love. Improvement takes time, and it is rewarding to see your improvement along the way.

After Ironman Florida 2002 in November I trained that winter to get ready for the 2003 racing season. I focused on my running since that needed the most improvement, and running is easier than cycling in rain, cold, and dark winter weather. In March 2003 I ran the Virginia Beach marathon in a new personal best time of 3:34, thirty minutes faster than my previous best. In May I raced the Gulf Coast half Ironman again and improved my time by fifteen minutes from the previous year.

In June I ran the Kona Marathon in Hawaii again, my third time running it as a fund-raiser for the ADA. I loved supporting the ADA, and they even asked me to speak at the pasta dinner to hundreds of people gathered for the race. That was my first speaking engagement. I loved it.

MAKE IT HARDER TO MAKE IT EASIER

Peter was always looking to make life more painful and training harder. One of the most evil tortuous devices he discovered and put on his bike and mine were called PowerCranks. The pedals on a bicycle are attached to two solid bars called the crank arms. Normal cranks arms work together, synchronized and connected in the bottom bracket, so when you push down/forward on one pedal the other pedal comes up behind you—a constant circular motion like blades of a fan.

Unfortunately this leads to an inefficient pedal stroke because most people simply push down on the pedals. The back half of the pedal stroke is just wasted unless you are wearing cycling shoes clipped to the pedals to pull up. But even cyclists that wear cycling shoes attached to the pedals rarely pedal efficiently in a complete circle. It is too easy to just push down and let the other foot and leg coast up the back side, especially when you are tired. Cyclists call that "pedaling in squares" or "mashing a gear." Your quads are powerful so pushing down with them is easier than pulling up with your hamstrings and hip flexors. The best professional cyclists pedal in circles, pulling up and pushing down to generate twice the power. But you have to force and train yourself to do that.

PowerCranks force you to do that. Replace your crank arms with these, and you are in for twice the workout. Each PowerCrank arm is independent. If you push down on one pedal, the other pedal does not come up. It just hangs there, swinging loosely. You have to pull it up on the back half of the pedal stroke with your foot attached to the pedal. It takes a lot of practice, but it forces you to pedal in complete circles, strengthening your hip flexors and hamstrings and abdominal muscles. PowerCranks are also extremely heavy, intentionally weighing about three to four pounds each—more than three times the weight of most crank arms—further strengthening and working those muscles. A one-hour ride on PowerCranks is like a three-hour ride on regular cranks.

I rode PowerCranks every day in training. I put a set on my road bike and my new triathlon bike. I rode them in group rides and solo rides. I rode four and five hours for eighty to one hundred miles on these torturous devices. The workout was grueling and more than double the effort to hold the same pace with cyclists riding regular cranks.

But after training on them all winter and spring, when I took the PowerCranks off and put on my regular cranks for the Gulf Coast half Ironman the following May, it felt like I had a rocket on my bike. My knees almost hit me in the chin, flying up effortlessly. When I pushed down on the front half of the pedal stroke I was so used to lifting my leg up on the back half that my other leg shot up and the bike propelled forward. I was pedaling in complete circles, pushing and lifting, generating power the entire pedal stroke. It was amazing. It also allowed me to rest my quads and use my hamstrings and glutes cycling, saving different leg muscles for the run.

Is there a training device to help your performance get better by making your practice harder?

COPY THE BEST

Somebody is always better than you. Find them and copy them. Ask to work with them. Compete against them and get spanked by them. Then you will get better. Whether it is someone that plays the trumpet better than you, a salesperson that always seems to close the sale or get the company sales awards, or the tennis player at your club who can torch your backhand like a cannon shot that breaks your wrist, there is a reason they are better. Learn from them. Often, they are happy to help you and flattered that you asked. If you compete with them and are afraid they won't want to give away their secrets to success, ask honestly and humbly. Remember, they used to be like you. They weren't born that good.

In triathlon, that meant finding the best in each individual sport and training like a swimmer, a cyclist, and a runner. I started riding every Tuesday evening after work with the local cycling club in practice races of between thirty and sixty miles. These were pure road cyclists—called "roadies"—who didn't swim or run. Cycling is what they did, all they did.

These Tuesday night rides were A, B, and C groups of between fifty and a hundred cyclists, segregated by ability. You did not ride in the A group unless you had racing experience, reserved for the best cyclists with USA cycling certification of pro and a Category ("Cat") 1, 2, or 3 license. Even though I was probably about a Cat 4 ability at this point, I had not done any USA cycling official races so my license was a Cat 5. I wondered if I'd ever be good enough to ride with the As.

The course we rode was always the same—a seven-mile loop on a seldom-traveled road around a long airport runway. It used to be the Donaldson Center Air Force Base in the 1950s but had been converted to a private airport for Lockheed Martin to repair aircraft. We had a police escort with blue lights leading the group to clear traffic for us.

Riding with pure road cyclists was great training and even harder because I used PowerCranks. It was like running in work boots while everyone else wore running shoes. I both hated and loved it. I dreaded it all day at the office with a knot in my stomach knowing the pain that was coming that evening at the Donaldson cycling slaughterhouse.

Without fail, every time on the first lap, I felt that I might not be able to handle the pain. At lap two (miles eight to fourteen) the pace would pick up and I would think, *Ugh, this hurts, I might not make six laps tonight.* By laps four and five about half of the hundred cyclists who had started an hour and a half and about thirty-five miles ago had disappeared. By lap six (miles thirty-six to forty-two) it was the fastest seven miles and I would burn all my matches with the remaining gluttons for pain as we powered and sprinted to the line.

Of course, being a triathlete, I always had to quickly throw on my running shoes and do a three- or four-mile run while the rest of the cyclists sat by their cars chatting, watching me run off with curious looks. My quads would throb for hours every Tuesday night when I collapsed in bed for a great night's sleep after a big bowl of pasta to prevent nighttime low blood sugar.

I loved this feeling. Weekly agony survived. I knew it was making me better.

One Saturday in the spring of 2003 Peter asked if I wanted to ride with him on a long training ride. I was flattered. That first time I was as nervous as a race. *Could I keep up with him for seventy miles?* I did, and after that we met every Saturday at 7 a.m. to ride sixty to a hundred miles together. I watched how he rode, his position on the bike, his pedaling cadence, how he paced himself, even his drinking and eating.

If you want to get better, copy and imitate someone better than you. I was studying everything. It was hard riding and really pushed me, and I think I might have pushed him a

If you want to get better, copy and imitate someone better than you.

little too. It's always better to have a training partner to keep yourself honest, and I'm sure he didn't want to slack off in front of me. It was also great to have company on long four- and five-hour rides. We talked about everything—my job as a lawyer, his life in Czechoslovakia and America, triathlons, women, the fat guy standing shirtless outside the mobile home in forty degrees, or the turkeys, fox, and deer we spotted in the quiet forests we passed through. We battled thunderstorms and rednecks in pickup trucks yelling and throwing things at us on country roads.

Dogs charged at us from houses, causing an immediate explosion in our heart rates to outsprint them as they barked and growled at our heels. I began carrying pepper spray and got good at spraying it in a charging dog's face at twenty-five miles per hour or planting my foot or water bottle firmly in the dog's nose. One time, a year later in 2004, a large dog charged us so fast it knocked Peter off his bike onto the road. He suffered bad gashes and ruptured a tendon in his knee, and it severely damaged his very expensive Italian racing bike. He could not race for several months. My day job as a lawyer came in handy when I got a claim paid by the dog owner's insurance company.

IRONMAN LAKE PLACID

I did my second Ironman in Lake Placid, New York, in July 2003. Lake Placid is deep in the Adirondack Mountains of upstate New York and the site of the 1980 Winter Olympics. The course is beautiful with rivers and lush greenery and long, hard, mountainous climbs on the bike course. You need big mountains to host the Winter Olympics. The transition area was the interior of the outdoor speed skating oval, where Eric Heiden won five gold medals, next to the hockey arena where the US team won the gold medal after defeating the Soviets in what is famously known as the "Miracle on Ice." The place is steeped in athletic history.

The weather on race day was horrible with strong wind and torrential rain from summer storms during the morning and afternoon for the bike and run. I did the swim in 1:06, four minutes faster than I had in Ironman Florida, so I was pleased, but the payoff for a good swim is minimal. The bike and run are where the real money is.

My blood sugar in transition (T1) was 180 mg/dl. A little higher than a normal 100 mg/dl but just what I needed after swimming 2.4 miles and getting ready to bike 112. I knew the racing would keep bringing it down. A worker in the transition tent gave me a puzzled look as I pricked my finger and dropped blood on my meter. *What? You've never seen someone do a blood test in transition?*

Rain fell throughout the bike. I felt strong for the first eighty miles, climbing and descending steep mountain roads, sometimes at forty-five miles per hour, and cruising along the rivers in the valley. It was a two-loop bike course so we traveled the same fifty-six-mile route twice. At about mile eighty-five I caught a few of the pro women, which was nice because, well, they were pros and I was not. My legs felt good and I was having no trouble keeping my cadence. It was cloudy and cool in these mountains of upstate New York. At mile ninety-five I approached the base of White Face Mountain. I had already been up this climb several hours ago on the first loop. Now there was only fifteen miles to go, all straight up the mountain back to the village of Lake Placid and the transition area. At the start of the climb I saw a few guys in front of me toss their bottles at the last aid station to shed extra weight. A full water bottle weighs about two pounds. I had just a few seconds to consider this before I passed the last aid station—you're penalized for discarding anything on the course outside an aid station. I felt okay and well hydrated, so I tossed my full bottle of carbohydrate drink at the last aid station and started the seven-mile climb up the mountain.

Big mistake.

PURIFIED BY PAIN

I hit the climb and started struggling. I had no power in my legs. I could spin my pedals in an easy gear, but I could generate no power. I had not been eating enough the last hour on the flats and rolling hills in the valley. The load on my legs was not hard in the valley, but starting this mountain climb a second time was like hitting a wall.

If the climb was not hard enough, the wind made it worse from a building afternoon storm, steadily blowing into our faces, pushing us back down the mountain like a weather god who did not want us to reach the top. Having worked my way to the front of the field for five hours and a hundred miles, I now started falling back from racers in front of me. I was suffering. My legs felt useless. My heart rate climbed to 165 to 170 beats per minute, above my anaerobic threshold. I could not generate any power. Athletes I had passed miles before were gaining and passing me, and it felt like they slugged me in the chest every time they did.

It was like that nightmare we've all had where someone is chasing you and you try to run, but your legs won't move. It was like I had blown seven cylinders in an eight-cylinder engine, sliding back down the mountain. My lungs gasped for air and my legs screamed. The pain began to consume me, both the searing, burning, scorching pain in my quads trying to generate power that wasn't there and the psychological pain of watching racers pass that I had spent a hundred miles getting ahead of. My mind was foggy and dazed. All I could think about was *pedal, push … keep going … don't stop.* My thoughts sputtered and stammered like a cell phone losing its signal. My lungs heaved and blood pounded through my head, throbbing in my temples and eyes. My quads were searing and burning. The wind howled down the mountain at me, pummeling my face and body as sweat dripped off my face.

It may sound demented, but if I hadn't been losing so much time, I would have actually enjoyed this for the sheer torture of it. I was paying the price of victory over my diabetes, suffering for a cause, and proving that I was stronger than diabetes, this mountain, and the wind. I thought, *You will not break me.* It reminds me of the scene in Mel Gibson's movie *Braveheart*, where he has the option to give in to the king or "be purified by pain." I could sit at home and give in to diabetes or be purified by pain climbing the mountains of Lake Placid. Give me the pain.

I finally made it to the top of the mountain and bike finish, dismounted at the line, and started for the racks of "bike-to-run" transition bags. As soon as my feet touched the ground, I knew I was in trouble. I was light-headed and dizzy, seeing spots and having trouble moving, like a head rush from standing up too fast or a blow to the head. I wobbled and had a hard time finding my transition bag with my race number on the rack among thousands of others, even though they were in numerical order. I couldn't count. I finally found it and dumped it on the ground in the changing tent. There were other racers in the tent getting ready to run the marathon. Even with my slow crawl losing time going up the mountain, I was still in the top quarter of the field. I pricked my finger and checked my blood sugar as I kicked off my cycling shoes, put on my running shoes, and stuffed some things back into the transition bag.

The display on the meter counted down the seconds … five … four … three … two … one … forty-seven.

Wow. A forty-seven blood sugar is dangerously low if you're sitting on your sofa watching TV. It's devastating if you're cycling up a mountain and need to run a marathon. I ripped off the cap and drank from a bottle of high-carbohydrate drink in my transition bag, some of it running down my mouth and chin. I bit into a Clif Bar. It was my responsibility to have a blood sugar meter, carb drink, and bars in my transition bag. I couldn't run around the transition area expecting (hoping) the race to have that for me. You cannot expect someone else to take care of your problem if you don't first do everything yourself. I sat there for a few minutes trying to recover and let those carbs digest, still a little dizzy. The clock was ticking. I was losing time sitting there watching athletes come in off the bike and run out for the marathon.

After a few minutes I stood and started out of the transition tent. Thousands of people were outside cheering the athletes starting the marathon. My legs were still a bit wobbly, but I jogged out of transition, holding the bottle of carb drink in one hand and clutching a half-eaten Clif Bar in the other. About twenty meters out of the transition tent I realized I still had on my cycling helmet. You aren't supposed to run the marathon with your cycling helmet still on. I ran back into the tent and handed it to the official who was just about to take my transition bag away. Low blood sugar confusion and exhaustion—this could be a long marathon.

The first five miles were a slow jog trying to get my blood sugar to come up. I resigned myself to just run the best that I could without worrying about time. I had made an inexperienced mistake with my nutrition. At mile ten I entered a stretch of road with large fields on each side. Dark clouds were overhead and an angry storm wind blasted across the road. The sky opened and poured rain sideways in sheets that pummeled my face and body. It was like running through a car wash. Even though this was difficult, just like on the bike, I looked up at the storm and thought, *I love this! This is why I trained. Make it harder! 140 miles. Mountains. Low blood sugar. Rain. Wind. What else have you got?* I felt like Lieutenant Dan in *Forest Gump* atop the mast of the shrimp boat in the hurricane, shouting at God, "Is this all you got? You call this a storm? Come and get me! It's you and me! You … can't … sink … this … boat!"

RUNNING BALLERINAS

Watching top pros running back in as I was still headed out to the turnaround—they were about two hours ahead of me—I noticed some of them had an odd running form. They took short, light steps, even if they had long legs. They looked like they were almost leaning forward. I am tall, 6'3" with long legs. I felt like I was taking long, clunking strides, with my feet landing in front of me on my heels. That was the way I had always run. But that's not how these guys looked. They looked like ballerinas tip-toeing down the road, their feet barely making a sound. *They must know something I don't. They look kinda weird, but they are two hours ahead of me.* I made a mental note to investigate this.

After twenty-six miles I crossed the finish line a bit disappointed, feeling like I still had energy in me. I wanted to be exhausted, totally spent. The low blood sugar had forced me to go easy and slow for about an hour of the race and sapped me of strength to push hard during the marathon. It was only my second Ironman, so I was still learning my limits and my nutrition. I finished with a time of 12:04:32, top third overall but still not very good.

CHANGE YOUR TECHNIQUE AND FORM

Soon after the race I investigated that odd running form I saw the elite guys doing. I found a video on the Pose Running Method. I never knew technique was important for running, but it is just like swimming, golf, tennis, or dancing. I thought you just ran like your legs naturally did, just do it more and longer. I didn't know you could change your running form.

I shortened my stride and brought my foot strike back under my body, landing on the ball of my foot rather than my heel out in front of me with my leg straight. Landing on your heel slows you down and sends shock waves up your legs. There is no elasticity in your heel, but there is in your calf, plantar fascia ligament that connects your heel to your toes, and a bended knee. That elasticity provides bounce and spring to propel you forward. The most efficient and fastest running form is for your foot to land under you like you are running barefoot down the beach or hopping up and down lightly on one foot, knee bent slightly, leaning forward. You can't hop on your heel. There's no spring and it causes jarring injury in your heel, shins, and knees. However, you don't want to bounce up and down running. That wastes energy. You want to use that elasticity to propel you forward, not up and down. Watch elite long-distance runners and you will see that their head stays level at a constant height, barely fluctuating up and down, like they are balancing a book on their head, with a slight forward lean at the waist. Their cadence is a constant rotating motion of their feet lightly touching under them, like a spinning wheel.

Over the next few months I started working on this new running form. I ran intervals in my socks on the soft outdoor track at Furman University and the grassy infield. On training runs I concentrated on shortening my stride like I was 5'8" rather than 6'3" and I leaned slightly forward. It felt weird, like I was tiptoeing down the road. I thought I must look silly doing this ballerina dance, but I'm sure no one noticed or cared. You always think people are looking at you when you feel self-conscious, when usually nobody cares. Don't worry about what others think. They are not paying attention to you. I was willing to look silly if that's what it took to improve. It would take time for this form to become natural, probably at least a year, so that I could do it by instinct and muscle memory in the latter stages of the Ironman marathon when I would be too tired to concentrate on it.

Have you tried changing the way you have always done something? Change your routine, form, habit, or technique in athletics, work, or life? It takes investigation and effort and time and a willingness to feel silly and uncomfortable until it is natural. You have to make changes to see changes.

You have to make changes to see changes.

GET CREATIVE—BORROW FROM MUSICIANS

Besides my running form I also needed to increase my running cadence—the number of times my feet hit the ground. More foot strikes means more opportunities to push forward, which means more speed. Shortening my stride would increase my cadence, but I still needed help to speed it up.

I tried counting my steps, but that got old fast. So I got creative. I thought outside sports. *What beats consistently at a regular cadence? Clocks? Yes, but I can't run with a clock, and it needs to be faster than one beat per second. Music? Yes, but I can't run for two hours listening to the same song. Hmmm, wait a minute! Music!* I visited a local music store and found a small, battery-powered metronome about the size of a beeper. Musicians use them to keep a steady tempo. It gave loud knocks on the tempo you selected. I researched and learned that elite runners have a cadence around ninety foot strikes per minute, about one every half second. I entered ninety beats per minute into the metronome and ran with this device in my hand, timing my feet to strike the ground with every knock. Running by people in the park generated odd looks from this loud knocking emanating from this device hidden in my hand. It sounded like I was running in wooden shoes. Sometimes you have to get creative and think outside the sport.

Another thing I did was to imagine I was running barefoot over hot coals. You wouldn't want your feet to stay on the hot coals long, right? You'd want to skim and float quickly and lightly across the coals, like a bug skimming across the surface of a lake. On long runs, when I was growing tired, I would chant to myself "Hot coals, relax your quads … hot coals, relax your quads." Then I would repeat that chant when I was tired in the last miles of the Ironman marathon. I also told myself to relax my shoulders and decrease tension in my upper body. I didn't want any energy being wasted on any part of my body that wasn't helping me move forward.

Think outside your sport, job, or area. What do others do in their area that you can use in yours? What is the metronome you can use for your running? Get creative.

CHANGE ANOTHER TECHNIQUE AND FORM

Just like changing my running form, I knew I needed to change my swimming technique. Technique is even more important in swimming. I took several stroke technique lessons from a local elite swim coach. I also watched videos from Total Immersion about proper swim technique: body balance and rotation, the catch, pull with high elbows, and glide. I watched underwater videos online of the world's best freestyle swimmers like Australian Ian Thorpe (the "Thorpedo"), a world-record holder and winner of multiple gold medals at the 2000 Olympics. I remembered how I had always played better golf after watching the Masters, mimicking the beautiful, smooth golf swings of the best pros. I imprinted Thorpe's swim stroke in my brain and repeated it during every swim workout. Catch ... pull ... rotate ... glide ... repeat.

It sounds counterintuitive, but fast endurance swimming for long distances requires smooth, graceful, almost slow strokes, like dancing with power. You cannot fight or overpower the water with fast, thrashing strokes. The water will win. You have to be efficient, make minimal splash and waves, slice through the water like a dolphin, and use it to propel you.

I did workouts in the pool just on proper balance, rotated on my side with my hands resting at my hips while I kicked slowly down the lane with one shoulder just above the water's surface like a submarine cruising into port. I was learning to keep my head, body, and legs balanced at the surface, so my lower body and legs did not sink and drag below me. Picture a motorboat on a lake with too much weight at the rear of the boat. The back end (the hull) drags in the water, pushing a huge wake, and the engine strains, slowing it down. But when weight is shifted to the front and the boat balances, it rises to the surface, glides across the top of the water, and increases speed with less strain on the engine.

Air is thinner than water. I needed to be a boat skimming across the surface and a fish slicing through below. Just like riding my bike with PowerCranks and running like a ballerina, these slow swim balance workouts looked and felt kind of weird, but I didn't care. This was making me better. For these workouts I had to swim when no other swimmers were using the lanes, because I was barely moving and would block them. So I would do it very early morning or late night or sometimes sneak out of my office at 10 a.m. and do it while grandmothers were in the pool next to me doing water aerobics. They looked at me strangely as I slowly passed back and forth. "Son, do you want to join our class?"

I reduced my stroke count, trying to get more glide with each stroke. Swim cadence is the opposite of running where I wanted to *increase* my running cadence. Endurance swimming is like golf—fewer strokes are better, as you get more from each stroke. Save energy and glide far and fast. I counted my strokes for each lap of the pool, trying to lower it. Gradually it started dropping, and my times did too. I knew I was swimming more efficiently with less energy and drag.

I did sets with short fins on my feet to get used to the feeling of fast movement in the water and streamlining my body. I did other sets using a pull buoy clinched between my knees so that I could not kick. Kicking your legs is important for speed and power when you are swimming short distances in a pool, but kicking hard for 2.4 miles in the ocean burns too much energy. The legs and hip flexors are large muscle groups needed for 112 miles of cycling and running a marathon. But I wouldn't be using my shoulders and arms after the swim so I could use them up now. Not only was I learning better technique but I was getting smarter about how to race.

I swam with paddles attached to my hands, strengthening my shoulders. I also used stretch cords attached to paddles in my basement, doing swim workouts at night while watching TV. I watched my technique in a mirror to have proper shoulder rotation and high elbows. This strengthened muscles in my shoulders and back—the ones that make a swimmer look like a V from their broad shoulders down to their slim waste. Eventually I found myself in races imagining I was back in my basement pulling on those stretch cords. Using stretch cords was also a great way to get in a swim workout at any time of day or night or in my hotel room while traveling. I will talk more about that when I discuss work-life balance and time management.

Are there aspects of your life or job that you can do more efficiently by avoiding wasting energy and time on things that provide little benefit, like kicking hard and splashing water without moving forward? Are you willing to look silly now so you can look great later? Are there tools like stretch cords and metronomes you can use to improve your work or sport or life?

MEDIA AND THE US NATIONAL TRIATHLON TEAM

The hard training started paying off. After Ironman Lake Placid in July I raced three half Ironmans preparing for Ironman Florida that November. I raced a half Ironman in Clermont, Florida, twenty minutes faster than my previous best for that distance. In September I raced a half Ironman in Oak Ridge, Tennessee, in another personal best time on a much tougher, hilly course, and the South Carolina half Ironman in a new personal best time. I was getting faster every race. Times were dropping. I was approaching the leaders, not scaring a win but finishing with them not too far in front.

In 2003 my Ironman racing started to catch the attention of the media. I was profiled on the cover of several national diabetes magazines, including *Diabetes Forecast*, published by the American Diabetes Association (ADA). I was extremely honored. That led to a few speaking requests from diabetes groups and more requests from the media.

I received letters and emails from people all over the US who were struggling with diabetes and from parents of kids with diabetes. I was honored that I inspired them and gave them hope. Suddenly my racing to prove to myself that I could conquer diabetes became something more. I realized that I was helping and motivating others. It made me want to race even faster.

In November 2003 I raced Ironman Florida in 10:29, an improvement of over one hour and fifteen minutes from my first Ironman race on that same course just one year before. In my final half Ironman of the year I had a great race and finished ninth and qualified for the US National Team for Long Distance Triathlon.

Wow, I thought. I could race for the national team the next year at the 2004 Long Distance Triathlon World Championship in Sweden. I started getting sponsors in the sport: Clif Bar for nutrition and Rudy Project for helmets and sunglasses. Pharmaceutical companies that made products for people with diabetes offered monetary sponsorships to wear their logos on my jersey.

It seemed liked all the hard work was paying off. Everything was going in the right direction. The next year would be full of success.

Oh, how right, and wrong, I was.

CHAPTER 12

WHAT DO I DO NOW?

Topic: Handling Change and Failure

I was excited to start the 2004 racing season. I trained hard all winter. South Carolina does not get snow like the Northeast, but it does get cold rain and ice in the upstate near the Blue Ridge Mountains where I live in Greenville—cold enough to be uncomfortable cycling and running outside for two to four hours. On some long Saturday rides in twenty-five-degree weather I had to wear every piece of cold weather cycling gear I had: winter gloves and liners; spandex leg warmers; under layers; long-sleeve jersey and a thick cycling jacket; wool socks; insulated covers over my cycling shoes; a thermal hat under my helmet; a hood covering my head, neck, and face; and glasses covering my eyes. Not a bit of flesh was visible. I looked like I was scuba diving. Cycling for hours in freezing wind will numb your hands and feet, so I put plastic bags over my socks to hold in heat, a trick I learned playing night football games as a kid. Sometimes my water bottles froze so I had to pour hot water over them at gas stations. My Clif Bars were frozen rocks.

These rides were painfully cold just like the ninety-five-degree rides in July were painfully hot. I loved them both—training when I feel like no one else is willing to do it. I was getting ahead of the competition. With little daylight in the winter I did a lot of two-hour rides on my bike on my indoor trainer in my basement after working all day at my office. I would soak towels dripping sweat on them on the floor with a fan blowing on me even though it was below freezing outside. I could have hooked my trainer to my house like a generator and saved money on my electric bill. Trainer rides are difficult on the butt and in some ways harder than riding outside because you don't get to change position, coast, or stand up. It is monotonous, constant pedaling. After a few months I was so desperate to ride outside I rode at 5 a.m. before work in the rain with lights on my bike.

That spring I did a few 10k run races and sprint triathlons before I raced the Gulf Coast half Ironman in May and finished almost thirty-five minutes faster than the prior year and an hour faster than the year before that. Two weeks later I traveled back to Florida to race the Florida half Ironman in Orlando. Racing two half Ironmans in two weeks would prepare me for some back-to-back races coming up that summer. About two hundred meters into the 1.2-mile swim in Florida, another athlete punched me in the face, knocking my goggles off. I briefly treaded water and grabbed my goggles before they sank to the bottom. I'm pretty sure it was unintentional, but I never saw who did it. Or maybe it was an alligator. There was no point in trying to figure out who it was. It is impossible to tell in the thrashing arms and legs. Just like life, you waste energy and time trying to retaliate and get revenge. It distracts from your race or your job. It's better to just recover and keep going. My eye throbbed, and I never quite found my rhythm in the remaining mile of the swim. I exited the water with a sore eye, a disappointing five minutes slower than my swim just two weeks prior at Gulf Coast.

Sometimes life or your competition punch you in the face. Use it as motivation to take out your revenge on what you do best. For me that was the bike.

I had a good bike—my winter training had paid off—and finished

Sometimes life or your competition punch you in the face. Use it as motivation to take out your revenge on what you do best.

the bike in two hours and twenty-two minutes, averaging 23.6 miles per hour, forty-seventh out of two thousand in the race with about thirty professionals.

I drew more blood in T2, ready to inject myself with my insulin pen if it was too high. In the frenetic intensity of T2 of a triathlon—hot and sweaty off the bike, ready to run, and the clock ticking—drawing blood and deciding insulin doses and whether to eat carbs or inject myself with a needle is not easy. In this flurry of activity I always have to pause and think clearly so as not to make a mistake. Little diabetes details, like over or underdosing or eating or leaving my meter or insulin exposed in the sun in T1 before the bike, can ruin my race. The meter will not function and the insulin is destroyed if either gets too hot.

Fortunately my blood sugar was fine at 150, so I felt good running about a 7:15–30 pace for 13.1 miles. I drank at every aid station to hydrate in the sunny Florida midday heat and squeezed gels in my mouth. I finished seven minutes faster than two weeks before at Gulf Coast despite my slow swim and a hillier course. Things were getting better. I was getting faster.

I was learning a lot of the tools to improve besides just slogging miles. I had been using a European device called a Compex electrical muscle stimulator that Peter had gotten from a friend who raced on the Czech national team. Euros always seem to have things not approved in the US, like cool devices to electrocute yourself. It sent volts of electricity into my muscles, tightening and contracting them or relaxing and massaging them, depending on whether I wanted to strengthen or recover. I used it mostly on my quads, abs, and glutes. It was painful but a great way to maximize time (if you can stand being electrocuted while you watch TV). Peter slept in a hypoxic tent to simulate altitude and increase red blood cells. Endurance athletes frequently train at high altitude to generate more oxygen-carrying red blood cells and then return to sea level for competition. But I wasn't ready to sleep in a plastic bubble yet.

I was confident and optimistic traveling to Coeur d'Alene, Idaho, for the Ironman on June 27. Everything indicated that I was going to have a good race in Idaho, and just a week later I would make my debut with the US national team at the Long Distance Triathlon World Championship in Sweden. I was ready.

CHANGES AND CHALLENGES AT MY DAY JOB

While my life as a triathlete was going well, the months leading up to Idaho and Sweden were a challenge in my law job. That year I was making a special effort to work hard at my firm all day and to train and race in my off-hours. I tried to keep my triathlon racing quiet and unnoticed. Since January 2004 I had been working long hours on a multimillion-dollar lawsuit involving a tragic hotel fire with several fatalities. There were over twenty lawsuits in state and federal court and I was lead defense counsel in all of them for a national hotel franchisor. The litigation required thousands of hours of research, investigation, discovery, depositions, motions, and hearings. We eventually settled most of the cases, but for ones that didn't settle several years later I would win an appeal before the United States Court of Appeals for the Fourth Circuit, *Allen v. Choice Hotels International*. In March 2004 I won another appeal before the South Carolina Court of Appeals in a different lawsuit I had been litigating for over six years, *Deloitte and Touche Consulting v. Unisys Corporation*.

Despite my successes I began to detect some criticism from a few colleagues about my life outside the firm. Some of it was subtle—disapproving glances when I exited the building to run while they went to lunch together.

Some of it was not so subtle. One day a fellow partner stopped me in the hall outside his office. Other than working at the same firm and being the same age, we did not have a lot in common. He lived his life according to strict rules. He was very religious, didn't drink alcohol, and had six kids that his wife homeschooled. I was not married, had no kids, and was dating a twenty-three-year-old model living in New York City who was fourteen years younger than me and the current Miss South Carolina USA (who would eventually be my wife). He sent work emails late at night and on weekends, constantly billing hours. I did workouts at night and on weekends. I had logos on my racing jerseys and a basic website to promote my sponsors and to inspire people with diabetes. That lawyer pulled my website up on his computer and let me know that he did not like it. I told him to live his life and I would live mine, but I knew from that point he would be working against me in the office.

Fortunately others were very supportive, but I still tried to be a lawyer by day and a triathlete in my off-hours. My secretary Kathy had been at the firm for many years. If I ever wanted to know something, she knew the goods. She was like a proud mom that ran interference for me and would secretly tell her friends on the staff whenever I was in a magazine. I appreciated her support and perspective.

I served on a national committee of the American Diabetes Association and traveled to meetings in Washington, DC, and San Francisco. I was speaking at events for the local ADA chapter, and the director surprised me one day at my office with a framed plaque of one of the magazine articles. That summer with the buildup for the Olympic games in August 2004 in Athens, Greece, I spoke at my local Rotary Club to two hundred business leaders about racing for a national team in Europe. The local newspaper *Greenville News* did a front-page story with a color photograph of me in my Team USA racing kit headlined "Jay Hewitt: Greenville attorney has will of iron when it comes to helping others."

I was pursing this aspect of my life while I could, before I was married or had children, and helping others while I tried to fulfill my duties at my day job. But at times I felt like I had to lead a secret double life. I felt like Clark Kent at the *Daily Planet*, disguised as a lawyer by day but secretly changing into a triathlon racing suit in a nearby phone booth.

IRONMAN COEUR D'ALENE—EXPECTING SUCCESS, SUFFERING DISASTER

I arrived in Coeur d'Alene, Idaho, in late June 2004, three days before the Ironman. It was a challenge packing for two weeks for two long-distance triathlons and travel across the US and Europe, with my racing bike and all of the racing and diabetes supplies and other clothes and items for international travel. Peter and I stayed with a host family provided by the race for professional athletes. They had a house on the beautiful Lake Coeur d'Alene so we did easy swims in the cold lake water, the same lake for the Ironman swim. On race morning we rode to the start on their ski boat—a cold, dark ride across the lake at 5 a.m.

Race day I had a good swim and exited the water ready for the bike. From my previous races I knew that the bike was *my* time. Get through the swim, keep the leaders in sight, and then use my strength on the bike to build up a lead on the fast runners who could outrun me in the marathon. I was ready to ride. This was going to be a great race.

The Idaho bike course has short, steep climbs and rolling hills, a challenging course different from the long descents and climbs at Ironman Lake Placid or the windy flats of Ironman Florida. It has about five thousand feet of climbing up and down a range of the Rocky Mountains that runs along the border of Idaho, Montana, and Washington. We rode into western Washington State and back. I had spent a lot of miles training on similar mountains near my home in the Blue Ridge Mountains.

I felt good for the first half of the bike, but the most significant issue was not the course or my fitness. It was nutrition and hydration. The Idaho air of the western US is arid and dry, unlike the wet, thick humidity that I was used to training and racing in the Southeast. In South

Carolina and Florida in June I would be coated in sweat, reminding me to drink, but in Idaho my skin was dry. I wasn't sweating and I didn't feel hot, so I did not drink enough. I was getting dehydrated.

I was also getting dehydrated because of my blood sugar. I checked my blood sugar at the special needs area fifty-six miles into the bike. Ironman allows athletes to place items in a special needs bag that the race transports out to the midpoint of the bike. Most athletes use it for their favorite nutrition or sport drink. You can place anything in there that is your "special need"—a favorite sport drink or bar, a teddy bear, a cheeseburger, or a picture of your wife or girlfriend. For me, it's my drink, bars, and a blood sugar meter and insulin. I was shocked to find my blood sugar there was 250 mg/dl, which was way too high, more than double the normal blood sugar of 100 mg/dl. In my bag I had packed a bolus (fast-acting) insulin pen in ice to prevent it from getting too hot sitting for several hours in the sun on the side of the road.

Now I had a decision to make, stopped at the side of the road. I was having a good bike, close to the front of the field. *Do I inject insulin to bring my blood sugar down and risk it dropping too low on the bike and the marathon like it had at Lake Placid? Or do I rely on my basal insulin dose already in my system and hope my blood sugar does not remain too high for the next fifty-six miles?* High blood sugar causes an upset stomach, slug-gishness, and weakness. And I would not be able to eat or drink any car-bohydrate during the remaining miles of the bike, dumping more carbs on top of my high blood sugar. But my muscles and cells desperately needed those carbohydrates and calories. High blood sugar also causes dehydration as your kidneys attempt to flush all of that extra glucose out of your blood, making you urinate. So I had a double dose of dehydra-tion—not drinking enough in the hot, dry conditions and my kidneys flushing extra fluid out of my body.

I decided not to inject insulin. I hoped that my basal dose would bring it down. I could not risk another low like in Lake Placid the previous summer. Low blood sugar in Lake Placid, high blood sugar in Idaho—both cause problems. Pick your poison. I picked high blood sugar.

I started feeling a little sluggish the final twenty miles of the bike. It was hard to know if it was dehydration, high blood sugar, not eating enough because of the high blood sugar, or just because I had biked ninety miles in the mountains of Idaho. When I finished the bike, my blood sugar in T2 had returned to normal. But I did not feel strong running the first mile of the marathon. I did not realize then that it was dehydration, and even if I did, it was too late to correct it now. It is hard to drink while running a marathon. My pace was slow and got slower. Athletes started catching me and passing me. The dry heat was debilitating because dehydration had reduced my blood volume, meaning less blood in my skin and epidermal layer to cool my body in the sun. Dehydration also had reduced my sweat volume, making it even more difficult to cool my body. My skin was dry and tacky with salt crystals on it from the sodium in my sweat hours earlier.

By mile thirteen of the marathon I knew my race was in trouble. By mile fifteen I was reduced to a slow jog. I felt nauseous and weak. I jogged slower and slower, then started walking, and then started wobbling. At about mile eighteen of the marathon I sort of sat down, sort of collapsed, on the side of the road. I did not want to stop. I could not believe my body was failing me. The course medics picked me up and put me on a stretcher. They transported me by ambulance to the medical tent at the finish line and placed an IV in my arm to rehydrate me. I was sick and nauseous from dehydration and exhausted from racing 132 miles.

I lay there on a cot in the medical tent thirty feet from the finish line as the top finishers began to cross to the cheers of the crowd. *That should be me*, I thought. *Everything seemed to be going right leading up to this race. Ironman Florida last November went well. My half Ironman races this year went great. I improved with each one. All of that progress and work ... now this.*

Failure and disappointment. At first I had just wanted to see if I could finish an Ironman. Then I started to become one of the best. Now here I was, back to the beginning, unable to even finish one.

ITU LONG DISTANCE TRIATHLON WORLD CHAMPIONSHIP, TEAM USA

Two days later I flew from Spokane, Washington, to Stockholm, Sweden, to meet the US national team. My first race with the team I did not want to tell any of the officials or other athletes what had happened that week back in the states—how I had struggled and stumbled and then collapsed just eight miles from the finish. It's not something you would expect from someone who just earned a spot on the national team, which is supposed to mean I was one of the best triathletes in the US, about to race against the best triathletes in the world at the International Triathlon Union (ITU) Long Distance Triathlon World Championship. I had not met any of the other athletes on the US team yet, although I had seen some of them at races and knew their results. None of them knew I had diabetes, and while I did not hide it, I did not announce it either. I did not want it to be an excuse. I would prefer they just find out, if at all, after they saw me race well.

I only had six days between these two races—not a lot of recovery time. And one of those days was spent flying across the globe. In July the sun barely sets in Sweden, with daylight lasting almost twenty hours from 3:00 a.m. until 11:00 p.m., making it even harder to sleep and recover from the jet lag and nine-hour time change from the western coast of the United States. With only about four hours of true darkness at night, I slept with blackout shades on the hotel windows and a mask over my eyes. I spent three days prior to the world championship scouting the course with the US team and doing light workouts to recover and prepare to race again. Fortunately the US team had plenty of support staff, massage therapists, doctors, and bike mechanics to handle all of the details that I normally have to handle myself at other races. My recovery progressed very well thanks to a lot of massages, bike spins, swimming, and nutrition.

CAN I DOPE?

One thing I had to do was get permission to dope. It's hard to believe, but insulin is banned as a performance-enhancing drug (PED) under the World Anti-Doping Code, so I had to file a Therapeutic Use Exemption (TUE) with the race doping control office. If I were found injecting insulin without a TUE, I would be disqualified. The staff physician for the US team filed my TUE, and we met with the race officials to verify that I indeed had diabetes and had a medical necessity to use insulin. Most Ironman races do not have the resources (money and staff) to monitor or test athletes for doping, but the ITU would be watching this world championship race closer.

It is virtually impossible to detect insulin use because it does not show up in a blood or urine test like other banned substances such as EPO, testosterone, growth hormone, and steroids. For insulin they have to find the injection devices and the drug in your possession. At the 1998 Tour de France a large haul of various doping products and syringes were found in a car of the Festina cycling team just prior to the race and the entire team was disqualified. Of course, it is ludicrous to believe that insulin gives me a performance benefit, but evidently some nondiabetic athletes have attempted to use it perhaps to aid in recovery. It is a hormone that transports carbohydrate (glucose) from blood to cells, so I suppose those cheaters were hoping to speed up their recovery process after workouts to train again the next day and get stronger and faster. I have never seen or heard any reports that any endurance athlete actually received a benefit by doping with insulin, but if any nondia-betic athlete wants to trade places with me, they can have my diabetes and insulin and inject it all they want.

The world championship was in a picturesque area of rural Sweden, about two hours north of Stockholm by car. The Swedes are beautiful people: blonde hair and blue eyes, clear fair skin, strong and broad shoulders. It must be the cold, dark Scandinavian winters. They looked like models walking in the streets, so it was beautiful people watching prior to the race. Triathletes from dozens of countries were in the city and countryside getting in final prerace workouts, along with thousands of spectators and raucous supporters from Europe and countries around the world. Two days before the race the athlete parade of nations through the city was a memorable event with the teams from each country wearing their ceremonial uniforms and national colors, carrying flags similar to the opening ceremony at the Olympics.

On race morning I felt proud with "USA" on my racing jersey, lined up shoulder to shoulder with the world's best triathletes at the water's edge, before thousands of spectators cheering and chanting for their countrymen in a linguistic stew of different languages. Hundreds of local age-group athletes were also there ready to race behind us on the national teams. Staring out at the sunrise over this large lake in Sweden, in the midst of all this noise and pageantry and prerace excitement, I thought about how far I had come. Four years ago I had run a marathon just wondering if I could even finish what I thought was the hardest thing I would ever do—just looking to test myself and see what limits diabetes would have on me. Now I was about to race some of the fittest athletes in the world representing the United States of America in the triathlon world championship. *Wow.*

Every athlete, every person, has a journey and challenges that are unique to them. The people around you often do not know yours or what you have overcome. I am sure that many around me that day had overcome things more difficult than type 1 diabetes: life in a difficult country, poor upbringing, health, and personal challenges. But it was hard for me to hold back the emotion and a tear at the start—a brief, calming, private moment, before I suddenly and violently thrust my body into the cold water to battle these men for four kilometers.

The ITU long-course distance is a total of 154 kilometers, or 96 miles, longer than a half Ironman (70.3 miles) but shorter than an Ironman (140.6 miles). It is a 4-kilometer swim (2.49 miles), a 120-kilometer bike (76 miles), and a 30-kilometer run (18.6 miles). It is considered an "ultra" or long-distance triathlon, popular in Europe. Once you get past the half Ironman distance, the ITU Long Distance and the Ironman both hurt about the same.

The water was a "refreshing" sixty-two degrees, but fortunately I was used to it from swimming the cold waters of Coeur d'Alene, Idaho, just six days before. My swim went well, and even though it was longer I actually beat my swim time from Ironman Coeur d'Alene earlier that week. I exited the water roughly in the middle of the pack. A quick check of my blood sugar in T1 told me I was a little below my target at eighty-five, so I chugged a few swallows of a high-carbohydrate drink as I headed out for the bike.

The Swedish air was wet and chilly in the low sixties, very different than dry, arid Idaho or the humid heat of my home in South Carolina. I wanted to set a fast pace on the first of three laps on this bike course of rolling hills through the Swedish pastoral countryside. The intensity of our race seemed to contradict the quiet fields of yellow flowers, green farmland, red barns with white trim, and rivers that I rocketed past. It looked like beautiful scenes from a children's fairy tale.

As I moved forward, catching the faster swimmers as usual, it was quite a spectacle to see colorful racing jerseys on athletes I passed from Germany, France, Denmark, Britain, the Czech Republic, and Australia. This was my first taste of the national pride that overflows in a world championship race. I felt a strange power of honor and obligation to go faster with USA on my jersey. For the first time I was racing for my country, not just for myself.

By the second lap the weather changed to a windy rain, making it chilly in the cool Swedish air. I was pleased that my second twenty-five-mile lap was only one minute slower than my first, and my third and final lap was only four minutes slower, despite the wind and rain and stopping to check my blood sugar on that third lap. I had maintained a consistent pace on this hilly course, averaging twenty-one miles per hour for seventy-six miles. I entered T2 fresh and ready to run.

But I would soon discover that just like not sweating in the dry Idaho air had deceived me to not drink enough, so too did the cool, wet Swedish air. You don't feel like you need to drink from a cold sport bottle when it's sixty-five degrees and raining.

I started the run feeling good, but looking back now I know that dehydration was moving in like a storm brewing in the distance. The run course took us out and back to the finish area on four laps, each lap approximately 7.5 kilometers (4.7 miles), which made it easy for spectators to line the route and cheer for their countrymen. My good bike had placed me in the top 10 percent of the field, and I set an easy 7:15–30 pace on the first lap. My first lap was over before I knew it and the crowd was growing larger and louder each lap as more athletes behind me finished the bike and headed out on the run.

Although it remained cool, I tried to drink at every aid station. The race was serving some sort of weird European sport drink that I had never used, but I had no choice but to drink it. I had tested it several days before the race to see if my stomach would reject it. You can carry your preferred sport drink in water bottles on your bike, but you can't run with those for eighteen miles. On my third lap my pace began to slow. I was experiencing the same uncomfortable feeling I had in the marathon the prior week in the US.

On my fourth lap, several miles out from the finish, I saw a young boy standing with his dad on a distant part of the course. He was holding a little Swedish flag on a stick looking down the road for approaching runners. There were not many around me as I approached.

He spotted my red and white USA jersey and shouted "Amare Reeka! Amare Reeka!" With the September 11, 2001, terror attacks happening just three years earlier, patriotism was still pretty high back in the US. I was just a piece of America passing before him. Despite my exhaustion and building dehydration, I smiled and held out my hand for him to touch as I passed. My teammates and I may be the only Americans he ever meets, so I wanted to acknowledge his cheers.

Two ultra-distance triathlons in six days began to bite on that last lap, but the energy of the crowd in the last half mile electrified the air. I was nowhere close to the lead and suffering pretty bad, but I still enjoyed the pageantry of the finish. Flags from each country lined the last hundred meters. Spectators wore their national colors with their faces painted like rowdy European soccer fans. Everyone was cheering and shouting in languages I did not understand. Near the finish, someone held a small American flag on a stick for me to grab. I could barely hear the race announcer above the raucous crowd, saying in English with a Swedish accent: "fwum dee Uuu-NIE-ted Steds ov Amareeekaaa... Yay Yewitt!"

I finished thirty-third out of eighty-one in the world championship. I was thrilled and proud to represent America but quietly disappointed in myself. Finishing in the middle of the pack was not a good race. I know I could have done better had I not raced an Ironman just six days before back in the US.

But something else was wrong.

I was in a lot of pain, different than I had ever experienced. The US team doctors examined me in the medical tent. I felt a sharp, piercing pain in my midsection and gut. I was nauseous. I felt like I had to urinate but could not. When I did, the small amount of urine was dark, almost brown, like coffee. The team doctors told me that dark-brown urine was a sign of the most severe state of dehydration. I had done it again—destroyed my race by dehydration, just like in Idaho.

That was two ultra-distance triathlons this year (this week) and two big disappointments, after all of that work and training—failure and disappointment when it looked like things were going in the right direction.

I had to figure this out.

IRONMAN WISCONSIN—ANOTHER FAILURE

Two months later I raced Ironman Wisconsin in Madison in late September. With only six days to recover between Idaho and Sweden, two months felt like two years. I was determined not to suffer dehydration like I had in my previous two races so I used this extra time to practice a new hydration strategy.

Ironman Wisconsin is a great course in the US for the crowd. Many races in Europe and Australia are packed with spectators because endurance racing, like cycling and triathlon, is more popular there than in the US. But the people of Madison, Wisconsin, come out by the thousands. I'm sure it's for several reasons—the start and finish are in downtown Madison, the state capitol and home of the University of Wisconsin with forty-three thousand students. Second, those students like to drink beer, as do many people in Wisconsin, the home of Miller Brewing and some of the best beer in the US. Third, there is no UW home football game on race weekend, so why not tailgate watching 2,500 Ironman athletes suffer all day? Any excuse for a party. I love their attitude.

I had a good swim (translation: nobody punched me too hard) and started the bike after running up four stories of a parking deck helix to the transition area at the top. Heart rate up! The bike course is the shape of a lollipop extending sixteen miles out of Madison, repeating a forty-mile loop twice, and then returning sixteen miles back into the city. The course is rural, with great views of farmland on rolling hills if you're in it for the scenery rather than the suffering. There is no single long mountainous climb to worry about; it's the endless short, punchy hills that gradually sap your legs. It has only three thousand feet of elevation gain, compared to over five thousand at Coeur d'Alene and Lake Placid, but it is important to follow a pacing plan and not get sucked into attacking the short hills when you feel good early. Standing up and hammering the short hills takes much more energy than trying to ride smoothly over them. Repeated bursts will wear you down much faster than a steady approach. Remember, you still have to run a marathon.

I stayed seated for most of the climbs and focused on keeping my pedaling cadence high above 90 rpm, not grinding a slow, heavy power gear that would drain my quads. I was not concerned about speed as much as I was keeping my watts and heart rate in check. But the most important thing I was focused on was blood sugar and hydration. I knew my legs could take it, but could the rest of my body? I was not going to get dehydrated again.

Wisconsin has one of the slowest bike courses on the Ironman circuit because of the relentless hills. That day only four athletes out of over 2,200 broke five hours, and three of them broke it by only a few seconds. I did not have a good bike, finishing in over five hours. Although dehydration was not a problem, I had an upset stomach, queasiness, and bloating on the last twenty miles. Perhaps I drank too much trying to avoid dehydrating. It is a fine line to approach but not cross.

Despite the disappointing bike, I started the marathon in the top hundred, still on target to break ten hours at the finish.

Just run a good marathon, move up through the field, and you will be there, I thought.

But that upset stomach really hit me running the first few miles of the marathon. By mile four my stomach was churning. I stopped briefly near Camp Randall Stadium, home of the University of Wisconsin Badgers football team, and threw up. I'm probably not the first person to do that there, with all the college students tailgating on too much beer and bratwurst, but I did it from too much sport drink and gels.

I tried running again, but a few miles later I stopped and threw up again. I tried to keep running, but my stomach was in revolt. I could not throw up anymore. By mile eight of the marathon, I was walking. I was still close to the front of the field with few athletes around me on the course and over two thousand behind me.

It is unusual for spectators to see an athlete at the front of the field walking. That happens often at the back of the pack, late in the marathon, after the sun goes down. Thousands of spectators lined the marathon route through the city. It was now early afternoon and many had been there for hours, eating lunch and drinking great Wisconsin beer in downtown pubs, waiting on the first athletes to appear on the marathon course after hours of swimming and cycling. They screamed and cheered, wondering why I was not running.

But I couldn't. My legs and lungs were fine. My stomach was not.

SHOULD I QUIT?

Have you ever considered quitting? Thinking, *Why am I doing this? Maybe I should just quit school … this job … this relationship … just walk out and disappear. This is not working like I thought it would. It is too hard.*

You can quit and no one will know, but you will know for the rest of your life. Don't quit. Keep going. Think about why you started. Think about what you can do differently, what you need to change.

You can quit and no one will know, but you will know for the rest of your life.

I thought about that as I walked the last eighteen miles of that marathon. I could have walked into the crowd and disappeared at any moment. Since I was not able to get to the finish line at Coeur d'Alene, I was going to get to this one, even if it meant I had to walk to finish in last.

Over a thousand athletes passed me as I walked those eighteen miles. Walking eighteen miles gives you a lot of time to think and ask questions of yourself. *Why are you doing this? What do you have to do differently? This is three races in a row that you have struggled.*

In fourteen Ironman and ultra-distance races and over twenty half Ironman races that I would do in my career, Ironman Wisconsin 2004 was by far my worst finish. But it is actually a race that I am proud of now. It took me almost seven hours to complete (walk) that marathon when I needed to run it in a little over three hours if I was going to break ten hours. I finished the race in 13:43:16, 1,197th place out of 2,200. I missed my goal by only … four hours. No matter how humiliating and tortuous it was to walk for eighteen miles and watch over a thousand people pass me, I was not going to quit. Failing three straight times at Ironman Coeur d'Alene, the ITU Worlds, and now Wisconsin was just like getting cut several times from my high school basketball team. I wanted both so bad but kept failing—my Sisyphean nightmare. The finish line kept moving farther and farther away.

I had Ironman Florida coming up in November, my last race of the year. I thought, *Do I really have what it takes to make it, to compete with the best? What do I need to change?*

I had to figure this out.

HANDLING FAILURE AND DISAPPOINTMENT

Failure happens in life. Everyone wants to succeed, but not everyone will keep trying after they suffer, feel humiliated, and fail. What is it that really drives you to keep getting up in the morning to go to work, to drive that car that is falling apart when others have nice ones, to keep doing that job that you don't like so your family can have a home and so your kids can have clothes and a future? Why do you keep trying to start that business after it struggles and fails when others seem to be succeeding around you? Why do you keep trying to work out, get in shape, lose the weight, get stronger and faster, when it hurts and you don't see results yet?

In 2013 American Taylor Phinney was one of the most promising young professional cyclists in the world. By age twenty-two he had already been to the Olympics twice, 2008 and 2012, and was US national champion twice in the cycling time trial. Phinney's star was on the rise. At 6'5" and 180 pounds he knew his limitations as a big guy that couldn't climb mountains with the little 5'8", 140-pound water bugs, but he could overpower them on the flats and sprint to the line if he could just hang with them long enough to the end. He knew his strengths and his weaknesses. I know how he feels.

In March 2013 Phinney was racing the seven-day Italian stage race Tirreno-Adriatico. The second day he was racing the hardest stage of the race, a stage he knew he could not win. He just needed to finish with the field and be ready for the next stage. Strategy. Pick your battles. The next day would be the time trial, his specialty, a stage that he could definitely win.

"I was just dangling," Phinney said in an interview in *The New York Times*. "We kept going over these really difficult climbs. I'd get back to the group and I would get dropped. I'd get back again, then get dropped." This was happening to one of the most talented young pros in the world.

Like the Ironman triathlon, professional bike racing is a sport that demands suffering—long suffering, for hours, in agony. But even the most determined souls can take only so much. How do you know when to quit and try again another day?

Soon Phinney was in a small group of a couple dozen riders who had fallen off the back of the main field. They still had eighty miles to go. In cycling this group is called the "gruppetto," a pack of cyclists struggling to keep up and just hoping to work together pacing each other to finish before the time cut even though they are on different teams. The weather was horrible, cold, and raining. The riders in the group were talking and it was clear that nobody wanted to finish. It was not worth the effort. Word began to circulate among them that they would not make the time cut. These riders were experienced; some had been pros for ten or fifteen years. Phinney had been pro at this level for only two years. The experienced riders knew when it was futile to keep going.

But Phinney wanted to try to finish, to beat the time cut to do the time trial the next day. "If I was going to finish, I was going to have to do it by myself," he said. Everyone else dropped out. He put his head down and kept pedaling, kept going alone. Do you ever feel like that? The main field was so far in front of him that the fans on the side of the road had left. "It was kind of embarrassing. The race has gone by, and people aren't expecting one rider slogging along by himself," he said.

He pedaled for six hours, twenty-two minutes, and fifty-four seconds and finished in 109th place, alone in dead last, fifteen minutes behind the second-to-last rider and thirty-seven minutes behind the winner. He missed the time cut and was disqualified. He would not be allowed to compete in the time trial the next day.

WHY DO YOU KEEP GOING?

Why did he keep pedaling? What was driving him to keep going, keep suffering, when it seemed pointless and embarrassing and when everyone else had quit?

"I would just think of my dad," he said. Phinney's father, Davis Phinney, has Parkinson's disease. Davis, one of America's greatest cyclists of all time, a Tour de France stage winner, and an Olympian, now battled physical challenges greater than any on a bike. "I knew that if my dad could be in my shoes for one day—if all he had to do was struggle on a bike for six hours, be healthy and fully functional—he would be me on that day in a heartbeat. Every time I wanted to quit, every time I wanted to cry, I just thought about that."

Phinney came in last that day. But he won. He gained more than if he had come in first: more fans and more knowledge about himself—knowledge that only comes when you push yourself to the edge of quitting and come back before you give in. Just one week later he finished seventh out of two hundred riders in the one-day Milan-San Remo race, a race so difficult that over a third of the field did not finish (DNF).

> **What is the thing in your life that will drive you to keep going when others all around you give up? Think of that thing at your finish line; that is your finish line vision.**

What is the thing in your life that will drive you to keep going when others all around you give up? Think of that thing at your finish line; that is your finish line vision.

Walking those eighteen miles of the Ironman Wisconsin marathon, I thought about all of the kids I had met with type 1 diabetes and their parents. They had seen me in magazines and sent me emails and attended my speaking engagements. They wondered the same things I did when I was diagnosed: Would diabetes control their life or limit them? Could they be an athlete, an elite athlete, or even just be normal? They told me I gave them hope because I was an Ironman triathlete. Not just an Ironman triathlete, I was one of the best and on the US national triathlon team.

But I had not finished with the best yet. I kept failing. I was supposed to finish with the best, in under ten hours, not in thirteen hours in 1,197th place.

I did not want to let them down. I had to figure this out. Ironman Florida was in seven weeks.

Nobody wants to fail. Yes, I recommended earlier in this book that you should risk failure, even seek it, and view failure as good. I want you to try something at which you might fail, setting a goal that had failure potential. But that is so that you challenge yourself, even surprise yourself with what you can achieve.

Years later when I had kids I enjoyed watching the animated film *Zootopia* with them, featuring the title song "Try Everything" by Shakira. I love to hear my daughters singing it and the lesson it teaches them.

> *I messed up tonight, I lost another fight,*
> *I still mess up but I'll just start again.*
> *I keep falling down, I keep on hitting the ground,*
> *I always get up now to see what's next*
> *Birds don't just fly, they fall down and get up.*
> *Nobody learns without getting it wrong.*
> *I won't give up, no I won't give in*
> *'Til I reach the end and then I'll start again.*
> *No I won't leave, I want to try everything.*
> *I want to try even though I could fail.*

ARE YOU WILLING TO MAKE CHANGES?

Change feels the same as failure. It is difficult to handle. Sometimes it is handed to us with no choice, imposed on us by some authority—the government, employer, teachers, parents—or by life. We don't like to change. But that is what makes us improve, chart a new course, find a new career, or find a better method. Change is inevitable. Growth is optional.

Change is inevitable. Growth is optional.

Charles Darwin said, "It is not the strongest or most intelligent that survive, it is the ones most responsive to change." Change gives you the chance to become something different. Use that chance. Use that change. Become something different.

Ironman Florida 2004 would be my fourth Ironman or ultra-distance triathlon in five months. No doubt I was in the best shape of my life. But no doubt I had little to show for it.

After my disappointments in Idaho, Sweden, and Wisconsin, I knew that fitness was not my problem; it was nutrition and hydration. With six Ironman and ultra-distance triathlons and nine half Ironmans under my belt (or my shoes), I had a lot of history to study. I studied my nutrition from past races and experimented on long rides and runs in the seven weeks between Ironman Wisconsin and Florida. I had to change something. If you want a different outcome, you have to do something different.

> **Change gives you the chance to become something different. Use that chance. Use that change. Become something different.**

I researched a new hydration strategy. Dehydration is defined as losing 2 percent of your body weight from sweating. But losing just 1 percent can significantly impair your performance by raising your body temperature and causing your heart to beat three to five times faster per minute. During exercise muscles generate twenty times more heat than at rest.

> **If you want a different outcome, you have to do something different.**

Your rate of sweat loss is individual and influenced by many factors such as age, temperature, genetics, gender, and fitness level. Fortunately there were still hot days in September and October in South Carolina to test my hydration in training that year. I weighed myself before and after long rides and runs to see how much weight I lost and measured how much I drank in sport drink and water. On some long (over three hour) workouts I lost almost four or five pounds, so at 180 pounds I was losing more than 2 percent of my body weight. I was definitely getting dehydrated.

TESTING AT THE GATORADE SPORTS SCIENCE INSTITUTE

A few years later, with the help of the US national team, I would have the benefit of laboratory testing at the Gatorade Sports Science Institute in Illinois. Their laboratory can simulate the playing conditions for any athlete: humid heat for an Ironman triathlete, dry cold for a cross-country skier, or perfect indoor conditions for a professional basketball player. At Gatorade I rode an hour on a stationary bike in the laboratory with the temperature over eighty-five degrees. They piped in warm, wet air like a steam room in the sun. It felt like Florida in August. I felt right at home.

I was instructed to maintain an easy consistent 210 watts (pushing the pedals) and a 145 to 150 bpm heart rate for the hour. They weighed me and took urine samples before and after and stuck patches on my skin to soak up sweat that they analyzed for sodium and electrolytes. They sealed a plastic bag over my left forearm and hand to collect several ounces of sweat. I drank Gatorade sport drink (of course) in a set amount that they carefully measured. After the bike and a ten-minute break, they continued the test with me running on a treadmill for another hour at my Ironman marathon pace, monitoring my heart rate and pace—a nice two-hour bike and run workout in the lab.

The results of that Gatorade test were interesting. My overall combined bike and run sweat rate for two hours was 2.2 liters (74 oz.) per hour. In two hours in the laboratory I generated 4.4 liters of sweat, over one gallon, and finished 3.4 percent dehydrated. Racing an Ironman for over ten hours you can understand how much fluid loss occurs just from perspiration—over five gallons! It is hard to believe that my body could fill five one-gallon milk jugs with sweat during the race!

They also determined that I have a high concentration of sodium in my sweat and thus need to consume additional sodium during my races. Sodium is the primary mineral lost in sweat and used in sports drinks for two reasons. First, sodium makes you want to keep drinking. Water and other low-sodium beverages dilute the blood sodium levels, eliminating thirst and your urge to drink, even though you may not be sufficiently hydrated. Second, sodium helps the body retain the fluid instead of it being excreted by the kidneys.

Dehydration also makes you overheat because of the decrease in circulating blood volume. This means the heart must work harder to pump enough blood to the skin to cool the body and enough blood to the muscles to deliver the oxygen and nutrients. It's like a car engine that is low on coolant and oil. Thus, the body loses some of its ability to cool, and the muscles will have to rely more on glycogen stores because there is less blood delivering nutrients. The body might be able to perform dehydrated for a two-hour football game or even a marathon, but it is only a matter of time before the body crashes and burns in something like an Ironman triathlon. I knew what that felt like.

Drinking enough to match sweat losses requires practice. The stomach must be trained to accept fluid the same way you train your heart, lungs, and muscles to handle exercise. I trained my stomach for several weeks after Wisconsin by eating and drinking different amounts of carbohydrate and water. I also tested my carbohydrate consumption. I changed my race nutrition, trying to figure out the nausea and upset stomach that stopped me at Ironman Wisconsin. I did not want to eat too much and overload my stomach.

The body can only empty, absorb, and oxidize between sixty to a hundred grams of carbohydrate per hour. Consuming more is not only unnecessary but will cause cramping, bloating, and nausea. That's what I experienced at Ironman Wisconsin that made me throw up. Because of my diabetes I have to carefully calculate how much insulin to inject the night before the race to handle the carbs I will be consuming (or set the basal rate on my insulin pump). If I get it wrong, my blood sugar crashes like in Lake Placid or balloons too high like in Coeur d'Alene. After testing several nutrition plans, gels, bars, drinks, and amounts on training rides, for Ironman Florida I made a new plan to consume between sixty and eighty grams of carbohydrate per hour from sport drink, gels, and Clif Bars.

I had a new nutrition plan for Ironman Florida. I had faced the failures. I had made changes. I was still determined. I was ready to try again.

CHAPTER 13

WHO HAS TIME FOR THAT?

Topic: Work-Life Balance

I get asked a lot: "How do you balance all of that—racing Ironman triathlons, type 1 diabetes, a full-time job, travel?" Once I got married and had children, I continued racing triathlons for several years and started my own speaking business. "Who has time for that?"

In previous chapters we talked about how to find motivation with your finish line vision. But motivation is only half of what you need. Motivation without balance leads to frustration and disappointment. You become a caged animal, wanting to run but trapped by the walls of obligations around you. No matter what age or stage you are in your life, you can't pursue your goals if it damages other important things: your job, your family, your health, or your schoolwork. You won't achieve (or enjoy achieving) your goals without balance. Fortunately, the opposite is true—you will achieve your goals better if your life is balanced. So balance is vital for success.

In the Ironman I have to balance three very different sports. I cannot reach the finish line if I only train or focus on just one or two. Life is the same way. In life, you no doubt have several different roles with different obligations and challenges, such as work, home, school, parent, spouse, community, and health. You must be able to perform all of them. Not equally well and not all at the same time or amount or priority, but you have to perform all of them.

Balance is also important for happiness. Don't we all want to be happy? People who are happy are more successful in their career, family, school, and life.

HOW DO YOU ACHIEVE BALANCE?

You can't do a good job if your job is all you do. Whether you are a busy working professional, a busy student, or a busy parent, those things that you *must* do are "your job." That is your first priority.

Never get so busy making a living that you forget to make a life. You make time for your work because you have to, so make time for your life because you need to.

You can't do a good job if your job is all you do.

I love graduation speeches. They were the original TED Talk before the Internet—a short speech by an accomplished person to an audience of eager graduates willing to listen, full of idealism and optimism about the future. The speaker looks back on his or her own life and career and gives lessons learned and mistakes made. The advice is real and honest in their own words.

Never get so busy making a living that you forget to make a life.

In 1991 the president and CEO of Coca-Cola, Brian Dyson, gave a commencement speech at Georgia Tech University. Coca-Cola was and still is a multibillion-dollar international company with intense competition, thousands of employees, and millions of shareholders to keep happy. You can imagine the pressure and responsibilities on a CEO of a company that size.

Ironically, Dyson first told the graduates that one of the keys to success is vision. He relayed the vision of the Coca-Cola founders and how Atlanta native Billy Payne's vision was able to convince the

International Olympic Committee (IOC) to award the 1996 Summer Olympics to Atlanta. Payne told the IOC selection committee how as a child he had dreamed of winning an Olympic medal and had never lost that dream, and he had a new vision that the Olympics would be held in Atlanta. Dyson would no doubt agree with the importance of finish line vision.

At the end of his speech, Dyson told the graduates to strive for balance. He said that life is like juggling balls:

> *Lastly, I would caution you that as intelligent and active participants in a dynamic society like America, you must bring balance into your lives. Imagine life as a game in which you are juggling five balls in the air. You name them—work, family, health, friends, spirit—and you're keeping all of these in the air. You will soon understand that work is a rubber ball. If you drop it, it will bounce back. But the other four balls—family, health, friends, spirit—are made of glass. If you drop one of these, they will be irrevocably scuffed, marked, nicked, damaged, or even shattered. They will never be the same. You must understand that and strive for balance in your life.*

This is not advice to drop your work ball. It is advice to keep your priorities right about which ball you save first.

Quality of life does not happen by chance.

Quality of life does not happen by chance. It requires planning and preparation. It requires organization and direction. To build a quality house, you must have a plan to construct it in the right sequence. You can't just hire a bunch of subcontractors all to show up the same day or random days and hope they build you a house with no plan to follow or what to start first.

To build a quality life you must have a plan and someone in charge. That someone is you. You are the owner, architect, and general contractor for the life you want to build. Where do you want it and how do you want it to look? You can't just live day to day and hope that happiness happens. You can't expect someone else—your spouse, your employer, your doctor, your government, or the god of your choice—to give you a happy life while you sit waiting and asking them to do it. You can still involve them and ask them to help you achieve it; just tell them what you want and start doing some of the work yourself.

To build a quality life you must have a plan and someone in charge. That someone is you.

In my life racing Ironman triathlons and managing diabetes while working as an attorney and speaker with a wife and children, I have learned and applied the following seven principles for work–life balance. I am not perfect at it and struggle to achieve it as my personal life and career have changed and grown. I have watched others do it even better than me. These are the tips I have learned.

1. MANAGE YOUR TIME

The most important key to work–life balance is time management. How many times have we all said, "I just wish I had the time to do that"? That is a close second to "I just wish I had the energy to do that." Fortunately, those two are related. That's why this chapter on work–life balance is titled "Who Has Time for That?"

The Ironman triathlon is an athletic competition about one thing: time management. It is not like other sports where you must score points or stop your opponent to win. All of the triathletes have exactly the same tasks in front of them—swim, bike

The most important key to work–life balance is time management.

and run—and the same distance to cover on the same course, but they don't all have the same equipment (bike, wheels, wetsuit, shoes, etc.), fitness, body, or experience. Some are great at swimming but not so great at running. I am really good at cycling, but I have to work on my running and get a lead on the bike ahead of faster runners. Some can do it in nine hours, some take twelve or fifteen, but each athlete knows their ability and races their own race, recognizing their strengths and weaknesses to get the job done. The best are the ones who can do it the most efficiently and strategically, without wasting time or energy.

Your life and work are just like the Ironman—different tasks in your day and week, and some you are good at, some you are not. Some you really enjoy. Others not so much. We do not all have the same equipment, skill, or experience in life and might not have exactly the same job or tasks, but each day we all have the day to complete it. You may be a busy corporate executive with meetings, phone calls, emails, and reports to study or a busy parent with a house full of kids and a full day of errands and chores and meals to fix. And maybe in today's working parent world you are both. Just like the Ironman, the best are the ones who can do the most without wasting time or energy.

Let's discuss some keys to manage your time and energy.

Time Choices

You always have time for things that are important to you. Think about how you spend your *extra* time. What do you "make" time for? TV? The Internet? Facebook? Talking on the phone? Texting? Video games? Eating? Sleeping? We all have the same amount of time in a day. Some things we have no choice but to spend our time on: work, family obligations, school. We are required to be there. But the rest of the time is ours. How do you choose to spend it?

You always have time for things that are important to you.

When I started racing short triathlons I realized quickly that in order to get better, I would have to train more. When I moved up to Ironman triathlons the training required even more time. It became a second job, twenty hours a week or more.

I had to make time choices and sacrifices. I chose training over sleep. I still got seven hours of sleep, but I got up earlier three days a week to be in the pool to swim by 6 a.m. before work. It was hard at first, but soon it got easier because the sleep I did get was so deep and restful from exercising that I needed less of it. I always felt physically better working out early to start the day and mentally better that I was ahead of everyone else who was just waking up.

I spent my lunch hour running or cycling from my office and then grabbing a quick shower in my building or at the track before returning to my office to eat lunch at my desk.

I sacrificed time after work in the evening. I ran or cycled rather than socializing with friends or going to happy hours. In the winter, when it got dark early, or during bad weather I trained in my home, riding my bike on an indoor trainer in my basement while watching TV or swim stroke training with rubber stretch cords. When I had my first child I rode the trainer after she went to bed.

On weekend mornings I did long bike rides (four to five hours) and runs (two to three hours) early rather than watching football games, playing golf, or sleeping late, and then I had the rest of the day for errands, activities, yard and house work, or time with family and friends.

You may have to give up some things that occupy your time. Are you willing to make sacrifices? Make time choices. You have the time. We all have the same amount of time. How do you choose to spend it?

Time Creep

Have you noticed how you set a budget or plan to spend your money this month or for Christmas or an event, and then gradually you spend a little bit here and a little bit there? You choose to do this little extra thing or something small comes up. It just slips away a little bit at a time—drip, drip, drip. We think each small purchase won't make that much difference, and it won't by itself, but soon all of those little expenses combine and ... where did the money go? We're out of money. That is money creep.

Time does the same thing. Each day we make choices to spend a few minutes here and ten or fifteen minutes there, and soon an hour is gone or the afternoon is gone. People call, text, or email you or stop by your office and suddenly you're in a quick conversation and ... where did the time go? You're out of time. That is time creep.

Learn tactics to prevent these small interruptions and delays. Some you can't avoid, but you may be able to deflect or redirect them to a better time. When I was eighteen I worked heavy construction as a pipe fitter's assistant on a high-rise office building. I was low man on the job site and everyone had the seniority to tell me what to do. If I needed to take a break or to get a piece of equipment for another foreman, walking through the job site was dangerous. Another foreman would always stop me and pile a new task on me. One day another guy who had been working my job a little longer gave me a tip. Never walk the job site empty handed. He told me to carry a small piece of cast-iron pipe or fitting on my shoulder and walk diligently on the project. That sent the signal that "he's busy doing something else; he's not available."

As a young lawyer I did the same thing. When I had something one senior partner wanted by the next morning, if I walked down the hall another partner would inevitably stop me or call me into his office to talk about his new assignment. You can't tell your boss, or fifty senior partner bosses, that you don't have time for them. So I never walked empty handed; I always carried a file with me—my piece of cast-iron pipe. I was always looking for more work, but I learned to receive and redirect their requests quickly. For instance: "Yes, I can help you with that. I am working on this project for [other senior partner] right now, but can I come see you in an hour or first thing in the morning?" My evening plans and other assignment were saved.

Plan and prepare for problems and delays. If they happen, you are not stressed. If they don't, you have extra time to relax. In the Ironman I carry a spare tube strapped tightly under my seat in case I get a flat tire. I only need one $CO2$ cartridge to fill that tube, but I carry two just in case one malfunctions. In fourteen Ironman and ultra-distance triathlons and over twenty half Ironman triathlons, I have flatted only one time in a race, but it saved me to be prepared that time. The other times I raced a lot more focused and effective (i.e., less stressed), not worried that I might have a flat with no spare.

I use this method when I'm flying to speaking engagements. Airplanes will not wait. I plan for something to delay me on the way to the plane—road traffic or a ridiculous line at security (seems everybody is TSA pre-check these days)—by building in extra time. Those delays do not happen most of the time, just like my tire does not flat in the Ironman most of the time, but it eliminates stress to be prepared when it does. And it's always nice to relax with a beer and a book waiting with extra time to board or return a few emails, texts, or phone calls.

Technology contributes to time creep. Technology makes our lives easier, but it also lures us into distractions. According to Shawn Achor, the author of *The Happiness Advantage*, "Technology makes it easier for us to save time but also easier for us to waste it. It is not the number of distractions but the ease of access to them." We can open our phones and plunge into dozens of apps in less than five seconds: Facebook, YouTube, eBay, sports, news, and electronic games. I am convinced that Candy Crush puts a hypnotic trance on some people, including my wife.

Technology has ruined planning skills. Before the iPhone was launched in 2005, life required more planning. We had to plan our afternoon to spend a few hours going to several stores to shop for the right item. Now we can look for that item on dozens of websites anytime—*always available, always tempting us.* We had to organize our day not to miss our favorite TV show. Now we can record every episode automatically on our DVR and watch it right now—*always available, always tempting us.* We took care of our responsibilities at school, work, or home first until the TV news at eleven or the newspaper the next day to find out what happened. Now we can watch game highlights and news twenty-four hours a day on smartphones and cable networks—*always available, always tempting us.* We had to call or visit friends to find out what is going on in their lives. Now we can monitor thousands of "friends" voyeuristically by the minute on Facebook—*always available, always tempting us.* All of these advances in technology are wonderful and convenient, but they lure us to just bob along without planning.

Put down your phone and cut the e-leash. Set the example for your children who have never known a life without TV, the Internet, tablets, and smartphones that there is more quality of life in person-to-person contact, reading a book, or just plain thinking. Share stories by telling them in person rather than by sharing them on Facebook.

Put down your phone and cut the e-leash.

At the time of writing this book, my three kids are all under nine years old. We go to the park a lot. I cherish that they want that simple pleasure of spending time with me on the playground. Before smartphones parents had no choice but to watch their kids and talk with them. The other day I saw a dad pushing his daughter on the swing with his left hand while his face was glued to his smartphone in his right. When she said, "Push me, daddy! Push me!" he would push, but he never looked up from his phone. I wanted to tell that dad no matter what is going on in his right hand, it is not more important than what's in his left. Soon she will not be asking you to go to the park or wanting you to push. Put the phone down.

In *The Happiness Advantage*, Achor recommends a twenty-second rule. Make it take twenty seconds longer to access a bad habit or a time waster. At the office hide your email and Internet icons on your computer so you have to click multiple steps to access them. When you are busy, forward your phone to voicemail so you do not know when someone is calling. Shield yourself from distractions and temptations that waste time and get you off task. Turn off the TV

Make it take twenty seconds longer to access a bad habit or a time waster.

when working in the house, close the curtains so you can't see activity outside, and wear earplugs or headphones with no music when distractions are around you. Hide your time temptations the same way you hide your food temptations when you are on a diet, keeping junk food and unhealthy snacks away from you, making it hard for you to grab and pop in your mouth. Studying hours each night in law school I hid myself from distractions by wearing earplugs to block out the sounds of my roommates. I covered the clocks in my apartment before I started studying so I would not be distracted by how long I had been studying or how late I stayed up. I woke in the morning not knowing what time I went to bed. How often do we beat ourselves up and moan about how little sleep we got, and it affects our attitude and performance the next day? Save yourself from yourself. Hide your temptations and distractions.

The opposite is also true. Make it twenty seconds easier to access a good habit. Pack your workout bag every night so you can take it with you on the way out the door like you take

Make it twenty seconds easier to access a good habit.

your keys and wallet or purse. Put your guitar in the living room, tuned and ready so you can grab it and practice easier. Keep that bike cleaned and ready to ride in the garage so you can jump on it and go. Keep healthy food in your house rather than junk food. Reduce the effort required to maintain habits you want to adopt, and raise it for ones you want to avoid.

Employers Can Reward Balance

Companies that reward a healthy work–life balance have found that it actually increases productivity and performance. In his book *Start with Why*, author Simon Sinek (also a great TED Talk from 2009 that has over twenty-five million views) offered a theory on why some companies are more innovative, influential, and profitable than others. One company, a commercial construction company in Baton Rouge, Louisiana, did it by actually rewarding work–life balance. The owner believed that his employees should work hard and then spend more time with their families. Every employee is required to clock in in the morning and clock out in the evening. That's not that unusual you may say. But here's the difference. In order to qualify for the bonus pool they must clock in *no earlier* than 8:00 to 8:30 a.m. and clock out *no later* than 5:00 to 5:30 p.m. Wasted time at work decreased. Productivity is high and turnover is low. Work–life balance is rewarded.

Have you ever noticed how much work you get done the day before you go on vacation? Don't meetings that are scheduled at 4 p.m. on Friday afternoon go a lot faster? Practicing law I tried to schedule all of my depositions to start in the afternoon rather than the morning because I knew the other lawyer would not waste time if he had to beat rush hour traffic or catch a plane.

Many companies start corporate wellness programs trying to help employees with work–life balance. But like horses and water, you can create a program and provide facilities to lead people to wellness, but you can't make them drink. They have to want it. Most fitness centers or walking trails on corporate campuses are utilized by less than 10 percent of their employees. Visit the local health club in January and then again in April to see how many kept their New Year's resolution. I use the fitness center in every hotel I stay in, but even in the largest hotels with hundreds of rooms at the busiest times I rarely see more than a handful of guests in there with me. You can't just provide a wellness program or a fitness facility and expect them to use it. You have to motivate them to use it and keep motivating them. As Zig Ziglar said, "Motivation is like bathing. You need a little bit every day." That's what this book and your finish line vision is—your motivation every day. The company leadership sets the example and creates the culture by encouraging wellness and doing it themselves.

2. MAXIMIZE YOUR TIME

Work-life balance requires not only that you manage your time but also that you *maximize* it. Do two things at once. But this does not mean multitasking. What most people consider multitasking actually contributes to stress and hinders work–life balance—talking on the phone to one person while typing an email to another, texting while in a conversation or meeting, scanning email and smartphones while eating a meal with your friends and family or while pushing your daughter on a swing. These forms of multitasking all require attention from your brain. Both tasks are competing for your attention—the email and the conversation—so either one get's ignored or (more likely) both get half of your attention and a halfway job.

> **Work-life balance requires not only that you manage your time but also that you *maximize* it.**

Just because you're doing a lot more doesn't mean that you're getting a lot more done.

Maximize your time by doing two tasks at once that do not compete

> **Just because you're doing a lot more doesn't mean that you're getting a lot more done.**

with each other. For example, in your house you can wash clothes in your washing machine while dinner cooks in the oven. The washing machine and the oven do not compete and can function perfectly at the same time. There is no reason to waste time waiting for the washing machine to finish and then going into the kitchen to put dinner in the oven. Duplicate that with tasks and desires in your life that can be accomplished at the same time without competing with each other. Here are a few suggestions.

Exercise and watch TV. You like to watch TV and you need (and hopefully will soon like) to exercise, so exercise while watching TV. I rode many hours on my bike on my indoor trainer in my basement while watching sports, movies, and news on TV. Invest in a treadmill, balance ball, stationary bike, or other equipment to use while you watch TV at home. Make a rule that you must be using that device the entire time of your thirty-minute or one-hour show. That gives your workout a goal. Even better, watch something with beautiful, fit people and use them as your finish line vision while you sweat. Early in my racing career I watched many hours of the Ironman triathlon while riding my bike on the trainer, dreaming about my next race. Watch inspiring movies like *Gladiator, Braveheart, Chariots of Fire,* or *Rocky* that get your blood pumping and fuel your motivation.

Exercise and socialize. You need to call your mother. So call her while you walk the neighborhood. Socialize with your friends and family by inviting them to go on a walk or bike ride with you or to the local health club. Sometimes my wife rode her bike beside me while I did training runs. Remember the goal to exercise at a labored conversation pace to burn fat? Invite someone to have that labored conversation! I pulled my infant and toddler kids in a trailer attached behind my bike. It's a great workout pulling the extra weight and they love the ride with dad.

Work and commute/travel. Make phone calls and listen to voice-mails while you commute to and from work, paying attention to the road by using an earpiece with both hands on the wheel, just like you are talking to a passenger in your car. Driving the interstate on long trips is a great time to schedule an extended conversation. Public transportation like trains and planes are even better because you can put 100 percent of your attention on your work while someone else does the driving.

Work and exercise. I spent many hours on my bike on long rides thinking about a client's case, a trial I had coming up, my exhibits, my examination of witnesses, and opening and closing statements. I needed quiet and solitude to do those things. I could have spent hours at my desk on weekends or late at night when no one was in the office, or I could spend it on my bike on long country roads or mountain climbs. The solitude of my bike was much more pleasant than my office. I carried a small notepad in a Ziploc bag (to protect it from sweat) in my jersey pocket and stopped frequently to write notes. Some nights I read depositions while riding my bike on my indoor trainer. I traveled with stretch cords and paddles so I could swim in my hotel room on business trips. Everybody's job and work is different, so be creative.

Do tasks and errands. We all have errands to run. Get your oil changed or tires serviced next to a grocery store, Costco, or Wal-Mart so you can do some necessary shopping while you wait. Get your car repaired at a shop or dealership that has Wi-Fi so you can bring your laptop and work. I wrote some of this book in waiting areas. Plan quick errands or phone calls while your child is in soccer, football, or dance practice.

Eat and meet and work. Network at chamber or industry lunches. Meet customers, prospects, or employees for lunch to discuss business. Run errands or exercise during your lunch hour and eat lunch at your desk while you work.

All of these things are just examples of accomplishing two things at the same time—things that do not compete with each other for your attention. Maximize your time.

3. HAVE A SYSTEM (SAVES YOU STRESS TIME ENERGY MONEY)

Systems create order and efficiency. Routines create stability. Tasks get completed on time. Things are done automatically so you have more time to do the things you enjoy. Systems take the stress and worry out of trying to remember to do things.

Your employer has systems so you can get more work done. Have systems so you can get more life done. Businesses have systems and routines. You have an office or cubicle assigned to you; you don't just come to work each day and wander around looking for an open spot to work. There is a payroll system so everybody gets their paycheck when expected; employees don't have to hope somebody remembers to write them a check or visit the payroll office and ask to be paid. There is a system for when a new customer walks in the door, calls on the phone, or contacts you online, and there's a system to process their order. There is a HR system to hire new employees, a system to reorder supplies, and a system to maintain equipment.

Your employer has systems so you can get more work done. Have systems so you can get more life done.

The great thing about a system is it works most of the time, and when it doesn't, you have comfort that it usually works and this time was just an aberration. You don't have to be a slave or prisoner to your system.

Have a system or routine to do your exercise early morning or during the day. Pack your workout bag and take it with you every day to work. Plan how long it takes you to drive to the health club, where you can grab lunch, dinner, or groceries on the way back to work or home. Leave the same time every day, managing the time creep so you can leave on time. When I ran from my office at lunch I packed my workout bag at night, took it to work the next morning, and carried it from my car into my office. That saved me an extra ten minutes at lunch walking from my office to my car to get my bag and back into the building to change. Ten minutes can mean a lot for lunch hour. Fortunately I had a shower in the basement of my office and deli in my building or I brought lunch from home and could be back to eat it at my desk in sixty to seventy-five minutes max. On Tuesdays at lunch I drove to the track at Furman University. The drive was ten to twelve minutes at midday, but there was no shower at the track so I found one at the tennis facility locker room next door.

I had a training system around my day working full time as a lawyer—two workouts a day, fifteen to twenty hours a week. Monday: swim early morning before work, and then run at lunch or in the evening. Tuesday: track workout or other run early morning or at lunch, group bike ride in the evening. Wednesday: swim early morning, bike at lunch or in the evening. Thursday: run early morning or at lunch and bike/run brick workout in evening. Friday: swim in the early morning or after work. Saturday: long bike ride and brick run. Sunday: long run in morning, and recovery bike in evening. Each workout was different from week to week to avoid repetition and to keep improving, depending on where I was in the season and my races coming up. Only one workout had a mandatory day and starting time—the Tuesday night group ride at 6 p.m. If I had to miss or got started late on some, I didn't stress because I knew the system was there.

Develop a system for your kids. At the time of this writing, I have three young kids under nine. Kids can affect work–life balance in ways good and bad. You want to spend time with them, but they also take time and energy, especially caring for young ones. One day I noticed my kids would bust into our house with wonderful enthusiasm and immediately toss and drop things anywhere and everywhere: shoes, bookbags, papers, toys, jackets—an explosion of debris.

"Do you do that at school?" I asked one day. "Uh, Daaaaad, no way! We have to put things in our cubbies, lockers, and the box on the teacher's desk as soon as we get there." Duh! Mind blown. My wife and

I started taking advantage of that system that they were used to from school. Place items in certain spots in our house as soon as you walk in the door. I realize that kids six or sixteen don't always comply, and you can't control or predict all of the challenges (and drama) that come from raising children, but having a system for things saves you a little time, stress, and energy and brings more balance.

Develop a system to manage your health condition. Diabetes requires constant, daily management of blood sugar. I keep blood sugar meters in many locations—my car, bathroom, desk in my office, workout bag, and airline carry-on bag and suitcase—so I do not have to remember to carry one with me. I keep Clif Bars in my car and workout bag and travel bags so I do not have to search for something to eat for low blood sugar. If you have a health condition that requires regular medication, equipment, and monitoring, think of a system and routine you could implement to make it easier for you to manage. Eliminate some of the stress of having to remember.

Develop a system to manage your money. As a child in the 1980s I recall my father sitting many nights after dinner, reviewing household bills and writing checks and balancing his checkbook. Fortunately today technology allows bills to be paid by automatic bank draft. You can view you bank balance online immediately without waiting for checks to clear mailed to fifteen different places. You can deposit checks with a photo on your smartphone. I'm still old school and like to receive and view some paper statements, but I know bills will be paid and investments are made automatically. More time for life. More balance.

4. TO HAVE THE TIME OF YOUR LIFE, MAKE IT THE RIGHT TIME OF YOUR LIFE

You do not grow vegetables in the winter. You do not go snow skiing in the summer. There is a right and a wrong time for things in nature and life.

Do not beat yourself up right now if you cannot find time to enroll in classes to finish your degree or race a marathon or start your own business. Right now may not be the right time in your life. I started racing Ironman triathlons before I was married and had kids and continued it after I got married and while my kids were too young to know I was out training. I had the time of my life because it was the *right* time of my life. I planned it that way. I knew it was the right time and I took it. I realized that if I didn't pursue it then the opportunity would be lost and gone. I cringed when I saw a man or woman my age with a job, a spouse, and kids forcing a time-consuming Ironman dream into their life that caused frustration and damage at work and home.

When is the right time in your life to pursue something? Is it now when your career is stable and you are single with extra time, or is it better to wait until your kids are older and out of the house? Now may be the right time, or now may not be the right time. It's okay not to do it now. Don't risk your job. If you're willing to take a risk, you also have to be willing to take a fall. It's worse to force it when the time is not right, but start planning now to do it when the time *is* right.

5. PLAN YOUR DAY

Planning your day not only helps you accomplish tasks, it reduces stress. Anything that reduces stress helps work–life balance.

During the first hour of the morning think about what you need to do that day. Write it down. Make a to-do list with your cup of coffee and refer to it throughout the day. You may have a separate list for work and for personal, or it may be one list. "Call client *x*. Get clothes from dry cleaners. Make hotel reservation for trip next month." Take it out of your brain and put it on paper or your smartphone. Throughout the day you can see it, add to it, and check things off. The feeling of crossing something off your list is a little moment of satisfaction. We all need those moments every day. Some items may spill over to the next day.

That's okay. Just save yourself the burden of trying to remember everything in your head. You just freed up brain cells to think of something more pleasant or daydream. Your to-do list is downloading stuff off of your brain's internal memory and storing it on an external hard drive.

Sheryl Sandberg is chief operating officer at Facebook and author of the book *Lean In: Women, Work, and the Will to Lead.* Her book and TED Talk created a national movement and discussion on women in the workplace. You can imagine that her day is busy running one of the largest technology companies in the world. You would think that she has an app on her smartphone with all of her tasks wirelessly synchronized with her brain so she never has to write them down. No, she does it the old-fashioned way, and if the COO of Facebook does that it gives you permission to do it too. She says, "I'm a big believer in thoughtful preparation. Everywhere I go, I carry a little notebook with my to-do list—*an actual notebook* that I write in with *an actual pen.* (In the tech world, this is like carrying a stone tablet and a chisel.)" Ironic advice from the person who runs the company that causes so many people to waste time. Make your to-do list to balance your life.

You can script your preparation, even if you can't script your outcome. As Eisenhower said, "Battle plans are fine—until the battle starts." Organize and control what you can. Whether its trying cases as a lawyer or racing an Ironman triathlon, neither go exactly as planned. Trials are fluid and unpredictable improv shows. Suddenly the judge rules that my crucial piece of evidence is inadmissible, or opposing counsel offers a witness I did not expect, or a witness changes his testimony on the stand. In Ironman triathlons the ocean water may be rough when it was calm all week, the bike may have strong winds, or I may get cramps in my quads or a flat tire, and the marathon may be hotter than expected or my stomach gets nauseous at mile 130. Of course, diabetes and blood sugar are always unpredictable. Your customer, boss, family, or opponent can throw a curveball in your plan for the day.

You may not be able to control your outcome, but you can control your preparation. Preparing for trial I had a list of all the witnesses, mine and the other side's, with their relevant points and testimony, the evidence I needed to get admitted, and the evidence of the other side to oppose and the grounds. I had a list of motions and supporting law to be made during trial. At trial I followed the plan but always had to think on my feet and react to the moment.

> **You may not be able to control your outcome, but you can control your preparation.**

Racing an Ironman I have a list of everything that goes in both transition and special needs bags and the items I need prerace and postrace for my bike, my apparel, my diabetes, my nutrition, and anything else. I use that list for packing and bring it to every race and revise it as needed. It gives me great comfort when packing to fly across the world and great comfort on race day. I've thought about it before and don't have to keep it in my head. Now I can just adapt and adjust as the day develops and wing it when I have to.

When Things Don't Go as Planned—A Marriage Proposal

Sometimes in work, sports, and life you still have to just "wing it," but winging it is a lot easier (and less stressful) when you are prepared. Some days do not go as planned. Like the day I proposed to my wife.

One week after we met in 2003 she watched me race a half Ironman triathlon in South Carolina. (It was kind of a first date, I guess. I know, romantic, but we had plenty of "normal" dates after that.) After dating a few years in 2006 I came up with a brilliant, memorable plan to propose to her *during* that same race.

> **Sometimes in work, sports, and life you still have to just "wing it," but winging it is a lot easier (and less stressful) when you are prepared.**

I had enjoyed good success, racing several years on the US national team, and had sponsors and invites to speak at diabetes events around the country. Two days before the race in 2006 I had to attend an event in Newport, Rhode Island, for the Joslin Diabetes Center Foundation. She attended with me. The plan was to fly to South Carolina the next day and propose to her during the race the next morning. I had the diamond engagement ring at home waiting. That was the plan.

The plan started to unravel traveling from Rhode Island the day before the race. After flight delays and cancellations, we were still sitting in Chicago O'Hare airport at 11 p.m. the night before the race. I'm sure I'm not the only one who has ever had flight delays at O'Hare. The race would start in South Carolina in eight hours.

"Do you really want to do this race?" she asks. A legitimate question—I had already done it three straight years and we were stuck in an airport eight hundred miles away eight hours before the race would start.

But she did not know the plan.

"Yes! I definitely want to do this race. It will be no pressure since I've done it before, blah ... blah ... blah," I said calmly, not wanting to give it away. I made up some other excuses why it was important. The flight finally got us to South Carolina at 1 a.m. We napped for two hours and drove an hour to the race site. Slight adjustment number one to the plan. Despite unplanned travel delays and no sleep before a half Ironman and marriage proposal, so far everything was still a go.

My plan was to do the swim and the bike and propose at the start of the half marathon run. I had the diamond ring stashed in my running shoe in transition. She usually stood in generally the same place watching this race (she was a professional Ironman triathlon spectator at this point). She said she would be at that spot so I could look for her in the crowd lining the route. I had also talked to her father, asking his permission to marry his daughter like a good Southern boy should. He was going to be at that spot with a camera to capture the moment. That was the plan.

I had a good swim and was having a great bike—a really great bike. As I passed mile fifty I started thinking about the proposal. Although my real focus for this race was to propose to her, I couldn't help but notice that I was very close to the lead. My competitive nature was kicking in at right about the time … I crashed.

A bike crash is rare in a triathlon, more common in a bike race where lots of cyclists are packed together. This is the only crash I ever had in a triathlon. Bad timing, right? I hit a patch of sand at about twenty-five miles per hour too close to the edge of the road and went tumbling and sliding down the pavement, asphalt, and bits of gravel and road debris ripping and thrashing my back and legs. Imagine falling out of the back of a pickup truck going twenty-five miles per hour wearing only a swimsuit. Fortunately I did not break any bones and was only a few miles from the transition area. But I was covered in blood on my back and legs, with gashes and open road rash wounds and tiny pebbles stuck in my skin. I pedaled the next few miles slowly into transition since my bike was stuck in one gear.

Adjustment number two to the plan. I had not planned on the travel delays (adjustment no. 1) or crashing my bike (adjustment no. 2), but everything was still a go.

The diamond engagement ring was right where I had hidden it, stuffed in my running shoe in transition. *Whew!* I grabbed it and ran out to start the half marathon. I poured water on my arm and back leaving transition, thinking, *Maybe I'll just propose and then drop out since Anna will be real close to the run start and I'm now covered in blood and hurting kind of bad and need to go to the medical tent.* Anna was supposed to be on the run course only about a thousand meters out of transition. I approached that spot and scanned the crowd, holding the box with the engagement ring in my hand. Blood ran down my arm from my elbow onto the box.

She wasn't there. I slowed and looked around. Spectators lining the route were looking and pointing at the blood on my back and legs. Her father was not there either. I had a choice. I could stop and quit the race, walk off the course, and propose all bloody wherever I could find her in the crowd, but that wasn't exactly the memory I was shooting for. Or I could keep running. I was close to the lead, so I kept running.

Adjustment number three to the plan. She's not there. Keep going.

I ran seven miles holding that diamond engagement ring in the jeweler's box in my hand with blood dripping on it, rinsing myself at aid stations with cups of water. Race officials, medics, and volunteers at the aid stations looked at me with a mix of shock and horror. The September air was hot and humid and salty sweat burned the open wounds on my shoulder and back.

After seven miles I returned to the transition area, completing the first loop of the run. I was still close to the lead when I saw Anna (finally). I approached her and stopped and proposed. She was a little confused, stunned by the proposal and that I was doing it in the middle of the race and that I was handing her a bloody engagement ring and that I was covered in blood.

She said yes. At least I think she did. I'm really not sure she said anything at all. It was kind of confusing. I don't think she knew if she was supposed to hug me or take me to the medical tent. But after a few minutes of hugs and kisses and chitchat, I was still close to the race lead, so she said, "Well, you might as well keep running." I had come this far and didn't really care about winning anymore, but I only had six more miles to run. I ran the last six miles slow and easy as an engaged man, still bloody and bruised but happy. The plan was done. After all the delays from crashing and proposing and lollygagging those last six miles, I finished in thirty-ninth place out of approximately four hundred. After

Sometimes the day doesn't go as planned, but just keep going. Even if you get a little bloody.

the race we celebrated our engagement at the emergency room. They removed the bits of asphalt and gravel embedded in my back and bandaged me up. Adjustment number four to the plan.

Sometimes the day doesn't go as planned, but just keep going. Even if you get a little bloody.

6. PLAN TO BE UNBALANCED.

There are many times in life when you *have* to be unbalanced. It is not only *okay* to be unbalanced, it is *required*. Prepare for those times. Don't fight it. In some periods of your life certain things have to take priority.

> **There are many times in life when you *have* to be unbalanced. It is not only *okay* to be unbalanced, it is *required*.**

Plan to be unbalanced in the first months or year of a demanding academic program: college, law school, medical school, business school. Dedicate yourself to the priority—your academics. Get off to a good start. You will not have as much time to exercise, socialize, relax, or spend with friends and family. Expect it. Tell your friends and family (and yourself) that before you start. It will be temporary, and you will have more time later to regain your balance. My first year of law school I noticed (and envied) how second- and third-year students appeared relaxed and seemed to laugh and play golf and talk about going out that night. They had fewer classes and understood how to manage the demands of law school. The ones who had worked hard their first year had a higher GPA and class rank and better prospects for a job. They told me to work hard the first year and I would be glad later. They were right. In my second and third years I had more time and my life became more balanced.

Plan to be unbalanced in your first six months to a year at a new job. You must focus on that job, learn the responsibilities, and establish your reputation at the company as a reliable, hard-working colleague. You will understand the culture of your employer and learn when is the best time to take time away from work to keep yourself balanced, and your boss and colleagues will not question your dedication. They will know that you will get the job done because you have already proven yourself reliable.

Plan to be unbalanced in the first years of your child's life. Your child needs and requires more of your attention and time during early years. Your child is dependent on you for things. That dependence decreases as he or she gets older. Not only does she need your presence, she *wants* it. Embrace that and enjoy it. Those days will be gone soon and you will regret not spending that time with them. Don't fight it and beat yourself up that you do not have as much time to socialize, exercise, or relax as you used to. Just make time to do it as much as you can to keep yourself going. You will have more time as your child ages and becomes more independent and capable to care for himself. Kids make other new demands on your time as they grow up (activities, carpools, drama, and expenses), but prepare for the extra time demands when they are young.

Equal balance is not the goal.

Equal balance is not the goal. Some things in your life will always require more time and more energy. Each day you will spend more time working and commuting (eight to twelve hours) and sleeping (six to eight hours) than anything else. Perfect balance is impossible. Work–life balance requires constant adjustment and flexibility. It is not easy. You have to make sacrifices and often do things that you do not want to do to have your job, family, health, and happiness. As Facebook COO Sandberg noted in *Lean In*, "Instead of pondering the question 'Can we have it all?' we should be

Perfect balance is impossible.

asking the more practical question 'Can we do it all?' And again, the answer is no. Each of us makes choices constantly between work and family, exercising and relaxing, making time for others and taking time for ourselves. Being a parent means making adjustments, compromises, and sacrifices everyday."

Plan and expect that there will be certain times in your life that you will be unbalanced. That is okay. Those periods will pass and it will get better.

7. PURSUE YOUR PASSION

There are many things in our lives that we *must* do. We feel unbalanced when we feel like that is *all* we do. Find your passion and pursue it, even if just in small doses. I pursued racing triathlons, which became my passion, which led to speaking. I saw that speaking was helping to change and improve lives, which became another passion and part of my career. I love it.

Pursue a healthy stress relief, not drugs, alcohol, gambling, or other destructive behavior. It is better to spend an hour three evenings a week in a health club than in a bar. Take an art class, learn to play a musical instrument, join a sports team, coach a youth team, or hike the trails of your state parks. Do something for others while you do something for yourself—race a local race as a fund-raiser for a charity. Volunteer. Do something for someone who will not be able to repay you.

In triathlons and life, whoever has the best time wins.

As hard and painful the workouts and races were in Ironman triathlon, I loved every minute of it. I was addicted to the pain and craved the work because it was my passion— the quiet bike rides in the mountains, the runs early in the morning, the zen-like swims. In triathlons and life, whoever has the best time wins. I dreamed of the finish line, but I loved every minute of the training and the race getting there.

We cannot just hope and pray that happiness and enjoyment will happen one day, in the distance, at the next station in life, at a new job, at retirement, or in some afterlife. We must work to make our lives happy now and enjoy the ride.

Have you ever left a funeral and thought, *What if that were me?* Imagine your retirement from your career or the day your children move out of your house. Will you look back and regret what you did not do? Write the eulogy that you hope someone will give at your funeral. It is a sobering, thought-provoking exercise. What will they say about you? Are you living and creating that life now?

Pursue your passion to help you balance your life.

CHAPTER 14

BLUFF THEM, BELIEVE IN YOU

Topic: Overcoming Doubt

I had a lot of reasons to doubt myself heading into Ironman Florida 2004. So far that year I had had good results in half Ironman races but fantastic failures in Idaho and Wisconsin and a mediocre showing for the US team at the Long Distance Triathlon World Championship in Sweden. My dream to race and finish with the best Ironman triathletes in the world and break ten hours was starting to seem a little … doubtful.

Have you ever felt doubt like that? Before giving a presentation at work? Before a big game or race? Before a test in school or a special event in your life? No matter how much you have prepared, has doubt started to creep in that maybe you are not as good as the competition, maybe you don't really belong with the best, maybe you are not that good?

There is a well-known psychological phenomenon called the imposter syndrome. Highly qualified, talented, and competent people are high achievers at work or school, even experts in their field, yet they sometimes feel like it is only a matter of time before they are found out for who they really are—imposters who are not good enough or even frauds. Sheryl Sandberg admits that she suffered from this. If there is anyone you would think would not suffer from lack of self-confidence it would be the Facebook COO, head of one of the world's most successful technology companies that virtually has consumed modern life, a person ranked on *Fortune's* list of the fifty most powerful women in business and as one of *Time's* one hundred most influential people in the world. Yet regarding her time as a Phi Beta Kappa honor student at Harvard she says, "Every time I was in class, I was sure I was about to embarrass myself. Every time I took a test, I was sure that it had gone badly. And every time I didn't embarrass myself—or even excelled—I believed that I had fooled everyone yet again. One day soon, the jig would be up."

If a person with those credentials and achievements can feel insecure and inadequate, it is okay for you to doubt yourself too. It is normal to doubt yourself. Don't think that you are the only one who feels this way, that everyone else is calm, cool, and confident while you are the only one who is a nervous wreck. Don't give in to those doubts. If you pursue only things that you know you can achieve, you will never achieve anything significant. And you will be really boring.

> **If you pursue only things that you know you can achieve, you will never achieve anything significant. And you will be really boring.**

I was starting to wonder if I really did belong with the best Ironman triathletes. I had invested a lot of time, money, and effort into this. It was starting to impact my legal career, with a few colleagues undermining me at the office. Would people start to think, *He wasted a lot of time pursuing this fantasy, but what does he have to show for it?* I had been on the cover of national magazines, qualified and raced for the US national team, but I had not crossed the line with the best. My confidence was shaken. *Do I belong? Have I reached my limit? Was that the best I could do?*

SURROUND YOURSELF WITH PEOPLE WHO BELIEVE IN YOU

In the movie *Good Will Hunting*, Matt Damon plays a twenty-year-old janitor from Boston named Will Hunting, who is an unrecognized mathematical genius. Working as a night janitor in the halls of the Massachusetts Institute of Technology (MIT), he solves a nearly impossible mathematical equation, posting the answer anonymously on a chalkboard after hours. He is discovered but still unsure of himself. He fears failure and rejects prestigious, high-paying job offers and a relationship with a female Harvard student played by Minnie Driver. He prefers to take the safe route, spending his free time drinking with his best friend (played by Ben Affleck), doing manual labor, and looking for trouble. It is only after his therapist (played brilliantly by the late Robin Williams) convinces Will that he believes in him and convinces him to confront his fears and believe in his own potential that Will pursues one of these opportunities. The tagline and lesson from the movie is "Some people can never believe in themselves until someone believes in them." The story is fiction, but the lesson is true. Find people who believe in you.

In the movie *Pursuit of Happyness*, Will Smith plays Chris Gardner, an entrepreneur father who invested and lost his life savings in a failed venture. The IRS garnishes his bank account. The city of San Francisco impounds his car and he is temporarily jailed for failure to pay over a thousand dollars in delinquent parking tickets. His marriage dissolves and he is left homeless with his five year-old son, spending nights in a homeless shelter and even a San Francisco BART subway restroom. Despite these failures, he still dreams big, of overcoming, of making money and succeeding, telling his son Christopher, Jr. one night:

> **Chris Gardner (Dad)**: Hey. Don't ever let somebody tell you you can't do something. Not even me. All right?
>
> **Christopher (Son)**: All right.

Chris Gardner (Dad): You gotta dream? You gotta protect it. [If] people can't do something themselves … they wanna tell you *you* can't do it. If you want somethin', go get it. Period.

Gardner eventually gets an unpaid internship at a San Francisco brokerage firm, never revealing that he has only one suit and lives in a homeless shelter, competing for a paid position against twenty more qualified applicants. At the end of the internship he wins the job. The movie is based on the inspiring true story of Christopher Gardner first told in a televised interview on *20/20* in January 2002 and published in his 2006 autobiography.

THE PYGMALION EFFECT–LEADERSHIP

My coach Peter was a good source of encouragement during my 2004 series of race failures. He was more than a coach now; he was a friend and a training partner. Keeping up with him on training rides was proof that I could cycle with the best, but I still had to swim 2.4 miles and run a marathon to reach the finish line with them. I knew he believed in me.

The Pygmalion effect is a psychological phenomenon that our belief in another person's potential can bring that potential to life. It comes from the figure in Greek mythology named Pygmalion who carved a statue of his ideal woman and longed so much for it to come to life that it eventually did. I suppose that was the first finish line vision. It is often called the Rosenthal effect, after a well-known experiment performed by psychologist Robert Rosenthal. Researchers gave intelligence tests to elementary school students and told their teachers which students scored the highest, but the teachers were not allowed to tell students their scores. At the end of the year, all students were tested again and these same students received above-average test scores. However, the secret was that these students had not received the highest IQ scores on the first test. The researchers concluded that a leader's expectations and belief can influence the achievement of followers. The teacher or leader may subconsciously behave in ways that facilitate the student's success, treating them differently, believing and expecting them to reach greater achievement, thus actually causing them to achieve.

That is a powerful concept for leadership in all aspects of life: business, athletics, academics, and family. People act as we expect them to act. They achieve what we expect them to achieve, which means that a leader's expectations about his followers can influence them to come true. We also need to lead ourselves and believe in ourselves, expecting to succeed. Remember our discussion in the chapter about finish line vision and expecting to succeed and how leaders like NC State coach Jim Valvano believed that his team could win the national championship (and even practiced cutting down the nets)? The expectations we have about our children, employees, team members, and other people we lead, even if never voiced, can influence their behavior and success.

Be like Pygmalion. Keep believing in yourself, your dream, your finish line vision, and work for it to come to life.

BLUFF THEM, BELIEVE IN YOU

But what do you do when it comes time to perform; when the job interview starts; or the presentation to a large audience, the sales appointment, the big game, or the race, and you are torn up with doubt, lacking confidence?

Bluff. Fake. Lie.

Yep. I just wrote that. Everyone has to fake confidence at some, often many times, in their lives—even high-level executives of multi-billion-dollar international companies. As Sheryl Sandberg, Facebook COO and Harvard graduate, admitted in her book, *Lean In*, "When I don't feel confident, one tactic I've learned is that it sometimes helps to fake it," she says. She cites research for this "fake it till you feel it" strategy, assuming a high-power pose and posture increases the dominance hormone level (testosterone) and reduces the stress hormone level (cortisol).

Feeling confident, or pretending that you feel confident, is necessary in all areas of life. Everyone does it, and so should you. People don't know you're faking it. People want to believe that you know what you are talking about, that you are one of the best, even if you are scared to death. Give them a reason to believe in you.

Bluffing is not being a fraud or an excuse not to work hard and prepare. Bluffing confidence is showing others—your boss, your job interviewer, your potential customer, or the competition—that you are capable and ready, even if inside you are nervous and about to puke.

Sometimes it's necessary to bluff just to get an opportunity. Opportunities and success are rarely offered. They are sought and seized.

Opportunities and success are rarely offered. They are sought and seized.

Heidi Klum is one of the most famous supermodels in the world. She has been on the cover of the *Sports Illustrated* swimsuit issue and spent thirteen years as a Victoria's Secret lingerie model and then became a successful businesswoman; fashion designer; and television producer, host, and judge on shows like *Project Runway* and *America's Got Talent.* You would think that she never lacked confidence or doubted herself. But growing up in a small town in Germany didn't prepare her for international stardom. After winning a national modeling contest she entered on a lark, she says in her autobiography *Body of Knowledge* that she spent the next two years trying to catch a break in a business dominated by skinny waifs and big egos. Ignoring the skeptics, as a teenager she boarded a plane to the United States barely able to speak English. "I was just one of thousands of new girls trying to make it as a model in New York, and every one of them looked fabulous. Every single day for three months I went on casting calls, sometimes as many as ten a day. Typically I'd wait in line and the client would look at my book, thank me, and send me packing. It sucked being such a small fish in a big pond."

Do you feel like this sometimes in your job or your life? Do you ever wonder, *How am I going to get my break, my chance?*

One day Klum went on a casting call for Victoria's Secret, the lingerie line that featured the most famous supermodels in the world. Those big names did the live Victoria's Secret fashion show that was broadcast on national television. When she showed up at the casting for the live show, she was out of her league. "I'd done a couple of small, no-name shows—new designers that needed a model—in front of a small audience. But I hadn't done anything big or anyone recognizable." She did not have the experience, and she was nervous and scared she was not good enough. But she wanted this opportunity to prove herself. This was her chance.

So she bluffed. She faked it. "When I showed up at the casting and they asked me if I'd done shows before, I ... lied. I said I had." When they asked her to walk, she kept bluffing. She walked proud and fearless, strutting back and forth, like she knew what she was doing, like she deserved the job. They hired her for the next show.

The bluffing didn't stop there. She admits that the night of her first Victoria's Secret live fashion show, "I was terrified. It was to be broadcast live around the world from the Plaza Hotel, with a feed to huge TV screens in Times Square. I was all nerves. Some of the most famous models in the world were roaming around backstage. The photographers were taking pictures of everyone but me, the new kid on the block."

But her friend and publicist had played another bluff card. Earlier that day she had planted a picture of Heidi on the gossip page, "Page Six," of the *New York Post,* proclaiming that Heidi Klum, the new Victoria's Secret model, had taken over the title of "The Body" from supermodel Elle MacPherson. Of course, that was not true, but as Muhammad Ali said, "I said I was the greatest before I knew I was." As the paparazzi were snapping photos of all of the other models, ignoring Heidi, her friend shouted, "Oh, isn't that Heidi Klum over there? She was on "Page Six" today!" Suddenly she was mobbed by paparazzi, asking her what it felt like to be the new "Body." She did the show nervous and excited and used that to launch her career. Even supermodels get scared, ignored, and overlooked and doubt themselves and have to bluff to get their chance.

In *David and Goliath*, Malcolm Gladwell discussed how the president of Goldman Sachs brokerage firm, Gary Cohn, bluffed to get his break. When he was twenty-two he was selling aluminum siding in Cleveland but was interested in stock trading after interning at a local brokerage firm in college. He graduated from American University with mediocre grades, not from a prestigious Ivy League school that set you up for positions on Wall Street. While visiting his company's sales office on Long Island, he convinced his manager to give him the day off to visit Wall Street. Wandering around the commodities exchange right as the markets closed, with traders exiting the floor, Cohn overheard a well-dressed man say he was heading to LaGuardia Airport as he rushed onto an elevator. Cohn jumped onto the elevator and said (lied) he was heading to LaGuardia too and asked if they could share a cab. Bluff number one.

The man happened to be high up at one of Wall Street's brokerage firms. It was luck but not so much. Cohn was strategic and smart trolling outside the floor of the commodities exchange, not randomly on the street. He put himself in the right place to find the right target, to meet the right people. You catch big fish in the right lagoons, not randomly out in the middle of the lake or sitting at home or at the mall.

Cohn admits that he lied to him all the way to the airport. That firm had just opened a new business buying and selling options, and this man was put in charge of it but did not even know what an option was. Neither did Cohn. Bluff number two. By the time they got to the airport, he had the man's number and had an interview the following week. In the interim, before the interview, he bought and read the leading textbook on options trading, repeating sentences until he was sure he understood them. Even more impressive was the hard work Cohn did preparing for the interview. One reason Cohn did not have stellar academic credentials was that he had dyslexia, like David Boies and Richard Branson, also chronicled in Gladwell's book. It took Cohn hours just to read one chapter of the options trading book. (Impressive because it probably would have taken me hours as well, and I don't have dyslexia.) But Cohn did what he had to do to get noticed, even if that meant bluffing to get the opportunity to prove himself. He had to bluff because this opportunity was not offered to him; he had to find it and seize it and work hard to earn the job.

Cohn and Klum's stories show that you may have to bluff to get your chance or fake confidence like you know what you are doing, that you deserve the finish line, but you still have to be prepared to do the job. You still have to earn it.

Humorous examples of women faking it in movies and TV are when Meg Ryan faked it to Billy Crystal in the deli in *When Harry Met Sally* and when Elaine Benes confessed faking it numerous times to Jerry Seinfeld. But that is a different subject.

It is usually important to bluff that you feel confident and strong. This is particularly true in sports to psyche out your competition, to not show any weakness. Boxers stare each other down at a prefight weigh-in and before the first bell. But sometimes in some sports the best strategy may be to bluff that you feel weak to sucker them into underestimating you. Coaches often claim that their team is struggling or has injuries.

My friend George Hincapie would use that strategy to win a stage of the Tour de France in 2005. George lives in my neighborhood of Greenville, SC. He finished the Tour a record sixteen times, and nine times his teammates won the Tour—Lance Armstrong from 1999 to 2005 (although these victories were later stripped), Alberto Contador in 2007, and Cadel Evans in 2011. He raced in the Olympics five times and is a three-time US national cycling road race champion. A record seventeen times he completed the grueling one-day races Tour of Flanders in Belgium and Paris Rubaix in France, both raced over narrow cobblestone and muddy farm roads of northern Europe in the cold rain where 70 percent of the field never even makes it to the finish line. He gives me a good workout when we do a casual training ride. He is a seasoned, savvy competitor.

In stage fifteen of the 2005 Tour he was in a breakaway with about a dozen riders in the hardest stage of the race—over a hundred miles with five climbs over the mountains of the Pyrenees, ending with the hardest, steepest ascent to the finish at the summit Pla d'Adet. With each climb the small band of leaders was losing members until there were only four left at the start of the final climb. Hincapie had completed eight Tours but had never won a stage. Winning just one stage of the Tour is a prestigious honor attained by few professional cyclists. It can vault a career. But you cannot fake it when you don't have anything left in the legs on the mountains of the Pyrenees. On the final climb he was battling three experienced climbers. Hincapie knew that the other riders were examining each other, as he was examining them, reading faces and body language, looking for who was suffering in order to launch an attack at the right moment and ride away for the win. But if a rider misjudges the competition and uses too much energy and cannot distance himself, he will burn his matches. It's a poker game pedaling up the mountain.

So Hincapie started bluffing. Not that he felt good but rather that he felt bad. "I began to feign fatigue and made it look like I was suffering a lot more than I was. About a quarter of the way up, I dropped back to the [team] car, telegraphing that perhaps I had had enough and wasn't able to keep up any longer." Hincapie's team director driving the car immediately began shouting encouragement. "Don't give up! You can do this! Just hang on! It's not much further. The other guys are tired and they're about to crack. You could win the hardest stage of the Tour!"

Hincapie leaned closer to the window of the car, pedaling up the side of the mountain, amidst the noise of thousands of fans lining the road screaming and yelling. He smiled and said barely above a whisper, "I'm not even feeling the chain." That is a cyclist's way of saying the pedaling is easy and his legs feel great. He'd faked out his own director. Believing that Hincapie was suffering, the other guys started attacking and pedaling hard, thinking they could leave him behind. They used valuable energy in these failed attempts, burning all their matches until they had nothing left. He'd bluffed them into attacking too soon. Hincapie rode past them to win the stage.

After he retired from racing, George and I have played as much tennis together as we rode, and we hang out at each other's houses with our kids roughly the same age, but the rides and talking with him in my career were helpful to learn from one of the best cyclists in the world. He is also an extremely nice guy.

Just like athletes might be scared or doubtful of their ability, you may be scared and nervous about your job. Maybe you can't remember the last time you had a prospect or lead or a sale. The worst thing you can do at your next sales call or opportunity is show how scared or nervous (desperate) you are. Customers want to buy if you give them confidence they are buying the right stuff from the right person. Show them you are confident, believe in what you are offering, and are worthy of their business.

Sometimes you have to fake it when people don't like you and you don't like them. Customers, coworkers, bosses, even your family in-laws, are all people we have to deal with in life and business even if you may not always get along with them. You display more courage and wisdom when you "grin and bare it" in these situations rather than lash out and display your true feelings. Sometimes it is necessary to fake it and not jeopardize your job or your family relationship. Take out your frustration on your next workout, not on your boss or family. I spent a lot of hours punishing my legs on the bike, venting frustration and stress from my job as a lawyer.

As a speaker I have faked it many times on stage. One time I spoke at an event in Hawaii and flew all night to Tampa, Florida, to speak at a breakfast event the following morning. I was jet-lagged and tired, but I faked feeling good for the audience. The client appreciated that.

Early in my speaking career I did a paid speaking engagement in San Diego, California, to a national association of sports nutritionists. I was speaking at 7:00 a.m. as the opening breakfast speaker. I was in the event hall at 6:30 a.m. ready to go, when I realized that I had left my presentation on a thumb drive in my hotel room, in a different wing of this large, sprawling convention hotel.

I spent the next twenty minutes sprinting several times back and forth to my hotel room upstairs (the first time I forgot my room key). Just before I went on stage I ducked behind a banner by the stage to wipe the sweat off my face with a towel. The audience had no idea.

It's okay, sometimes necessary, to bluff them. Just believe in you.

CHAPTER 15

HOW BAD DO YOU WANT IT?

Topic: Achieving Your Dream

I walked around the race site before Ironman Florida in November 2004 with a humble respect for the event. I did not want to anger the Ironman gods. They had shown me that they could crush me this year. I quietly registered and checked in my bike and gear in the days leading up to the race, but I did not hang around the race much. I did not want to be around the other competitors. I was over the expo pageant and the body off. It started feeling like being around law students in the days before final exams. I wanted to keep my mind clear and positive and just focus on what I had to do for my race, my exam.

As it had been all year, my goal was to break ten hours. That was starting to feel strangely similar to my goal in high school to make the basketball team and getting cut twice. *Do I keep trying for this? Can I do it?* Ten hours is the line separating good racers from elite racers. My times at this race had dropped previous years from eleven hours and forty-six minutes to ten hours and twenty-eight minutes, but cutting another half hour was not going to be easy. With my trouble in Ironman and ultra races this year I was not going in the right direction. Ironman Wisconsin just seven weeks before was thirteen hours and forty-three minutes. I was only four hours off.

The practice swims in the Gulf of Mexico days before this race were brutal. The surf was so rough it was almost impossible to get through the breakers. One wave slammed me so hard it ripped my goggles off my head, never to be seen again. Good thing I brought extra; always have a backup. Word around the race was that officials would cancel the swim if the ocean remained this rough on race morning. They cancel the swim for storms and rough water because officials and safety teams on the water and divers underneath cannot watch all 2,200 people in those conditions and determine if you are in danger or just battling the rough water or your competitors—or if you are a type 1 diabetic with low blood sugar. People do drown in the Ironman, usually from heart attacks, but it is often unknown what precisely caused it. Even the fittest athletes in the world are not immune to that. Tragically, the day before this race an athlete from Sweden died while on a practice swim in the rough water on the course.

I had changed my new nutrition plan and even cut out caffeine three weeks before the race—no coffee, tea, or carbonated beverages. At 6'3" and 180 pounds and frequently exhausted from multiple daily hard workouts, the small amount of caffeine I consumed never kept me awake at night, but I was willing to give it up if it would make a difference on race day. You never know unless you try.

Two nights before the race I ate a large meal of pasta, bread, and salad. I injected the normal dose of fast-acting insulin to get those carbs into my cells and stored as glycogen as soon as possible, not floating around in my bloodstream. I sipped water consistently for three days prior to the race, but I did not want to drink too much and dilute my body of electrolytes and sodium. Hyponatremia is a condition that occurs when the sodium level in the blood is too low. Some athletes (and nonathletes) mistakenly cause that by drinking too much water constantly throughout the day. But I could not sip a sport drink to add electrolytes and sodium, because those sport drinks also have carbs that would increase my blood sugar—always the blood sugar balancing act. The evening before the race I ate a smaller amount of pasta and bread and a larger portion of salad. Less pasta meant less carbohydrate, meant less insulin, meant less risk of my blood sugar being off on race morning. Hopefully these "lesses" would lead to less time on the race clock.

Before bed I had to take my injection of long-acting basal insulin. This dose was a big decision. If I took too much, it could cause low blood sugar during the race. If I took too little it could cause me to have high blood sugar. I had been back on injections for about a year rather than an insulin pump. Eliminating the pump gave me one less thing to keep up with during the race. But the main reason was that I had developed chunks of scar tissue in the infusion site area (my upper buttocks) caused by the large gauge needle to insert it every three days. I had muscles and low body fat from years of training. Jamming a large needle there hurt like bloody hell. This knot of hard scar tissue disrupted and blocked the insulin absorption from the pump. I was taking at least a year off the pump for that scar tissue to dissipate before trying it again.

That night to avoid low blood sugar during the race I decided to cut my basal insulin dose to fifteen rather than the twenty that I normally injected on nonrace days.

I would find out that was a mistake.

Unfortunately, when I awoke on race morning at 4:00 a.m. my blood sugar was 260 mg/dl, which was way too high (normal is approximately 100 mg/dl). Now I had a problem. The race started in three hours. I needed to eat breakfast for carbs and calories, but dumping that on top of already elevated blood sugar would make it go even higher. I could not risk low blood sugar during the swim. With nervous apprehension, I injected just three units to cover my breakfast, and nothing as a correction dose. I had to make a guess.

I guessed wrong. Two hours later at 6:45 a.m., fifteen minutes before the cannon blasted and the swim started, right before I entered the starting area on the beach, my blood sugar was 320. *Ugh. Oh no.* Now it was dangerously high. Nausea and sluggishness, muscle weakness, and, of course, eventual dehydration that I knew well, all could start happening. I know healthcare professionals often recommend not exercising when blood sugar is this high, but I have never had a problem starting workouts with a high blood sugar. I don't like it, but I knew that the swim should bring it down. But I have never started with one this high. I had another decision to make fast. *Do I inject a small amount of fast-acting insulin to help it come down, but risk it dropping too low swimming in the ocean over the next hour?* I could handle the high blood sugar better than the low blood sugar. The race was about to start, athletes were congregating on the beach, and the officials were about to close the transition area. I had to leave my insulin now.

I chose not to inject anything.

With these blood sugar battles before the race had even started, things did not look good for this race. All the work I had done to adjust my race nutrition and I was already having trouble. *Stay positive, Jay. It's a long race.* Standing on the beach with 2,200 other athletes, staring out at the ocean waves, the countdown started.

"Athletes, one minute!" the race announcer boomed over the PA system. The sound echoed off the high-rise condos behind us lining the beach. Thousands of spectators crowded the beach, dunes, and buildings and filled the grandstands.

Music boomed loud, and the crowd screamed and cheered with adrenaline-pumped excitement like the final minutes before a football team races onto the field or the warm-up laps of the Indy 500. Two helicopters circled overhead and one swooped down just above the surf about fifty meters in front of us. The pounding noise and wind from the rotors added to the roar of the crashing waves, the wind, the music, and the crowd. Photographers and videographers leaned out of the helicopter, pointing cameras at us, waiting to catch the carnage of thousands of athletes charging into the surf and crashing into the waves and on top of each other.

In the distance I could see a large boat a little over a half mile off shore. Florida is a two-loop swim. We swim a half mile off shore, turn and swim back to shore, run up on the beach across a timing mat, and then run back into the ocean to do the 1.2-mile loop again. Large, orange, inflated buoys bobbed and disappeared in the ocean swells about every five hundred meters to keep us on course.

"Athletes, thirty seconds!" AC/DC's "Thunderstruck" blasted over the loudspeakers, but it was hard to hear much over all the noise. At least they had good music for the start.

I had studied the surf prior to the race to see which way the current was pushing. I positioned myself to the left of the field. I knew the current would push everyone to the right, away from the buoys and the turn boat, making it more distance to cover and harder to turn left into the current out at the turnaround. I wanted to start as far left as possible to account for this drift. I had learned this from a few Ironman races.

The final seconds ticked down, but it was even more nerve-wracking because we could not see a clock. We just had to wait for the cannon to blast and the battle to be on, like bugles and a commander shouting "Charge!" to the troops to attack the hill. It felt like the tense prebattle scene in the movie *Gladiator*, those anxious moments of calm as Russell Crowe walks among the men lined up saying, "strength and honor," before the violent assault.

In this intense, loud environment, hearts pounding, athletes inching closer to the line in the sand, water touching our toes, wind blowing, waves crashing, helicopter roaring, I paused a moment. I took a deep breath and said a few words to myself. *Remember why you are doing this. Be strong. Be smart. You have earned this.*

Boom! The cannon blasted.

The ground shook as thousands of athletes ran, charged, and vaulted into the surf. Elbows flew, knocking guys into me on both sides, some leaping over the first waves, some tripping and falling into the knee-deep water. I ran until the water was too deep and dove. I knew from many races that the first five hundred meters of a mass start is the most important time to separate myself from this stampede of people. You have to swim five hundred meters hard and fast, like a short-distance swimmer in an Olympic final, and then scale back into a smooth, fast rhythm for the next two miles. My heart rate went from fifty beats per minute standing on the shore to 150, to 170, anaerobic, in one minute. The waves knocked me back and I rolled over and dove back into them. I felt hands hitting my feet, and I windmilled my arms to pound the water, driving me through the surf out to sea.

After about a hundred meters I had cleared the breaking surf and was in a bit of open water. I took a breath to my right side, turning my face to the right, and opened my mouth to suck in air and ... BAM! A hand punched me in the jaw, knocking me underwater. I never saw the guy. It almost knocked me out. My face went down, and I sucked in a mouth full of ocean water. If I had been standing my legs would have wobbled and I would have fallen like a boxer on the mat. I gasped and choked out the ocean water and threw my arm forward. I had to keep moving. Someone swam into me from behind, pushing me underwater again. I had stars in my eyes. I was still in the scrum of people that I knew would eventually fall back and thin out after a few hundred more meters. I had to keep swimming hard to separate myself from them and get on the feet of some fast swimmers to pace me. I just followed the feet and bubbles in front of me. I thought of Dory's cheery line from the children's animated film *Finding Nemo*: "Just keep swimming, just keep swimming!"

Eventually I found some fast feet and settled into a good rhythm. My heart rate decreased and I concentrated on swim technique. Glide, rotate shoulders, catch, pull, high elbow, repeat ... glide, rotate shoulders, catch, pull, high elbow, repeat. I imagined myself using the stretch cords in my basement, grabbing the water and pulling it back, thrusting me forward. After about fifteen minutes I was a half mile off shore, but there is no clock out there so we don't know our time and you don't want to look at your watch. The Gulf water was beautiful and clear blue, unlike many of the cloudy lakes and rivers we swim in. At the final turn buoy before the boat I could see scuba divers about twenty or thirty feet below looking up, watching for athletes having trouble. Turn buoys are always dangerous because the field comes together to make the turn, and it is easy to get pushed under the buoy and trapped in the ropes. At the farthest point in the course athletes are fatigued, having swam a half of a mile, and particularly on the second lap, having swam a mile and a half.

I turned left at that buoy directly into the current. Now I was also facing directly into the 7 a.m. sun barely above the water's surface. I was blinded. My goggles were slightly fogged and clouded. I lifted my head to glance quickly at my direction every few breaths, but I could not see much and just hoped the feet I was following, and the feet they were following, were going in the right direction. After a few minutes I turned left at another buoy to head back a half mile to shore. Running up the beach I saw the race clock as I crossed the timing mat. Thirty minutes. That was a good time for the first lap. If I did the same on the second lap I'd hit my target of sixty to sixty-two minutes. I knew the fastest swimmers in the field could do it in fifty to fifty-two minutes, but I could spot them eight or ten minutes in the swim because I could catch and pass them on the bike.

The next lap of the swim went well. I was in the front of the field with lots of good swimmers and open water to just focus on technique and form, saving my legs for the bike and run. I finished the swim in 1:02, exactly on target, seven minutes faster than this race last year. I liked that time on the clock, but the real indicator of where I am in the field is when I enter the transition tent. If it is deserted then I know I'm ahead of the field. If there are more guys in there, it means my time was not that great relative to the field and conditions.

The transition tent was deserted—only a few guys in there, scurrying and rushing to throw on their cycling shoes and helmet and heading out for the bike. It was eerily quiet. With virtually the entire field behind me still in the ocean, it felt like a swarm of bees was behind me about to attack this area, but now it was calm, like the eye of a hurricane.

I was pumped. I dumped out my transition bag and threw on my cycling shoes. I dried my hands and quickly got a test strip out of the vial and stuck it in my blood sugar meter. It is hard to grab a tiny test strip in a rush, and the strips cannot get wet. I pricked my finger and dropped blood on the meter while I threw on my cycling helmet and strapped my race number belt around my waste, anxiously waiting on the number that popped up on my meter. *Dammit! Error message!* The strip must have gotten wet, or I had put blood on it too fast. The race clock kept ticking. A few more guys entered the tent, and a few others ran out for their bikes. I got another strip out of the vial and stuck it in the meter and waited for the icon, ready for the blood drop. I pricked my finger again and squeezed a drop on there.

187. *Whew.* That was a relief. My blood sugar had dropped from 320 to 187 during the swim. I had made the right call not to inject insulin for that 320 or I might have been floundering around in the ocean on that second lap with a blood sugar level in the thirties or forties or lower. I did not drink any of my carb drink or eat any carbs in transition and ran out for my bike.

I always lose a minute or two in transition doing the blood sugar check, but you have to do whatever you have to do for your race. That's what I have to do. I'll take that time. If I'm not willing to do that I would be sitting on the sidelines watching others do the race without me.

I always lose a minute or two in transition doing the blood sugar check, but you have to do whatever you have to do for your race.

THE BIKE—USE YOUR STRENGTH

The Gulf wind on the bike was strong and seemingly always in my face. I settled into a steady pace and focused on my nutrition plan—drink, drink, and drink. I did not drink my usual high-carb drink in T1, which I thought in the past had overloaded my system and caused high blood sugar at the bike midpoint. There were very few cyclists on the course for the first thirty miles. Most were behind me from my good swim. I started passing the good swimmers and felt great.

Drafting is a big problem at Ironman Florida because of the flat course and the strong winds with no hills to separate the cyclists. After about forty miles I was overtaken by a couple of draft packs of five to eight cyclists, all sucking the wheel in front of them about four or five feet back. The minimum distance to be legal from the cyclist in front of you is seven meters or twenty-one feet. These guys could have given each other back rubs. I noticed many German and Swiss names on the race numbers as they went by. I know that European race marshals do not enforce the draft rules as strictly as in North America. It was tough to let these guys go, but I wasn't going to join them and cheat by drafting. I had to have faith the draft marshals would catch them and start handing out time penalties and have faith in my run. I could lose the race now by pushing too hard too early. I had to pace myself. *Be smart, Jay. Let them go. There's still seventy miles to go. Save your energy for the last thirty miles of the bike and then the marathon.*

During the first half of the bike (fifty-six miles) I ate four Clif Shot gels, squeezing one in my mouth every twenty minutes, each about 110 calories and twenty grams of carbohydrate. Clif Bar was now sponsoring me, and I was happy to use their gels and bars. I drank two twenty-ounce bottles of my sport drink and two other bottles, one of Gatorade Endurance and one of water that I got from aid stations every twenty miles. I also ate two half bananas that I grabbed at those aid stations. It's nice to have something different than bars and gels, but it's hard to grab a soft half banana out of someone's hand and peel it while riding your bike at over twenty miles per hour. I had learned to slow down and grab them easily, timing my arm motion to match their delivery. I tried to stay disciplined to keep drinking and consume between sixty and eighty grams of carbohydrate, approximately 350 calories, every hour. Of course, I did not inject any fast-acting insulin for these carbs. The basal insulin from the night before with the hard exercise should be enough to keep my blood sugar under control. I hoped.

By the special needs station at mile fifty-six I was often riding alone. That was a good sign. I knew I was close to the front of the field now. I felt good and was excited about what might be happening today. I stopped very briefly and grabbed my blood sugar meter out of my special needs bag handed to me by a race official. There were over two thousand bags on the side of the road, baking in the Florida morning sun, each numbered and separated by race numbers. I jammed fresh bottles of my sport drink into my bottle cages as I checked my blood sugar and waited on the number to pop up on my meter. The anticipation sometimes feels like watching a spinning slot machine. *What's it going to be? Do I win? … Bing!*

275. *What? Oh no. Not again! Just like Ironman Coeur d'Alene!* That was not good news. I was surprised because I had avoided the high-carb drink I'd used in other races. I had ridden fifty-six miles at twenty-three miles per hour and carefully consumed just the carbs I thought I needed, but the basal insulin injected last night had not been enough.

This was now a consistent pattern of high blood sugar at the bike midpoint that I would later figure out was caused by my adrenaline while exiting the water because of the crowd and the excitement starting the bike. Adrenaline spikes are the natural fight-or-flight phenomenon occurring in humans since the saber-toothed tiger chased the caveman. In times of excitement or anxiety, your liver dumps glucose into your blood for quick fuel to fight or run for your life. Or race an Ironman. Or give a book report. Or run from the monster in the woods—whatever you do in your life that gives you nerves, excite-

Adrenaline blood sugar spikes are natural, unpredictable, and impossible to prevent. For a person with diabetes, they are a big pain in the ass.

ment, and anxiety. Adrenaline blood sugar spikes are natural, unpredictable, and impossible to prevent. For a person with diabetes, they are a big pain in the ass.

After this race I would stop decreasing my basal insulin dose for race day in order to counteract this anticipated adrenaline spike. I realize that not reducing my basal insulin dose before an Ironman triathlon is counterintuitive to most people familiar with diabetes. After this race starting in 2005 healthcare professionals and diabetes specialists would gasp when I would tell them that I did not cut my basal rate. But this came from careful study over the years of racing and lots of trial and some error. The basal dose is not a fast-acting insulin, so it was not going to make my blood sugar crash suddenly. Rather it would be a slow slide that I could prevent by just feeding the basal with carbs I needed anyway.

But at this point I had another decision to make fast, just like that high blood sugar right before the swim. I had fast-acting insulin in my special needs bag that I had carefully packed in an ice pack. It was about 10 a.m. in the Florida sun with temperatures already warm in the mid-eighties. A race official stood next to me, wondering what I was doing, what was taking me so long, why I was not getting back on the course. A few guys I had passed a few minutes before zoomed past me.

Think, Jay. Think. Do I inject insulin to bring it down so I don't have the problems I had at Coeur d'Alene and Wisconsin? But how much of those problems were caused by high blood sugar and how much was caused by just mistakes drinking or eating that upset my stomach. What if I overreact now and inject insulin and it drops like Lake Placid last year?

I pondered these issues for a few seconds standing there at the side of the road, with the clock ticking. I could see more guys approaching on their bikes in the distance.

I chose not to inject any insulin. I probably only spent two or three minutes slowing down, stopping to check my blood sugar, and contemplating my options before getting back up to speed, but it felt like I spent twenty minutes on the side of the road.

I had to just hope that my blood sugar would come down on its own from the exercise and the basal dose in my system, like it had during the swim. But I was not going to make the mistake of dehydrating myself in this race. For the next thirty miles I drank only water. That was a gamble I had to take to stay hydrated but to deprive myself of vital calories and carbs so my blood sugar had a chance to come down. I hope I made the right bet. In the Ironman it is often not the fittest or most talented athlete that wins. It is the one who makes the right decisions. Stay disciplined to your plan, but be able to adapt to the moment.

In the Ironman it is often not the fittest or most talented athlete that wins. It is the one who makes the right decisions. Stay disciplined to your plan, but be able to adapt to the moment.

After cycling about thirty more miles I started drinking sport drink and consuming Clif Shot gels again. I was now past mile eighty and only had about thirty miles to go. I had to get calories and carbs in me for the marathon. It was approaching noon and the sun was beaming down with the temperature now close to ninety degrees. I started drinking heavily (sport drink, not beer, but a beer would taste pretty good). The total of nine twenty-ounce bottles of liquid I drank during the full 112 miles totaled almost one and a half gallons. I hoped that was enough not to get dehydrated.

The aid stations in the second half serve other purposes than just hydration. I grabbed a water bottle at each and squeezed it on my helmet, face, body, and legs—a refreshing shower in the heat. My body was covered in sweat and salt from my perspiration. Because I knew that I was close to the lead, I also did not want to waste precious time to stop and pee, so that little nature's necessity happens at twenty miles per hour about a half mile before the aid station, when no one is behind me. I had done that in a few other races and it takes some practice to keep everything going in the right direction, but the time saved is worth it when you are close to the lead—another reason for that quick water bottle shower.

I was riding alone for many stretches of the second half. It almost felt like a solo training ride and I loved it, hammering with a smile on my face. The consistent thumping of my pedaling cadence echoing off my hollow carbon disk wheel sounded like a train barreling down the tracks. I concentrated on a steady pace, keeping my heart rate below 150. Around mile ninety I began to catch some of the professional women and men. The pros started the swim fifteen minutes ahead of the rest of the field so if I was catching some of them I was having a great day since they had a head start and most pros also outswim me. Miles 100 to 112 I started mentally and physically preparing to transition to the marathon, getting in some final hydration and nutrition and switching to a faster, lighter pedaling cadence to loosen up my legs and get ready to run.

I finished the bike in 5:02:57, an average speed of 22.2 miles per hour, three minutes slower than the previous year, but I knew the wind was stronger this year. I did not know it at the time but I found out after the race that Peter rode 5:01:38, so my bike time was equal to some of the top pros even with my time spent standing on the side of the road checking blood sugar.

The transition area was eerily and pleasantly empty again, just like after the swim. Hundreds of bike racks stood vacant, like thousands of empty parking spaces in a giant parking lot at the mall. Virtually all 2,200 bikes and athletes were out on the course behind me. It was quiet except for the crowd surrounding the transition, cheering. I ran into the transition tent.

My blood sugar in T2 was 170. It dropped a hundred points in the last fifty miles of the bike without me injecting extra insulin, even though I had consumed almost two hundred grams of carbohydrate in those two and a half hours. I had made the right call not to inject insulin at the special needs area. I just hoped I had hydrated and eaten enough calories and carbs to run a good marathon. I popped a salt tablet in my mouth for more sodium, grabbed some Clif Shot gels, threw my helmet in my bag, threw on my running shoes, and took off on the marathon.

THE MARATHON

Running the first mile of the marathon I did some calculations in my head. I was on pace to break ten hours, but I know a lot can go wrong running twenty-six miles. If I could run a 3:30 marathon, just an eight-minute pace, I would break ten hours. I had run marathons that pace before but not in the Ironman. My Ironman marathons that year were walking, vomiting, and DNF disasters. I did a quick body checkup. *How do my legs feel? Is that pain in my calf just a pain or is it a cramp that won't go away? How is my back? What is my heart rate? Does my stomach feel okay?*

While I gave myself this running physical, I was pleasantly surprised to see the first mile marker. I glanced at my watch. 7:15 … 7:16 … 7:17. That was a good pace for the first mile—faster than my target. *Don't push it too hard, but run well while you can. You will slow in the second half. Gain time while you feel good. Faster runners are coming off the bike chasing you.*

The first seven miles flew by. At times I felt like I was running on one of those moving walkways at the airport, cruising by at twice the speed of everyone else. My legs felt great. My turnover was good with quick powerful steps. I was passing a few runners every mile, which is unusual for me since running is my weakest event and even more so because everyone at this position in the field (top hundred) is a great runner.

There were over sixty professional Ironman triathletes in the race, and I was catching and passing some of them.

I caught myself smiling several times. *I can't believe I am up here. I have worked so hard for this. Is this real? A dream? Don't wake up.* I recognized some of the guys on the course—pros and top amateurs. I had seen them on TV, in magazines, and on the stage getting awards at the race banquets. I knew them, but they did not know me. It was like I was crashing a private party of triathlon elite. I felt like they must be thinking, *Who is this guy up here?*

I concentrated on a steady pace, glancing at my heart rate, 145 … 147. Perfect. I made sure to drink at least one cup of Gatorade and water every mile while running through the aid stations and squeeze a Clif Shot gel in my mouth about every three miles. The Florida sun was bright and beaming down at approximately 2 p.m. The course was straight on flat roads lined with beach houses and some large condo buildings as high as twenty stories along the beachfront. Occasionally we crossed the main drag that was lined with restaurants and shops selling beach towels, chairs, and knock-off Budweiser T-shirts with sayings like, "This Butt's For You." I made a mental note to come back and get one of those. This was my third time at this race so I knew the marathon course well.

It was hot now, close to ninety degrees, but it felt hotter running on the black asphalt roads radiating heat up at me. The thick, humid air was still and steaming. Any ocean breeze was blocked by buildings and trees. At aid stations every mile I grabbed a cup of ice and stuffed it under my cap and let it cool my head as it melted while running the next half mile along with the cold wet sponges that I wiped on my arms and shoulders.

Ironman Florida is a two-loop marathon, like the two-loop swim course—a 13.1-mile half marathon run twice—making it less roads to close and monitor. That means that after 13.1 miles you are very close to the finish line and—psyche!—sorry, you have to turn around and head back out for another 13.1 miles. So cruel. That is such a tease and you have to prepare yourself mentally not to lose your focus and get dejected seeing the finish line just a hundred meters in front of you. There is an opening to head down the finishing chute, but you get turned away. It feels like you don't have a ticket into that exclusive club to go down that lane where glory and relaxation and an IV are waiting. Turn around and go run another thirteen miles. You've got a lot more pain to endure.

BLUFFING

For the last mile finishing the first loop I had been following a guy in front of me. There were very few of us on the course on the first loop and I could see him clearly up ahead. I was pretty sure he did not know I was behind him with the bends and turns in the road. He was the rabbit and I was the greyhound trying to catch him. I was slowly gaining on him, stalking him. It was starting to hurt.

We were nearing the end of the first loop, right by the transition area and finish line. He was about a hundred meters in front of me when he rounded the turnaround and started heading back toward me to begin his second lap.

I had been chasing him for several miles, pushing myself to gain on him, but now I was hurting. But I did not want him to know that.

So I bluffed. As he approached me heading the other way, I thrust my shoulders high and relaxed my face. I closed my mouth like I was breathing comfortably through my nose. *Just out for an easy twenty-six-mile jog with plenty of energy still in the tank. I feel great!* I picked my knees up high and showed good form as we passed each other. I didn't turn my head, but I glanced at him behind my sunglasses to see how he looked. He looked relaxed and strong. *Damn.* Hopefully he's bluffing too.

Once I was safely behind him and approached the turnaround I crossed the timing mat at the half marathon point and glanced at my watch heading back out of another thirteen—one hour and forty minutes. I felt good, easily holding about a 7:40 average pace. Crowds were lining this portion of the course near transition and the finish line.

I stopped briefly at the special needs area and grabbed another blood sugar meter out of my bag. It was eighty-six. It scared me that it was probably going to keep dropping. I took five quick swallows of my high-carb drink in my bag, about fifty grams of carbohydrate. I carried the bottle in my hand and started running again. This stop cost me about a minute and a half, time and distance I had to make up on the rabbit I was chasing.

Now the course was more crowded with runners on their first lap. After about a mile and a half I caught back up to my target. I slowed down, hiding behind a few first lappers. I felt like a hitman trailing a target in a spy movie, hiding in the crowd, waiting for the right moment to go for the kill.

A sharp turn was coming up in two hundred meters. I picked up my speed about thirty meters behind him and went by him fast and kept pushing. I could feel my heart rate climbing and glanced quickly at my watch. I didn't want him to see me doing that. Heart rate, 150 … 155 … 160. My pace increased to 7:30 … 7:15 per mile. I held this pace for about two hundred meters and never looked back until I turned the corner and glanced quickly over my shoulder. He was not going to chase. I slowed to catch my breath and about collapsed from the effort. This exercise reminded me of hundreds of interval runs I had done in training.

I settled back into my rhythm, counting the mile markers: 15 … 16 … 17 … I was passing a lot of first lappers, which is misleading because their pace was slower and they were thirteen miles behind me. I had to keep pushing the pace—my pace.

Running those last ten miles was like a dream—and a nightmare. I was up close to the lead, a place I had never been before. I was chasing some of the top guys in the world, and some of them were chasing me.

If I could hold this pace another ten miles I would break ten hours. *Could I do it?*

EMBRACE THE PAIN

The pain in my body was building. My lungs were burning like battery acid poured down my throat, trying to suck every bit of oxygen I could get out of the hot Florida air. The humid beach air was thick and heavy, like running inside a warm muffin. I had been racing for over 130 miles and eight hours. It was after 3 p.m. I could not expand my lungs enough. It felt like a belt was wrapped around my chest, squeezing me, suffocating me.

My quads had sharp, piercing pain, like someone was jamming a knife in them with each step. Lactic acid burned in the muscles like towels soaked in gasoline twisted tightly around my quads and hamstrings and then set on fire. I kept chanting in my head, *Hot coals, relax your quads … hot coals, relax your quads,* like I did in training. My face masked this constant pain, hiding behind the sunglasses over my eyes. *Don't give into the pain. Fight it. Don't acknowledge it.*

Battling this pain is both physical and mental. You can't let it get in your head, like a disease trying to overtake you. You have to keep it in your body where you can fight it. Once it is in your head it has found the bridge to the mothership and it has the control. Keep battling it. Embrace this struggle, whether it is in athletics, academics, or your career. You are pushing yourself beyond where most people are willing to go. That is where success lives.

I kept thinking about the finish line, the last one hundred meters, the

> **Embrace this struggle, whether it is in athletics, academics, or your career. You are pushing yourself beyond where most people are willing to go. That is where success lives.**

crowd, the music. That same finish line vision I had been to many times but never this fast. I had visualized it hundreds of times in workouts in the pool, on my bike, and on long runs. That image, that vision, that moment, was what I was suffering for.

As excruciatingly painful as this was, I loved it. I wanted this pain. I needed this pain. I wanted to be in this place. I had a purpose for this suffering, which is what makes it worth it. I was going to that dark place that few people ever go or push themselves to test. I was chewing on it now, grinding it into my teeth and swallowing it burning down my throat.

Two-time Ironman World Champion and ITU Long Distance Triathlon World Champion Chris McCormack said, "The pain is a slow process. You feel it coming from a long way off. When the gun goes off, you think, *I feel good*. Then the fatigue starts to come, and then the body rebels. It's a raw reality: your will against the agony that's setting in. When that happens, your mind can go to crazy places. But I've always found it blissful. I hate the pain, but I love it, too."

"It's part of the wholeness of being a triathlete, and it's totally real. It's you versus you. If you can be at peace in your mind and accept the pain, then you can see it as part of the whole amazing experience. You don't *play* triathlon. You play soccer; it's fun. You play baseball. Triathlon is *work* that can leave you crumpled in a heap, puking by the roadside. It's the physical brutality of climbing Mount Everest without the great view from the top of the world. What kind of person keeps coming back for more of that?"

I was that kind of person. Just two months ago I had felt the slow, plodding pain of struggling to finish in over thirteen hours. This was the ferocious, white-hot fury of pain to finish under ten hours. This is the kind of pain I love. I love it because it is so powerful, always a worthy adversary, always there to challenge me to overcome it. Some days it destroyed me, and some days I endured it and grabbed it by the throat and choked the life out of it and stomped on it at the finish line, proving that I was stronger that day. Sending a message to pain, and my diabetes, "You are messing with the wrong guy!" Real pain is going your entire life never knowing what overcoming pain like this feels like.

Real pain is going your entire life never knowing what overcoming pain like this feels like.

Jens Voight was a German professional cyclist for seventeen years until he retired in 2014 at the age of forty-two. He was known to sacrifice himself on seemingly fruitless solo breakaways, holding off a pack of 150 professional cyclists for mile after mile, sometimes soloing to a win, other times being swallowed by the peloton before the line. Few cyclists have displayed such a desire to suffer so intensely, solo, and for so long into his forties.

In a column he wrote for *Bicycling* magazine in August 2013 Voigt said, "Pain is good. I like the feeling because it proves you are still alive—because you are aware of something, even if it's a sensation most people consider bad. I like to constantly talk back to the pain when it is shouting at me to slow down. The more pain that comes your way when you race, the better you are doing. Pain is my favorite enemy. We keep watching each other and waiting for the other one to show weakness, to give in. The pain and me, nothing can keep us apart. It keeps me going. It keeps me young."

To improve in anything, you must be willing to endure the pain, the discomfort. It's not just physical pain in athletics. It's pain of striving for anything in life.

I know how he feels. To improve in anything, you must be willing to endure the pain, the discomfort. It's not just physical pain in athletics. It's pain of striving for anything in life.

Author Daniel Coyle discovered this while visiting and watching world-class performers in sports, art, music, business, and math. In

The Little Book of Talent he said, "I saw the same facial expression: eyes narrow, jaws tight, nostrils flared, the face of one intently reaching for something, falling short, and reaching again. This is not a coincidence. [It's] a feeling that can be summed up in one word: struggle. Most of us instinctively avoid struggle, because it's uncomfortable. It feels like failure. However, when it comes to developing your talent, struggle isn't an option—it's a biological necessity. Your brain works just like your muscles: no pain, no gain."

These last miles I thought about my slow walk at Ironman Wisconsin just two months before and the disaster of my DNF at Ironman Coeur d'Alene in June. Now I was this close to the triumph of breaking ten hours, beating some of the best triathletes in the world. I needed to meet and overcome those disasters to have the strength and will to meet and overcome this pain and reach my dream.

Rudyard Kipling's beautiful poem "If" was written in 1895 as fatherly advice to his son, John. Some of the last stanzas are:

If you can dream—and not make dreams your master;
If you can think—and not make thoughts your aim;
If you can meet with triumph and disaster
And treat those two imposters just the same;
If you can fill the unforgiving minute
With sixty seconds' worth of distance run,
Yours is the Earth and everything in it,
And—which is more—you'll be a Man my son.

I had met with disaster racing several times that year, and when I was diagnosed with diabetes over thirteen years ago. Now I was approaching triumph. Filling that unforgiving minute with sixty seconds' worth of distance run is not quitting when it gets hard. It is unforgiving because when it is gone, it is gone. The hour is gone, the year, the decade, the life ... is gone. Did you fill it with sixty seconds' worth of distance run?

HOW BAD DO YOU WANT IT?

At mile eighteen of the marathon, mile 132 of the race, I saw Peter running toward me going the opposite way. He had made the final turn-around and was heading for the finish. A guy who held the world record for a double marathon, running fifty-two miles at an unbelievable 6:22 pace, a professional winner of multiple Ironmans, and I was just a few minutes behind him. Just two months before at Ironman Wisconsin I finished *five hours* behind him. His face was focused and masking pain behind his sunglasses, a poker face I had seen many times on training rides together. He smiled when he saw me. Some races he never saw me because I was too far behind him. He knew the struggles I had had, the hours we had spent training together for two years, the improvement I had made, and my failures this year. He knew the challenges I faced with my blood sugar and diabetes.

Teachers, coaches, doctors, and parents help us in life by giving us instruction and techniques to improve. They tell us how to do things better and give the right pointers during competition and games to help us win. Perhaps that is your role and you do that for others. Peter could have done that at this moment. He could have said something about my form or technique or to drink or of something we had done in training. He could have told me how far the guy I was chasing was in front of me.

But he knew that did not matter at this point. Nothing else mattered. I was in pain and fighting for my dream. And I was close. The last eight miles would be a battle of my body and the demons in my head both trying to make me slow down. He knew how it felt to hurt like that. All that mattered was what he yelled to me as we passed.

"How bad do you want it?!"

Then he was gone, running the other way.

Those words sank into me as I fought the pain overtaking my body. They echoed in my head and went straight to my soul.

Are you a student in school, studying night and day, wondering if you can study again tonight, staying awake another hour and then another, avoiding TV and fun with your friends, trying to make that grade on your exam to get accepted into another academic program or to get that job after graduation?

Are you a working parent getting up for work every morning for months, years, leaving the house while your family sleeps, then coming home late after your kids are in bed, missing their games and activities, working from home nights and weekends, trying to pay for the house, clothes, college, health insurance, and maybe a vacation for your family?

Are you the parent taking care of your family and house everyday, doing laundry, cooking meals, driving that same old car another year, saving money and depriving yourself of things and trips and fun that everyone on Facebook seems to "check in" about, so your family, kids, and others you care for can have clothes, opportunities, or gifts?

Are you the athlete working out every day, getting beat by better players or teams, coming back again and again, trying to compete with the best, to make the team, the playoffs, the championship, the finish line?

Are you facing a serious health condition, a crisis, working hard to overcome it but wondering if you have the strength and will to keep fighting?

How long have you been doing this? How many times have you tried and failed? Do you keep going?

We all hit these moments in life. And it doesn't matter how much we have trained or prepared now. That training and preparation got us to this point, but all that matters now is ... *how bad do you want it?*

I got to mile twenty of the marathon, mile 134 of the Ironman. Only six miles to go, just a little 10k run I had done hundreds of times. I was beyond pain at this point. I was sure my blood sugar was low because I could feel the tingling in my lips and legs. I grabbed whatever I could at an aid station—pretzels, cookies, and a few orange slices—

and stuffed them in my mouth. *Carbs, give me carbs!* It is a buffet of carb snacks at an Ironman marathon aid station, and if they were selling it, I was buying it. I did not want to eat anything, but I had to get something in my system or I would not make it six miles. I had to walk a few steps trying to pick up a paper cup and a cookie. *Don't enjoy this walking. Don't notice how good this feels to take a break from the pain. Get back in the fire!* Running again I tossed back a few swallows of flat Coke and Gatorade from paper cups, trying to chew and drink and run. I was sick of anything sweet from hours of sport drink and gels. I pushed pretzels into my mouth, trying to breath around them.

Just past mile twenty-two, two guys came up behind me. I could feel them hovering over my shoulder, hear their breathing and tapping of their feet. They pulled even with me to pass, like two cars on the interstate coming up behind you and passing on the left. I'm sure they had been assessing my running form as they approached me. I glanced at them as they eased ahead. They were those good runners that are in the field. I had gotten ahead of them on the bike and it took them twenty-two miles to catch me in the marathon. They were still running strong at close to a seven-minute pace. We only had four miles to go.

I wanted to reach out and grab their jerseys as they went by. They glanced at me as they passed as if to say, "Who is this guy?" They did not know me, but I recognized them—a guy from Germany and one from the US. I had seen them in magazines and on stage receiving awards after races. But there is no talking at this point in the Ironman marathon. I was in too much pain to fake anything. I got in behind them, trying to match their pace as long as I could. Once you let one pass, it's easier to let the second, then the third, and then soon you're going backward. Your mind gives up and you start accepting it, the momentum of defeat takes over, thinking, *Well, I might as well stop trying; it's over now.* It's sort of like giving in to temptation, cheating on a diet or a commitment to break a bad habit. My mind did not want to give up. *Keep fighting!*

But my body was in trouble.

I ran with these guys, staying about five feet behind them barely hanging on, staring at their backs, locked into their pace like a dog on a leash to keep me moving. Occasionally they glanced over their shoulder and saw me still there. My heart pounded in my chest. I don't know how my form looked, and I didn't care. I was going to stay with these guys and make them beat me. I was not going to let them go or I would die trying. If you cannot win, make the guy in front of you break the record.

We got to mile twenty-four, mile 138 of the race, only two miles to go. The crowd was lining the route to the finish now, screaming and cheering.

> **If you cannot win, make the guy in front of you break the record.**

I have never felt pain like this before. My legs were on fire, tight knots in my quads and calves. My lungs burned and my chest heaved. It felt like lactic acid was coming out of my eyes. I could barely see.

People often ask me, "Why do you do this?" Why would I punish myself this way? Why would I suffer everyday in workouts, addicted to the pain, and then do it again the next day, all building for race day when I know the pain is going to be even worse? What is the logic of this? The value is situations like this, in this race, what I learn about myself. All kinds of qualities come out, some voices questioning myself telling me to stop and some pushing me to keep going. Which of these voices will win? The ultimate question is—is it worth it? Is your finish line worth it to you to keep going, keep suffering, and do it again until you reach it? Only you know because your finish line is unique and personal to you, but you will find out only when you push yourself to that point you have to answer that question. When you do, enjoy that moment. Congratulations. Most people never get that far. Most people never want something that bad, and fewer are willing to work for it. You have joined an exclusive club of artists, athletes, students, entrepreneurs, parents, and others working for a dream. Welcome to the club. At this point you will discover things about yourself and earn success that you never knew.

Inside of two miles to go now, these two guys started to pick up the pace, slightly pulling away from me, battling each other. They were experienced racers and had held some in reserve for the last miles, using the crowd to pick them up.

You can lose a lot of time in two miles. If I started walking now I could lose twenty or thirty minutes. If I stopped I may not get moving again, just like Ironman Coeur d'Alene five months ago.

Watching these two guys start pulling away, it felt like my dream was pulling away with them, slipping through my hands. I wanted to reach out in front of me and grab it and hold on. I was so close. I was screaming at my body—*Go! Move! Pick up your leg!* It felt like I was running in thick sand.

Then, with the crowd yelling, everything seemed to go quiet, and I heard the words Peter had said to me a few miles before: "How bad do you want it?"

WHEN DO YOU EARN YOUR FINISH LINE?

You don't earn your finish line on race day. You earn it every day, when no one is watching.

I earned this finish line. I earned it when none of these people were watching me in the pool at 5 a.m. before work or riding my bike alone for a hundred miles on country roads and in the mountains. I earned this finish line running eighteen miles in the rain early in the morning.

You don't earn your finish line on race day. You earn it every day, when no one is watching.

If you are a student, you earn your finish line all the days and nights you are inside studying while your friends are at the mall, outside playing, or watching TV and playing video games.

If you are a working mom or dad, you earn it all those hours your spend late at night or early morning while your kids sleep, doing your job, emails, reports, and proposals.

If you are a stay-at-home parent, it's the time you spend rushing to the gym and grocery store, cleaning the house, doing laundry while your kids are in school or day care, running with them in the stroller, or budgeting your money to buy and fix healthy meals.

If you are a small business owner, no one saw you mortgaging your home to start the business, balancing the books, cleaning the bathrooms, and working two shifts because one of your employees quit.

If you are a person with diabetes, you earn it checking your blood sugar, choosing to eat healthy foods and not eat dessert, and exercising rather than watching TV.

How bad did I want it?

I wanted it for the twenty thousand times I had stuck myself with a syringe to give me injections of insulin four or five times a day for fourteen years. I wanted it for the times I was flopping on the floor with hypoglycemia, unable to stand or move. I wanted it for the fifty thousand times I had pricked my fingers dropping blood on a meter five to ten times a day. I wanted it for the kids with diabetes and their parents who had seen me in magazines and written me emails or stopped me after I spoke at diabetes events, saying with a tear in their eye that if I could do the Ironman and make the US national team, then they knew their child with diabetes would be okay.

But I really wanted it for that one moment in time, to be more than I thought I could be that day I was lying in that hospital bed in 1991 and that doctor stood over me and said, "You've got diabetes, and your life is going to change."

She was right. My life did change.

A fire erupted in me. I raced with those two guys the last two miles of that Ironman. The crowd got deeper and louder. I don't remember much about those last two miles—I was in the black pain cave of death—but I remember the last hundred meters. I could hear the crowd and the music over a half mile away. It was exactly like my finish line vision always is.

The last hundred meters I saw the people packed in the grandstands lining both sides and behind the barriers. I stuck my hand out to slap their hands as I ran down the carpet. Music was booming and the crowd roared. I saw the huge clock above the finish, ticking off the seconds. I could see the race announcer at the finish, holding a microphone and looking at me coming. Another guy leaned into him flipping though the pages of a book with athlete numbers, looking somewhat confused. They were trying to figure out who I was. I had never been this close to the lead before. I was an amateur beating half of the professional field.

I saw the time on the clock and I started crying. Tears flooded my eyes. The announcer yelled, "From the United States of America … Jay Hewitt!" I raised my arms and crossed the line in nine hours, forty-seven minutes, and fourteen seconds (9:47:14).

I stopped running, took a few steps, and collapsed into the arms of an official waiting behind the line. I could not stand or walk. I could barely speak.

I had broken ten hours by almost thirteen minutes—two hours faster than I had done in my first Ironman at this race two years before. I was now one of those guys, one of the best in the world that day.

They carried me into the medical tent—it seems like I always end up in the medical tent—with my arms draped over the shoulders of two people holding me up. Departing from their usual procedure, they did not even bother to have me step on the scale. Checking your weight is like the boarding pass to enter the medical tent. If you haven't lost much weight from your prerace weight taken days ago at registration, they will have you wait in a chair while they assess your condition, asking you questions about your discomfort, pain, and symptoms. They didn't even ask me any questions. They brought me right in and laid me down on a cot and put an IV in my arm to start rehydrating me. A nurse looked at my chart and then looked at me, somewhat incredulously. I had seen that look before in the Ironman medical tent.

"You've got diabetes?" she asked. She seemed shocked and a little concerned. She called over the doctor. The Ironman medical tent is like a military MASH unit. I had been in there when it was full. But now it was deserted. There were only a few athletes in there, some of the top pros who had finished just in front of me. I beat thirty-four of the sixty professionals in that race. I, the amateur, the guy with diabetes, beat half of the professional field. The other thousands of amateur athletes were still out on the course.

They have a lot of equipment in the Ironman medical tent—IVs; equipment for heart attacks, seizures, and convulsions; a mini-ICU for athletes who have collapsed on the course. They could restart my heart, but they couldn't check my blood sugar. They did not have a blood sugar meter. They never do. They don't expect people with type 1 diabetes to be doing this race. I told the nurse to send someone outside and find Anna who had my blood sugar meter. When the nurse finally returned with my meter, my blood sugar was seventy. That had made those last miles even harder.

It felt so good to lie down. As I lay there on the cot with an IV in my arm, tears of joy in my eyes, and too weak to lift my body and head, I thought about how wonderful and ironic the circle of life is.

Almost fourteen years ago I was on a hospital bed with an IV in my arm, tears in my eyes, and too weak to lift my body and head, when that doctor said, "You've got diabetes and your life is going to change." That was the worst day of my life.

Now this was the best day of my life. And they both ended the same way.

"If you can meet with triumph and disaster and treat those two imposters just the same . . ."

If I had never had that day fourteen years ago, I never would have had this day.

The circle was now complete.

CHAPTER 16

FIND YOUR NEXT FINISH LINE

Topic: Setting New Goals

After Ironman Florida 2004, Peter seemed almost as happy as I was. Since my time of nine hours and forty-seven minutes (9:47) beat over half of the sixty professionals racing that day, he wanted me to keep improving and try to turn pro. I had even beaten his time when he won the Great Floridian Ironman the previous month in nine hours and fifty-five minutes (9:55). But while every Ironman race is the same distance, they are different courses and weather, so it is unfair to compare times even on the same course in different years. Most male pros routinely finish in the nine-hour range and below, sometimes drifting over the ten-hour mark in certain races with tougher conditions.

I was flattered but did not consider his suggestion seriously. I was thirty-seven years old. Most pros were at least five or ten years younger than me and with ten or more years of triathlon and endurance racing experience. I had two. Endurance athletes usually hit their peak between the ages of thirty and thirty-five. After that the aging process begins to sap muscle strength and aerobic capacity. Age and diabetes were not on my side.

And I could not afford to quit my day job. Being a pro triathlete is not the most lucrative or even comfortable career. Even the top pros don't make a lot of money, and I currently had the best of both worlds. I was racing as an amateur with paid sponsorships from several diabetes pharmaceutical companies and product sponsorships from sport companies Clif Bar and Rudy Project for all the bars, gels, sunglasses, and helmets I could use. And I loved racing on the US national team. The idea of quitting my job as a lawyer so I could train and race full time to improve enough to turn pro just to be eligible to win a few thousand dollars in race purse a few times a year did not seem like a wise career move at thirty-seven.

PROFESSIONAL SPEAKING—MY NEW PASSION AND FUEL IN LIFE

After my success at Ironman Florida I was committed to racing, but I also was starting to prepare for new events in my life and career. Just like in a triathlon, in life you have to work hard on the event you are doing but at the same time keep your eyes down the road and be prepared to transition to the next one—new products or new positions in your career, changes in your family like kids, home and college expenses, and retirement planning.

Just like in a triathlon, in life you have to work hard on the event you are doing but at the same time keep your eyes down the road and be prepared to transition to the next one.

When I made the US national team, I started getting media attention and sponsors and speaking requests. My first couple speaking engagements—okay, more like my first ten—were for free, as in, notta dolla. They were mostly diabetes charities, schools, and local civic clubs who had heard about me racing triathlons with diabetes and wanted me to inspire their groups. I got good responses, but they had every reason to be excited and no reason to be disappointed because the bar (i.e., the fee) was set pretty low, as in $0. But I felt like they got a lot more than they paid for, and I enjoyed it.

As part of one of my sponsorship contracts, in February 2005 I spoke at a meeting for LifeScan Inc., a Johnson and Johnson company that manufactures and sells blood sugar meters. This was my first "paid" speaking engagement. I had spoken many times to business groups as a lawyer but never as an athlete or a motivational speaker. I interviewed the managers of the company and prepared a message for this audience of 1,500 energetic, highly educated medical salespeople at their national meeting in Palm Springs, California.

I spoke for an hour about setting goals, overcoming obstacles, discipline, and hard work to succeed. I loved it, and the audience seemed to like it too. They gave me a standing ovation. I was overwhelmed. It was so fulfilling to motivate an audience, to hold them in my hand and take them on a journey with stories and lessons they could apply in their own life. It was so different than the rule-dominated (i.e., boring) presentations I had to do as a lawyer. The law is all about what you *can't* do. Here I could talk and inspire them about what they *could* do. I could not believe how fulfilling it was to touch and influence their lives with my message. I could see happiness in their faces when they approached me for autographs and photos and to talk about their goals. No one ever wanted a photo with me after I spoke as a lawyer. *And you mean I can get paid to do this?*

I was hooked. I wanted more moments like this, just like I had wanted the moments of the Ironman finish line. Speaking became my new finish line. I started thinking how I could speak more and, maybe if I was good enough, get paid to do it. One of the attendees at the meeting was Laura Billetdeaux, an organizer of an amazing nonprofit called Children with Diabetes, a growing online community of families from all over the US and the world. She asked me to speak that summer in Orlando at their national conference to eight hundred parents, kids, and vendors all connected to diabetes. I loved it. I felt like I was making a difference helping people and being an inspiration. It fueled my life like triathlon did.

I joined the National Speakers Association (NSA), the trade organization for professional speakers and attended the national convention in Atlanta that summer. I was blown away. Those speakers were amazing. Their delivery and messages showed me what a real professional speaker sounds like. They entertained, they inspired, they informed. I wanted to do that.

BEAUTY AND THE BEAST

In May 2005 a television crew from WGN-TV in Chicago filmed me for a documentary. This was before the days of hundreds of reality TV shows on dozens of cable channels. The crew came to my half Ironman in Orlando, Florida, and followed me for several days and during the race. Later that month I raced a half Ironman in St. Croix, Virgin Islands, a beautiful tropical paradise known for "the Beast," a climb twenty-one miles into the cycling course, the most severe and difficult climb in the triathlon world. It is almost one mile long, straight up the side of a mountain with an *average* gradient of 14 percent and a maximum of 21 percent. For perspective, a gradient of over 8 percent is considered severe in professional cycling events. The famous Tour de France climb of L'Alpe d'Huez has an average of 8 percent with a maximum of 13, and Mount Ventoux averages 7 and maxes at 12. The Beast is like riding your bike up a mile-long escalator.

Scouting the course riding it before the race I saw a guy fall off his bike and slide back down the road, his bike tumbling backward. I felt like I needed ropes and a belay. *How did they pave this thing? Isn't this why they make chair lifts?* Fortunately on race day I made it up the Beast and all fifty-six miles of the bike and thirteen miles of the run without falling over. I think my quads stopped hurting sometime in 2008.

The next month in June 2005 I got some revenge on Ironman Coeur d'Alene. It was not a great race for me, but at least I finished this time, unlike the year before. Sometimes you have to take small victories.

It reminded me that just because I did well in my last Ironman seven months ago, the Ironman gods don't give you a free pass. They all hurt. You have to earn it every time.

PHYSIOLOGICAL TESTING, PERCENT BODY FAT, AND VO2 MAX

Always looking for more information to improve, that summer I did some physiological testing at Meredith College Human Performance Laboratory in North Carolina. I love this stuff. It's the science for the sport. They tested my body fat percentage, lactate threshold, and V02 max. My body fat was 6.1 percent. The average for males my age of thirty-eight is 18–24 percent. While that number was interesting, it did not really help me race faster. The real numbers I was interested in were my V02 max and my lactate threshold. Those numbers I could use in training and racing.

The VO2 max test is quite painful. You either run on a treadmill or cycle on a stationary bike, gradually increasing to maximum effort and heart rate while wearing a mask over your face to register your oxygen uptake. The mask looks like you are part of a chemical spill HAZMAT team. You feel suffocated with it blocking your face, wheezing like Darth Vader, when your body needs oxygen more than ever smashing maximum wattage on a bike just before you pass out. The test lasted just fourteen minutes and forty-two seconds. Believe me, I was counting those last seconds.

Every few minutes the evil torturer wearing a white lab coat casually pricked blood from my ear lobe to test lactate acid building up in my circulatory system, while he increased the resistance on the bike. Dr. Waterboard, PhD, watched my heart rate increase each time he turned up the wattage, while I tried to maintain a constant low pedaling cadence of just 60 rpm. It didn't hurt for the first few minutes, but gradually he kept cranking up the wattage until I started to display signs of straining.

As I started sweating, he stood next to me periodically asking in an annoyingly calm voice, "How does that feel? Can you do more?" If I gave a nod, he cranked up the wattage. It reminded me of that famous interrogation scene in the 1976 suspense thriller *Marathon Man* where Laurence Olivier calmly asks Dustin Hoffman "Is it safe?" over and over, then each time drilling his mouth with dental equipment.

My heart rate climbed to 182 beats per minute, a number I had never seen on my heart rate monitor in training, I guess because one more beat and my heart would explode. I held that number as long as I could, grinding the pedals. *Okay, I'll talk! I'll tell everything! Whatever it is, I confess!* I was about to pass out when he mercifully stopped the test.

I slumped over the handlebars, gasping. Dr. Frankenstein smiled with evil pleasure. I expected him to scream at any moment "He's aliiiiiiiive! He's aliiiiiiiiive!" *Not for long, Doc.* He looked over my numbers with much more interest in the data than me clinging to life.

He reported that my lactate threshold, sometimes called the anaerobic threshold, was between 155 and 160 bpm. That is the point in exertion when your body passes from the aerobic (straining but sort of comfortable) heart rate zone into the uncomfortable anaerobic ("this kind of hurts and not sure how long I can do this") zone.

The test also confirmed that my body consumes the highest percentage of fat at a heart rate between 126 bpm and 150 bpm, just below my anaerobic threshold. Once my heart rate hit about 160 bpm, fat use dropped off significantly—my heart was beating too hard and exertion was too intense to have time to break down fat as a fuel source. Above 165 bpm and fat use stopped completely. This test confirmed that I needed to race with a heart rate of between 126 bpm and 150 bpm to be able to metabolize fat stored in my body as fuel (i.e., the labored conversation pace I discussed earlier).

The VO2 max measurement was also important. VO2 max stands for maximal oxygen uptake. It refers to the maximum amount of oxygen your body can utilize in one minute. It is a measure of your capacity for aerobic work—how big your aerobic engine is, how far, long, and hard you can go before you blow up, crash and burn, hit the wall, and collapse from exhaustion.

According to the Cooper Institute of Aerobic Research in Dallas, Texas, average VO2 max for males my age in their thirties is 35.5 to 40.9 ml/min/kg (milliliters of oxygen per minute per kilogram of body weight), 45 to 49.4 is excellent, and above 49.4 is considered superior. My V02 max that day registered 54.79. In another test two years later I registered 61.5. To quote the profound *Caddyshack* groundskeeper Carl Spackler (played by Bill Murray), "So at least I got that going for me. Which is nice."

There are many factors contributing to increasing aerobic capacity, primarily quality training and genetics. My parents were not endurance athletes so I did not have a lot of genetics helping me. Of course, another method is doping with the banned substance synthetic erythropoietin (EPO). EPO is the hormone produced by the kidneys that stimulates the production of those vital little oxygen-carrying sherpas, the red blood cells. Doping with EPO creates more red blood cells, which improves delivery of oxygen to the working muscles, which in turn allows you to run, bike, or dance faster and longer and at higher speed and intensity. Rumor has it that Lance Armstrong once registered a VO2 max of over eighty, but he may have had a little help from EPO since he admitted to doping with it for much of his career.

DANISH JELLYFISH

In August I raced my second ITU Long Distance Triathlon World Championship for Team USA in Denmark. It was always the highlight of my year to put on the jersey of the United States and race in Europe. The race was in the port city of Fredericia on the Baltic Sea. The icy waters of the Baltic Sea may be great for shipping to the North Sea but not so comfy for swimming. I thought the only time you swam in the North Sea was if you fell off an oil platform.

Cold ocean water was not the only problem; jellyfish were everywhere. But this is a triathlon, and they don't race these indoors. These squishy little guys are part of the race. The mass start was even more frenetic and pummeling than most Ironmans I race in North America, probably because this was a world championship and they were all good swimmers. Or maybe we all were just trying to get warm. I felt like an ice cube crashing into bodies in a triathlon martini, shaken not stirred. One nice byproduct of this thrashing was all of the jellyfish stayed away for a while, no doubt avoiding the human blender suddenly invading their waters. About halfway through the swim my hands began to cramp in the cold—sort of like keeping your hand in a cooler of beer for thirty minutes at a tailgate. I felt like I was swimming with only three fingers. The water was dark and visibility was poor, but when my hand thumped a jellyfish I knew they must be all around me. Wearing a swim cap, goggles, and full wetsuit the only skin showing was on my hands, feet, and face. I felt a few jellyfish bumping my head and shoulders as I continued swimming and then a suddenly sharp stinging pain on my face. I quickly pulled one away that clung to my cheek and nose. At that point I decided to hang close behind the feet of a guy in front of me, my jellyfish blocker.

Here's a helpful tip I discovered. If you get stung in the face by a jellyfish, just keep your head submerged in cold saltwater while you swim another five hundred meters. After the swim in T1 my hands were too cold to draw any blood for a blood sugar reading and it was hard to put on my cycling shoes. Once I got on the bike and got some blood flowing back in my face that little smooch from my jelly friend started to burn.

If you get stung in the face by a jellyfish, just keep your head submerged in cold saltwater while you swim another five hundred meters.

The bike course had big crowds lining it around the city center and lots of varying terrain outside of the city. I was making good time on the bike as I always do and felt great. The wind was strong and either dead in my face or gloriously at my back. Now I know why I'd seen pictures of those classic Danish wooden windmills. The wind blows strong here. Unfortunately, I had a crazy high blood sugar of over four hundred on the bike. High blood sugar during the bike midpoint was becoming a recurring problem for me.

The run was four undulating loops of 7.5 km densely packed with spectators cheering along city streets, waving Danish and other country flags. My high blood sugar made for a queasy run of over eighteen miles. I finished in 7:06:21, 131st out of 650 overall—not a great result but okay for the world championship. I had quit beating myself up about a poor finish caused by blood sugar problems now that I knew from Ironman Florida the previous year that on the right day I could beat the best. Some days the blood sugar behaves, some days it says, "Not today, Jay." My blood sugar was 140 at the finish, and I quickly injected a few units of insulin and began eating and drinking for recovery. I also got to see the Crown Prince of Denmark at the finish. Triathlon and cycling are popular in Europe. *I wonder why the US president never shows up at our races?*

THE RACE ACROSS ... WHAT?

It was in Denmark that I got an email from a young American cyclist with diabetes named Phil Southerland who was forming a team of cyclists with diabetes. I was interested in learning more and we planned to talk when I got back to the US. A few weeks later Phil and I had a phone conversation.

"What races do you plan to do?" I asked.

"Just one right now," he said.

"One?" He wanted to set up a whole team just to do one race? That was odd.

"Yeah, it's next summer 2006," he continued. "It's called RAAM."

I paused for a moment. This was starting to sound weird. I knew most major bike races in the US and the world. I'd never heard of that one.

"What's RAAM? Where is it?" I said.

"It's in the US. Well, kind of all over the US I guess." I think Phil was starting to enjoy this now that I know him. He's a bit of a wise-ass, like a cocky kid, which to me he was a kid, barely twenty-three, almost seventeen years younger.

Phil probably could sense my skepticism, or at least my confusion. "It's the Race Across America," he said finally.

"The race across what?" For a minute there I thought he said America, as in the United States of that—that country that I fly across all the time in an airplane. It was kind of funny that I thought he had said that.

Yes, he did say that. The Race Across America. He was going to call it Team Type 1. I had heard of the Tour de France but never the Race Across America. Probably because America is a lot bigger than France and no one wants to race across it, except some endurance freaks who first did it in 1982 racing from Los Angeles to New York City, and ABC television covered it as a freaky event for the classic *Wide World of Sports*. They had also covered another freaky event that year—the Ironman triathlon in Hawaii. And like most insane ideas, soon others wanted in and it became an official insane idea and race. They call Race Across America "RAAM" either for abbreviation or, as I would soon find out, that's what you feel like happened to your butt after you ride your bike three thousand miles across America. Team Type 1 was going to be a cycling team and be a positive example for people with diabetes, so I agreed to join the team next summer for RAAM. I could still race Ironman triathlons on my own.

I raced Ironman Florida again that November, now my fourth straight year doing that race. My result was not a good as the previous year. The night after the race I developed a sore throat and cough, followed by sinus congestion and sneezing for several days. I guess I was coming down with a cold on race day.

I was also disappointed because for the first time my parents had come to see me race an Ironman. Given my poor result I'm sure they left with more questions than answers on why I put myself through this ten-hour, 140-mile torture, but I was proud for them to see it in person, to see how hard their son was willing to work for something he believed in—the same way they had seen me work to make my high school basketball team, or good grades, or build a career. I owed that determination to them. I hope it made them proud.

A CRASH

With the Race Across America (RAAM) coming up in June, in the early part of 2006 I needed to race my bike more to build cycling fitness. My plan was to race RAAM in June, Ironman Lake Placid in July, Ironman Florida (my fifth time) in November, and finally the ITU Long Distance Triathlon World Championships for the US team in late November in Australia. I was also planning on proposing to Anna and starting a family and a speaking career.

That was the plan. 2006 looked like it might be kind of busy.

That plan got messed up on a cold, rainy day in late February. I was in a bike race in South Carolina for top amateur and local pros from the southeast. Cycling teams came in from Virginia, the Carolinas, Georgia, and Alabama. It was sixty miles in the rain and cold, about forty degrees. I was not thrilled about racing in this weather, but at least I did not have to swim before or run after it. I did not have an official USA cycling Pro or Category 1, 2, or 3 license that was necessary for me to do this race, but the race director was my friend Rich Hincapie, brother of George

Hincapie, a veteran of nine Tour de France winning teams. Rich let me race because he knew my cycling ability from a lot of rides together. The course was the same Donaldson Center route I trained on every Tuesday night with top local cyclists in the summer.

After about fifty miles the speed was up and teams had their leadout men at the front of the peloton to ramp the pace up and drop guys off the back. I was positioned close to the front of the main field, not planning to do anything crazy, happy to just sit in the group and use this for good speed training.

I could tell that the pace and the weather were starting to hurt some guys. You can always see it in the way they move on their bikes, with erratic movements and standing and sitting on short climbs, when top racers comfortably do things with ease by remaining seated and moving with the flow of the field. I didn't have any teammates so I was happy to hang in the pack and enjoy the leg muscle blood-boiling, throat-burning, heart-pounding pain that is cycling thirty miles per hour in a cold, wet road race in February.

As we were descending a slight hill at approximately thirty-five miles per hour with about three miles to go, suddenly I heard the unmistakable sound of metal clanging and a yell and saw a flash of color and bodies in bright cycling jackets about ten feet in front of me go down. It happened in a split second. There was nowhere for me to go, sandwiched in the pack with guys to my left, right, in front, and behind. It's like a crash in a NASCAR race with the entire field charging for the finish. About twenty guys and I slammed into the first to fall, vaulting us into an explosion of bodies and bikes tumbling down the asphalt at thirty-five miles per hour. I was launched into the air and landed on the road and rolled and slid down on the wet pavement. I never saw what caused it. Maybe the wet pavement contributed to the crash, causing someone in front to slip, but at least the wet pavement helped me slide on the asphalt. I was also fortunately wearing a thick cycling jacket and long tights because of the rain and cold so I did not have much road rash or blood—just ripped clothing.

I sat in the road stunned, processing what had just happened in the blink of an eye. My helmet was cracked, so it probably saved my life. A message to everyone cycling: always wear a helmet. My heart raced and adrenaline pumped in my body so I really did not feel any pain. Yet the road looked like a bomb had exploded in a cycling store. Guys were sitting and laying on the asphalt, bikes were everywhere on the street, with equipment and water bottles strewn about. My front wheel was bent in an oblong deformed shape where I had slammed into a racer downed in front of me that launched me into the air.

> My helmet was cracked, so it probably saved my life. A message to everyone cycling: always wear a helmet.

My legs looked and felt okay, but I felt a little tension in my right shoulder. I could not lift my right arm. I knew what that meant. A broken clavicle (collarbone) is the most common cycling injury. I hoped that it was just fractured. A visit to the emergency room that day and then to an orthopedic surgeon confirmed more than just a fracture. The bone had snapped in two, and my right shoulder hung down below my left. I had surgery two days later on March 1. The surgeon wrapped sutures around the bone to fuse it back together and lift my right shoulder up. I would be in a sling for six weeks. I was pleased that I did not separate or damage my shoulder joint. That would have ended or severely damaged my swimming for triathlons.

My surgeon told me no running for six weeks, which would have been hard to do anyway wearing a sling. I could not lift my right hand past my face so no swimming either. Since I am right handed the most simple tasks—brushing teeth, washing my hair, and writing— were difficult. He also told me not to ride my bike because I could not straighten my right arm to put my hand on the bars. No way I could ride outside. But I had to ride across America in three months. I could not afford a month and a half off the bike. Don't tell my surgeon, but I started riding my bike on my indoor trainer a few days after my surgery, propping my elbow in the sling on a bike stand next to me so I would not tear the sutures loose. I rode indoors like this for six weeks, sometimes for three hours at a time. After a month of this I was a caged mouse on a spinning wheel about to lose my mind.

I managed to work well as a one-armed lawyer and did not miss any time from work. I could type on my computer and do most paperwork with my arm in a sling, albeit perhaps a bit slowly. In mid-April I started physical therapy to straighten my arm that had been bent in the sling for six weeks. I had not lifted my arm above my face since the crash. My right shoulder and upper back muscles were locked in position, stiff and immobile. Race Across America was coming up in early June—just six weeks away.

KEEP SOME THINGS TO YOURSELF

The entire time I was riding my bike on the indoor trainer with my arm in a sling, my new cycling team was sending training schedules and workouts for the team to prepare to cycle three thousand miles. I was afraid that if they found out I had broken my clavicle and could not ride for six weeks right before the race, or at least could not do the normal road cycling outdoors, they might ask me to drop off the team and find a replacement. I would not have blamed them. A cycling team, just like any team, needs all its members to be ready on race day.

So I bluffed. I never told them I broke my clavicle. The team members were from all over the country so we had emails and occasional conference calls, but we did not meet in person. For six weeks I rode my ass off on that indoor trainer, dripping gallons of sweat onto the floor with my arm propped beside me. I did leg presses and strength training at the gym that I usually only did in the offseason, pushing weights while my arm and shoulder rested stationary. I did not talk a lot about my training other than to say that things were going well and I was getting ready.

In May with only one month before the race I was finally able to ride outside, holding the handlebars with both hands, and I trained even harder. The weather was warm and it felt exhilarating to be riding outdoors. I rode at night on deserted roads with reflective gear on me, a light on my helmet, and Anna driving the car behind me for the headlights on the road. I had to get used to riding at night because RAAM is a twenty-four-hour race, day and night, and I needed to log some miles after working in my law office all day. I swam and ran some, just to rebuild that fitness, because Ironman Lake Placid was coming up the month after RAAM. It was not ideal training. Things in athletics, life, and business often do not go as planned. Sometimes you just have to make it work.

> **Things in athletics, life, and business often do not go as planned. Sometimes you just have to make it work.**

RACE ACROSS AMERICA (RAAM)

The Race Across America was an amazing experience. It was great to be part of Team Type 1 to inspire people with diabetes. It was also great to be on a team at all, where my performance was necessary, even vital, for everyone's success. Triathlon is an individual sport. Yes, racing for the US national triathlon team is a team, but once the cannon goes off in a triathlon, we all race individually. My individual performance does not affect the results of another triathlete on the US team. In the Ironman I am all on my own. I cannot draft behind another cyclist blocking the wind. I cannot accept outside assistance during the race, not from a friend, fan, family, or coach. No one outside of the race can hand me nutrition or a bottle, change my flat tire, or do anything to help other than cheer, or perhaps my coach can say, "How bad do you want it?"

Cycling, on the other hand, is a team sport when raced at the professional and elite level. Yes, there is an individual winner of the Tour de France, but he cannot win unless his teammates help him along the way, ferrying water bottles to him from the team car, pacing him, and shielding him from the wind allowing him to draft, and when mechanical problems inevitably occur—a flat or a broken this or that on his bike—his teammate or crew is right behind him in the team car to hand him a new bike or wheel in seconds. Pro cyclists can even hang onto the team car moving at twenty or twenty-five miles per hour while a team doctor examines and nurtures a wound or a mechanic tightens a seat post or derailleur on his bike. There is lots of team support in cycling.

Our primary team sponsor was Abbott Laboratories, a medical device company that made blood sugar meters and a new continuous glucose monitor that they would be testing on us during the race. However, I was under my third year of a sponsorship contract with LifeScan, Inc. in my triathlon racing. LifeScan was a big competitor to Abbott in the blood sugar meter market. The team really wanted me to ride for them, but I could not jeopardize my LifeScan sponsorship by wearing their competitor's logo plastered on my chest. So I negotiated a compromise with the team that I would wear a customized kit—in cycling the shorts and shirt are called a kit—without the Abbott logo. It looked a little odd to have a big white space where everyone else had a logo, but I doubt anyone noticed. And I kept my sponsorship with LifeScan.

The 2006 Race Across America was over 3,000 miles from Oceanside, California, to Atlantic City, New Jersey. The race now finishes in Annapolis, Maryland. The Tour de France is approximately 2,200 miles around France, raced over three weeks and divided into twenty-one individual daily stage races. By contrast, RAAM is a constant twenty-four-hour race from sea to shining sea, pedaling a prescribed route through southern California and the desert of Arizona, over the Rocky Mountains, across the plains of Kansas and the Mississippi river, Illinois, Indiana, Ohio, over the Appalachian Mountains of West Virginia, and through Pennsylvania to the finish line on the boardwalk in Atlantic City. The race never stops until you reach the Atlantic.

As my teammate Phil Southerland wrote in his excellent book, *Not Dead Yet*, the route out West "sounds like a Johnny Cash song: Salton City, Prescott, Flagstaff, Durango, Alamosa, and Montezuma." Who can get from the Pacific Ocean to the Atlantic Ocean first, following the prescribed route and rules of the race? It is the ultimate cycling endurance and sufferfest and a great way to see the country and get a little exercise. It was perfect for me.

RAAM has been described as "excess bordering on insanity," "a breeding ground for champions," "a testing ground for elite riders," and "a shining example of the strength of the human spirit." It has been labeled "the most grueling endurance event in the world" and *Outside* magazine once ranked RAAM as the world's toughest endurance event. Over the 3,000-mile race it was thirty degrees when we summited Wolf Creek Pass, Colorado, pushing the pedals and gasping for oxygen climbing up to 10,857 feet before screaming down the other side of the mountain at almost fifty miles per hour. We rode through hundred-degree, dry, baking desert heat in Arizona and the sticky, wet steam of humidity crossing the Mississippi River. The race is always the second week of June to capitalize on the longest daylight hours in North America.

Late one night somewhere in the flatlands of Kansas my teammates Phil Southerland, Joe Eldridge, Bobby Heyer, and I were cycling together through a blinding summer thunderstorm, trying to perform a 2:00 a.m. team time trial. Lightning was hitting the ground all around us, starting fires visible in the distant open prairies and farmland. It was a long, flat, straight road that seemed like it stretched all the way from Colorado to Missouri. You could land the Space Shuttle on this thing, but I'm sure they wouldn't do that in a windstorm like this. It might blow their 165,000-pound spaceship around. So we did it on fifteen-pound bicycles.

The roar of the wind and rain became so loud in my helmet I could not hear the loudspeaker on our team car behind us or the radio earpiece in my ear. I had to lean sideways into the wind to keep my bike from being pushed off the road. We could not see anything but the night blackness and sheets of rain pummeling us. I chose to just keep my head down and stare at the wheel in front of me or the white line on the road when I pulled our train. Suddenly, blue flashing lights of a law enforcement vehicle raced up from behind us and blocked our path. The officer jumped out of his vehicle and yelled at us over the thunderous noise to stop and head back the other direction immediately.

A tornado was up ahead. If we had kept pedaling we might have had that feeling we were not in Kansas anymore, Toto.

We had to have at least one rider on the road at all times, but we often had three or four depending on the terrain, wind, or whether it was open road suitable for drafting with several riders, or mountains or congested urban areas that was a waste to have more than one guy riding. It was like we were carrying a baton across the country. We had eight riders on our team, which we internally divided into two teams of four called our red and blue teams.

For most parts of the country each rider rode for twenty or thirty minutes all out as fast as he possibly could and then recovered for about an hour in the trailing van while another rider or two rode, then repeat. Think of doing a thirty-minute spin class with no warm-up or cool-down at maximum effort, maximum heart rate, and pushing maximum watts to exhaustion, then sit for an hour, then repeat—over and over, for three thousand miles. Each team of four rode eight- to ten-hour shifts.

Our other four teammates—Troy Willard, Linda Demma, Steve Holmes, and Pratt Rather (the blue team)—would ride while Joe, Phil, Bobby, and I (the red team) climbed into the RV after our shift, took a dribble shower, and ate boiled chicken, rice, pasta, or some other bland protein and carbohydrate concoction. Then we tried to nap for a couple hours, wobbling down the road in an RV with four aching bike racers and several crewmembers to get ahead of our blue teammates.

To her credit, Anna volunteered for the crew, as did her brother Daniel, and both did a great job helping with everything from navigation, food preparation, bike mechanics, and virtually anything a team of eight cyclists could need riding night and day across America. The entire crew traveling for this expedition was between fifteen and twenty, depending on where we were on the route.

We had to obey all traffic laws and stop at all stop signs and traffic lights. Of course, stopping all of the time and dodging traffic on an open road cost us time on our average speed. The route used roads of all kinds, except interstates, and our navigator and crew gave us directions in our earpieces or over the loudspeaker from the car behind us. Before each stint we studied the topography for the next three hundred miles to know if we had climbs or flats, open roads or congested towns, and we made choices between time trial or road bikes and adjusted our gear ratios and mind-sets accordingly. We saw sunrises, sunsets, and moonlit nights and wildfires and wildlife in thirteen states across the country.

One night in West Virginia at about 3:00 a.m. I was hammering alone down a dark, winding, country road in a wooded area, pedaling up and down rolling hills with my mind either asleep or just dreaming of the Atlantic Ocean ... and a cheeseburger and a cold beer. I rounded a downhill curve over thirty miles per hour and suddenly a large possum was directly in my path. I had no time to swerve to avoid it. I am sure I would have crashed attempting that and I'd already had one violent crash that year. One of us was going to die that dark summer night. I chose the possum.

I gripped the bars firmly and jerked my front wheel up slightly off the road and did a little bunny (possum?) hop and slammed into, over, and on top of the possum and kept pedaling. The only sound I heard after the violent impact of my wheel against possum flesh and bone was the screams of approval from the crew in the car following about fifty feet behind me. I think it was a quick death. At least I woke up the crew while I pedaled across West Virginia.

For much of the race we were chasing a team of professional mountain bikers sponsored by the ski resorts Beaver Creek and Vail, Colorado. Of course, these mountain bikers were riding road bikes in this road race. They shot into the lead as soon as the horn sounded on the pier in Oceanside, California, and we chased them all the way across the country. At times it felt like Burt Reynolds in the movie *The Cannonball Run*. Because they were pro mountain bikers they could climb the Sierra Nevada and Rocky Mountains like, well, they did that for a living. We finally caught them in Missouri after the country flattened out. We held that lead until West Virginia when we ran into America's next mountain range, and the two thousand miles of cycling in our legs started to bite. Then we chased them again to Atlantic City.

We pedaled our bikes 3,042 miles and crossed the country in five days, sixteen hours, and four minutes, averaging 22.36 miles per hour. Unfortunately, every minute, every second, counts because we lost to the Vail team by three minutes. Their time was five days, sixteen hours, and one minute with an average speed 22.37 miles per hour. We rode our bikes three thousand miles across an entire continent and only three minutes separated us. My teammates and I, and our crew, were exhausted. On the podium at the end of the race I had to wear a new, clean, team jersey so in the picture I am holding my hand and arm across my chest to cover the Abbott logo. I had seen Michael Jordan, the face of Nike, wear an American flag draped over the Reebok logo on his shoulder on the medal stand of 1992 Olympics, so there was precedent for this. LifeScan didn't pay me what Nike paid Mike, but the amount was probably proportional to what it meant to both of us, so I decided to be like Mike. I was so sore and sleep deprived after a quick meal that I slept for eighteen straight hours in my hotel room.

I had great cycling legs after RAAM but not much swimming or running in me recovering from my clavicle surgery, so I was not ready for Ironman Lake Placid a month later. I did a one-armed swim, had a great bike, and did some run training in the marathon. I pulled out at mile 127, mile thirteen of the marathon, because it was clear that I was risking injury to keep running. Withdrawing is a hard decision to make. I learned that climbing Mount Whitney. It's not worth it to damage your body, your job, or your relationships just to reach your finish line. Be smart and you will get there on the right day. And it's a lot more fun when you do.

> **It's not worth it to damage your body, your job, or your relationships just to reach your finish line. Be smart and you will get there on the right day.**

I spent August and September 2006 training and preparing for my marriage proposal to Anna in October. You will recall from an earlier chapter the details of my bloody proposal during an October half Ironman after my bike crash in that race. It sounds like 2006 was full of bike crashes, but it's part of the cycling when you put in a lot of miles. For a cyclist it's not a question of *if* you crash but *when*. Bike crashes are rare in triathlon races because we cannot draft or ride in packs, and that was my only crash ever in a triathlon. A month later in early November 2006 I raced Ironman Florida very easy (translation, slow) since I was leaving for Australia right after it for the ITU Worlds in two weeks.

G'DAY MATE!—WORLD CHAMPIONSHIP IN AUSTRALIA

The 2006 Worlds in Australia was amazing in a different way than races in Europe. Australians are sporty people, with a vibrant spirit. Every time one says, "G'day mate" you want to swim with the sharks on the Great Barrier Reef, surf Bondi Beach, and then go for a run and have a cold Foster's. I knew many Aussies from racing with and against them for years. They are also some of the best triathletes in the world.

The race was in Canberra, the capitol of Australia, about a three-hour drive south and inland from Sydney, surrounded by undeveloped land called "the bush." The race was November 19, which is springtime in Australia so the weather was unpredictable like spring in the US. It was cold the week we arrived and even had snow flurries and then baking hot and dry over ninety-five degrees a week later on race day. This area of Australia is dry and arid, with red rocks in the barren bush land between the cities. On a training ride on the bike course a few days before the race about twenty miles outside of the city I passed a dead kangaroo—or wallaby, I did not stop to check—hit by a car like we hit deer in the states.

The swim was in the crisp waters of Lake Burley Griffin, a beautiful lake below the Australian Parliament House in downtown Canberra. The bike course was extremely challenging, hot, and hilly—just the way I like it. It was four laps of about twenty miles each into the bush once we left the city. Unfortunately the bike course had only one aid station—one!—so that meant conserving drink until we looped back into town every twenty miles to get fresh bottles—not good in this ninety-five-degree *Man vs. Wild* Australian blast furnace. Spectators were too smart to travel out to the bush so out there it was just the athletes on the open road, with scrubby trees, rocks, and no buildings or signs of humanity. They don't put these pictures in "Visit Australia" tourism brochures. Huge black flies buzzed around me as I slowly climbed the killer steep grades, the same flies that buzzed around dead kangaroos, so maybe that was telling me something.

I had an okay bike but got dehydrated as many athletes did from that one water station *Survivor* challenge they put us through in the outback. Starting the run the heat hit like a wall. The thirty-kilometer run course was on dirt and asphalt paths around the lake and through the city, a ten-kilometer (6.2-mile) loop run three times. Hot, hot,

hot, almost a hundred degrees! The ITU is the international governing body for triathlon, a different organization from the private for-profit company that runs Ironman. Since this was my third ITU World Championship for the US national team, I've learned that the ITU officials are a bit more strict than Ironman officials. Ironman has amateurs paying hefty entry fees (over $500) to race, so they do not want to be unduly harsh on the athlete hands that feed them. The ITU runs races only for pros and international competition, including the Olympics. It is not interested in making sure you enjoy your race. One ITU official in Australia even threatened to penalize me for having my jersey unzipped on the run. I suppose that would be a fashion penalty.

For this race the ITU had little plastic water tubes rather than cups, so I spent the run ripping them open with my teeth and sucking out the water like a kid sucking a freezer pop. That was a lot more trouble than it should have been for a world championship race. My blood sugar held up fine, but like many I was fighting a losing battle with the heat and dehydration. I finished fortieth, right in the middle of the pack—disappointing but about what I expected for this world championship with my crash-filled year.

PAY BACK YOUR FAMILY

After the race Anna and I spent ten days traveling in Australia. We hiked rainforests and snorkeled in the Great Barrier Reef north in Queensland and toured the beautiful city of Sydney. We were not planning it, but we even managed to see the symphony orchestra in the famous Sydney Opera House only because we were standing outside on a patio admiring the view when a concert let out for intermission. When the crowd started moving back in we found ourselves caught in the wave and got swept right into the concert hall. Okay, I might have allowed us to get swept up. We were a little underdressed and Anna was paranoid the entire second act that we were going to get thrown out no matter how many times I told her to act natural. But it was worth it to see a performance in the iconic Sydney Opera House. I assume the statute of limitations on concert crashing has expired if I ever get back to Australia.

Australia is fourteen hours ahead of the US east coast, so it was odd to be a full day ahead of everyone back in the States. That meant I knew who was going to win all of the US basketball and football games, and I made a bunch of money in the US stock market too. We left Australia in early December and the weather was warm, approaching summer in the Southern Hemisphere. It was strange to have Christmas decorations and music in the stores with everyone wearing shorts, like a Christmas in July in the US.

2006 had been an interesting year, with some surprises and challenges—a cycling crash and surgery, Race Across America, getting bloody engaged, and traveling to race in Australia.

But now I was preparing to make some major transitions.

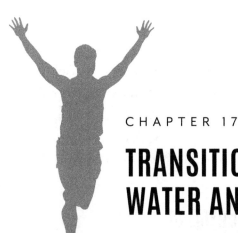

CHAPTER 17

TRANSITIONS: BREAD AND WATER AND ... DIAPERS

Topic: Making Transitions

What makes the sport of triathlon unique and fun are the immediate transitions required between three very different individual sports to reach the finish line. Imagine a competition where athletes played golf, rock climbed, and kayaked to the finish line, with no breaks in between.

The sport requires and teaches you to adapt and prepare for something different coming up. Life also requires transitions, and you have to prepare to make those to your next stage. I was preparing for transitions in my racing, my job, and my family.

I ran the Boston Marathon in April 2007. The crowds in Boston are fantastic with over five hundred thousand spectators lining the route,

> **Life also requires transitions, and you have to prepare to make those to your next stage.**

making it one of the largest crowds to view a one-day sporting event in the world. The race is always on Patriots' Day, the third Monday in April commemorating the Battles of Lexington and Concord, the first battles of the Revolutionary War. The city of Boston shuts down for the marathon and Patriots' Day. The Boston Red Sox traditionally hold a day game starting late morning so that the crowd from Fenway Park leaving the game can cheer late finishers of the marathon running by. I ran the marathon slow and easy, helping pace some other runners doing it at a fund-raiser for the Joslin Diabetes Center and because I was trying to save my legs for something more difficult starting later that week.

TOUR OF VIRGINIA PROFESSIONAL CYCLING

Three days after running Boston I was at the Tour of Virginia bike race for Team Type 1. The Tour of Virginia was a professional race with seven stages over six days through the mountains of Virginia. I did not like running a marathon and cycling a six-day stage race in the same week (since 2004 it seems these back-to-back races have become a pattern), but they won't reschedule them for me. *Dear Boston Athletic Association, I've had something come up. That's a bad week for me now. Can we move your marathon to … saaay … next month?*

Besides running the Boston Marathon earlier that week, another challenge I had was that our first child was due in three weeks. I was nervous about both—leaving this close to the due date and the pain this bike race was sure to inflict. I had scheduled a week away from my law practice for the race, so if I did not go, there was not much I could do at home watching the days click off the calendar. I would not have gone if Anna had objected, but she encouraged me to go, saying it was no different than a husband going on a business trip. I would only be about a four-hour drive away and both our parents lived in town.

Arriving in Virginia, I scanned the names and faces of 180 professional cyclists at the riders' meeting prior to the race. Some of them I recognized from magazines and cycling websites, veterans of European grand tour (three-week) stage races and other world tour and US races. Defending champion Brent Bookwalter would soon go on to race for the UCI World Tour team BMC and finish the Tour de France, Giro Italia, and Vuelta Espania grand tours multiple times. I saw Alejandro

Borrajo of Argentina who had finished top ten in stages of the Giro. Future US cycling and world tour pros Phil Gaiman and Ben King were there. King would win the US Professional Road Race Championship three years later. I felt like a towering hulk at 6'3" and 180 pounds with my muscular shoulders and arms from swimming standing next to most of these guys under 5'9" and barely a buck forty, with thin, wispy arms and bony shoulders from doing nothing but cycling for a living. You don't want to carry arm and shoulder muscles up mountains if you are a cyclist. These scrawny little guys looked like coat hangers in shirts.

If running the Boston Marathon five days ago was not already making my legs feel mushy, the thought of keeping up with these little dudes climbing the mountains of Virginia did. Race director Matt Butterman told *Cycling News* before the race that "not only is this the largest but also the strongest field in the race's history. There's depth and talent on the start list that we haven't seen before."

He wasn't talking about me. I am also sure that I was the only one who had just turned forty years old and had an office day job and a wife expecting a baby in a few days. I stood at the start house of the opening time trial with guys twenty years younger than me. But time trialing is what I do in triathlons, so I was anxious to give it a go.

Unfortunately, this time trial was just a prologue, only eight kilometers or about five miles over rolling hills. *Only five miles? I need another 107 to get in a groove!* I exploded my heart rate and legs on this little opener and was pleased that I placed in the middle of the field. *Okay, not bad. Maybe I have a chance to hang around this week.* I did not tell the riders watching results around the finish that I was really not a pro cyclist, just a triathlete and lawyer who ran the Boston Marathon last week and old enough to be their dad.

The second stage was a criterium in downtown Lynchburg, Virginia. A criterium is a short road race in a city on a circuit that racers travel multiple times. It is great for spectators because cyclists do multiple laps, whizzing by at extremely high speed. There is a lot of pushing and shoving in criteriums, and it is the closest thing to full contact cycling, with a lot of crashes. That's why criteriums are more common in US cycling than in Europe where the traditional long road race reigns. In the US it seems if you want spectators to show up for anything—football, NASCAR, and bike races—you need to offer the chance for high-speed collisions and crashes. I had raced a local one as a beginner six years before when I was just starting to cycle and got lapped by the other amateurs in the field. Might as well do my second in a pro race.

The course was a one-mile rectangle with hills at both ends. One we climbed and the other we descended, with two long straightaways, raced around to the left twenty-five times like a NASCAR track. It was like racing on the top and bottom rows of a football stadium. *Cycling News* described the uphill as a "grueling climb" of about two tenths of a mile. *Oh boy. Can't wait. Let's do it twenty-five times. Bring it on!*

And then, unfortunately, it was brought on.

One hundred and eighty guys were packed onto this course, and when the gun went off it seemed like every one of them, except me, wanted to be at the front. The field exploded off the start line like a shotgun packed with bicycle buckshot. BAM! *Hey guys, can't we warm up here?!* It was madness. I was very familiar with pack riding from years of doing it every Tuesday night at practice races at home and a few other local races and rides. But the quality of these riders was a few—okay, several—levels above some of the local pros and elite amateurs I had raced with at home. Eleven-time Tour de France veteran Christian Vande Velde describes positioning in a bike race as "a dance with close to two hundred other partners. You can't force it. You have to flow and be graceful."

Who can be graceful when your heart is coming out of your throat and it feels like someone attached jumper cables to your feet? Oh yeah, and hang onto the handlebars and shift gears, and tap the breaks delicately while you dance.

After about thirty minutes of dancing I was having trouble hanging in the pack and still had another ten laps to go. I kept drifting to the back of the field. That's when I began talking to myself.

I: Why did you run the Boston Marathon five days ago again?

Myself: Because it's the most famous marathon in the world!

I: I hope you're happy with yourself now.

Myself: Shut up. It was your idea to race this pro bike race!

I: Now we're both going to die.

Myself: At least we go down hard and fast, slamming into death screaming and yelling rather than sitting on a couch watching others live their dreams.

I: It's still going to hurt.

Dive bombing down the hill multiple times and taking the screaming left turn with 180 guys around me at over forty miles per hour trying to stay upright on barely a half inch of rubber, I had visions of my crash in the bike race last year that vaulted me over the bars and snapped my clavicle. One of the twenty-five times down this hill a cyclist just in front of me, but to the outside, had his tire roll off his wheel rim because we were leaning into the turn at such high speed. It sent him and several guys onto the asphalt in a crash of bodies, bikes, and yells, sliding into the barriers lining the course. That's criteriums. Cycling roller derby, hockey, and arena football. Sounds fun, doesn't it?

I managed to stay in the main field for a little while longer, yo-yoing off the back for a few laps until, as cycling television commentator Phil Liggett would say, "the elastic snapped." I was dropped. Now I was in trouble. I had several laps to go and I risked getting lapped and pulled from the race and not allowed to start stage three the next day. I found a few other discarded racers dropped from the group and we worked together even though we were on different teams. Fans cheered for us, like we were a group of little seals chasing a giant killer whale, or maybe the whale was chasing us. They always seem to like the determined little underdog who refuses to quit. Or maybe they just like to see suffering.

After the race a cyclist was quoted in *Cycling News* saying, "It was 800 watts coming up that last hill." That would be the one that we climbed twenty-five times. I'm not sure how accurate that wattage is, but I know it hurt. Watts are measured by power meters attached to the pedals, recording the combination of how hard a cyclist pushes the pedals and how fast he turns the crank arms (rpm). Elite pro cyclists will usually average 250 watts drafting in the pack and may push between four hundred to five hundred watts up a steep climb. The closest equivalent for a noncyclist would be to load multiple forty-five-pound plates on a leg press or squat rack at the gym and push it back and forth as fast as you can for an hour.

After a few more laps some of the guys in my little group dropped back, exhausted or to drop out, and I was left to race the last few laps alone like that monster of my childhood nightmares was chasing me. I've heard a quote by former professional cyclist Floyd Landis describing this suffering alone in a bike race. "It only feels like you're dying. You don't actually die." That's good to know. I crossed the finish line safely behind the winner, Alejandro Borrajo, in just over fifty minutes with more relief than I had crossing some Ironman finish lines in ten hours. Twenty-five miles in fifty minutes with an average speed of 30.6 miles per hour, including twenty-five times up that "grueling" climb where my speed averaged only eleven miles per hour, so our average for the other sections of the course was over forty miles per hour.

Like I said, madness. *Can we do this again tomorrow?* On to stage three.

Of course, pushing maximum watts and adrenaline for fifty minutes spiked my blood sugar over 300 mg/dl, similar to sprint triathlons, even though I did not eat or drink a thing in the race. There is no time, or need, to eat or drink in a criterium. My mouth was too busy sucking in oxygen anyway.

I can only imagine that pushing maximum watts every two minutes might be what contractions feel like to women in childbirth (at least that's what I've been told), so I was glad I got a sample of that to understand what my wife was getting ready to endure. We just didn't know how soon. She was starting to feel some rumblings and signals, and we did not know it then, but our daughter would be born in a few days, ten days early. I knew it was close and I had that on my mind starting stage three the next day. *Just see how far you can go and don't die.* If she went into labor during a stage I would just turn my bike south and ride it three hundred miles home as fast as I could. Just like Race Across America, right?

DRUGS ... OR BREAD AND WATER?
ETHICS AND DOPING CULTURE

One of the guys I had noticed in the race was hard to miss, covered in tattoos from his neck to his feet. I've never understood the desire for tattoos—talk about a permanent decision you might one day regret— but this guy took it to another level. It was hard to tell where his colorful cycling kit stopped and his painted skin took over. He could have ridden naked, like one of those models with painted swimsuits in *Sports Illustrated*, except he did not look like a swimsuit model. I had seen him on cycling websites and knew his results were impressive. Last year he had won the 2006 Criterium National Championship. He was a powerfully built guy with broad shoulders compared to other cyclists, and I wondered how he could climb and ride so well in steep mountain courses like we were facing in Virginia.

Then in 2008 he would be suspended by the United States Anti-Doping Agency for using EPO during the 2007 season, when I was racing against him at the Tour of Virginia. Maybe that was how. At one point doping was part of the cycling culture and many other sports. I knew that many top-level pros still did it. The previous year Floyd Landis had won the 2006 Tour de France but had his title stripped three days later when he tested positive for using another banned substance: testosterone.

My friend, neighbor, and cycling buddy from Greenville, George Hincapie, rode seventeen Tours and was teammates with Lance Armstrong for all of his record-setting seven straight Tour wins from 1999 to 2005. In his book *The Loyal Lieutenant,* George describes racing early in his career in the 1995 Vuelta Espania three-week stage race when his roommate received a "special package" one night. The next day, Hincapie said, "After having struggled every single day up until that point, he [his roommate] was in the breakaway. That solidified my sense that I couldn't compete on a level playing field without some assistance. The best way I know how to describe it is that I felt it was my only choice. I really did. If I wanted to be a professional bike rider, with all that entailed, in 1996 I felt I'd reached the end of my options of racing clean. The only way to compete on a level playing field with my rivals was to do what they were doing." He ultimately acknowledged using performance-enhancing drugs during part of his career and had several results and victories voided by the United States Anti-Doping Agency. He eventually stopped using them and worked behind the scenes trying to convince other professionals to stop as well.

I want to be clear that I disagree with the decisions of these athletes, but it is unfair to criticize them as cheaters without also criticizing and blaming those who encouraged and profited from it as well. It was quietly accepted by cycling's governing body and race organizers, even though those bodies won't admit that. Neither would Major League Baseball acknowledge when Mark McGwire and Sammy Sosa were chasing Roger Maris's single-season home run record in 1998. The only things bigger than McGwire's sudden growth of steroid-infused, herculean muscles were the ticket sales, television viewership ratings, and ad revenue. Major League Baseball loved it. They created a culture for baseball players to do it because the league was making money off of it.

So were the cycling leagues. The UCI (cycling's international governing body) and the ASO (the owner of the Tour de France) loved the benefits of Lance Armstrong wining the record seven straight Tours from 1999 to 2005. *The New York Times* reported that US television viewership of the Tour de France dropped over 50 percent in 2006, the first year after Lance Armstrong had retired and was not in the race. All those viewers and popularity from 1999 to 2005 meant increased television broadcast fees for the race owner and higher sponsorship dollars for cycling teams and races. Suddenly Nike was selling cycling apparel and shoes for the first time. Everyone is happy when the athletes are breaking records and bringing in viewers and revenue. Perhaps most telling that everyone was doing it is that when Armstrong was stripped of his seven Tour victories in 2012, the Tour did not award those titles to anyone else. They did not know how far down the standings they would have to go to find a rider who was clean.

At the 2007 Tour of Virginia I did not like that tattooed, doped-up, big guy kicking my ass up and down the hills of Virginia, but I'm pretty sure he probably would have done that just on bread and water too.

Stage Three was 107 miles in the mountains from Bedford to Covington, Virginia, over two category three mountains and one excruciatingly long seven-mile category one climb to the finish.

The moment the flag dropped for this third stage I was trying to survive—again. Seems like there's a pattern here. The first hour of a professional bike road race is extremely hard as cyclists try to get into an early breakaway. Once that breakaway is established, and the peloton realizes that no one dangerous is in it to steal the stage or gain time for the overall race lead, the peloton relaxes and everybody slows down a bit. It is contrary to training where we always warm up before hitting it hard.

About one hour into this stage I was hurting. *Will you breakaway masochists just get on with it so we can slow down?! Let those guys go!* The average speed was almost thirty miles per hour over rolling hills. We passed elementary schools where the entire school was out cheering us. I would have cheered too if I could get out of class for a bike race passing by.

As I hung onto the group, sucking the wheel in front of me, there was a momentary lull in the pace. A guy next to me said, "Hey man. What's that on your arm?"

I had started wearing an Omnipod insulin pump in late 2006. I wore it on my tricep, and it stuck out underneath my jersey sleeve.

"It's an insulin pump." Pedal. Pedal. We went around a curve and descent, and then it leveled out again and I continued. "I have diabetes."

I glanced at him quickly, but it is dangerous to take your eyes off the cyclists in front of you. He gave a surprised tilt of his head and raised his eyebrows. "Wow. Okay. Good job man."

With all of the focus on this race, I had actually forgotten that I had diabetes, or really, that the other riders didn't. It was such a part of my life and routine with Ironman, I was surprised when others looked at me strangely checking my blood sugar or wearing an insulin pump. I didn't mind that reaction. I kind of liked it now that I was competing at this level. I tell kids with diabetes not to hide it or be self-conscious about it. Other kids will look up to you if you manage it well and keep competing with them. I wanted everyone to know that I was competing just like them, not making excuses or wanting special favors or letting diabetes hold me back, proving that I am stronger than it is.

I tell kids with diabetes not to hide it or be self-conscious about it. Other kids will look up to you if you manage it well and keep competing with them.

After about thirty miles we started climbing the first mountain. A few breakaways had tried and failed to stick, but the constant attacks and surging splintered the peloton as soon as we hit this climb. Riders were already starting to drift back and string out on the slope of the climb. You can't draft in the group when the road goes up. Gravity hits us all. I joined a group and we battled up that first mountain together, but one thing about mountains is that there is always another one. Climbing the second mountain, about halfway through the stage, there were a lot of us battling to keep pace. The leaders were well up the road. It was here that the cold realism of reality started to hit me, or maybe it was the hot boiling lactic acid in my legs. *If I don't stay with the group I'll never make the time cut on my own.* There was still the final climb after this one, a seven-mile beast that was even steeper. If I did not finish within about twenty-three minutes of the leaders I would be cut, disqualified.

At the base of this second climb race officials on motorcycles had given time splits from the leaders to those of us in grupettos off the back. The last split I had seen was over twelve minutes, and that was fifteen minutes ago. Climbing this second mountain the officials had now quit coming back to us, the team cars were well ahead of us, and the dreaded broom wagon was not far behind us. The broom wagon even has brooms attached to the front bumper—the ultimate insult, to sweep road debris off the course, like discarded riders left as roadkill. The message it sends is clear: you guys better pack it in.

Clearly they did not know whom they were dealing with. *I'm not quitting, dammit!* Several riders in my group gave up, quit pedaling hard, and drifted back. I kept pedaling up ... up ... up. I passed a few more slowly pedaling up the road, waiting for the broom wagon. That should give me some more time while they loaded up. The casualties on this stage were increasing, giving me a moment of comfort that I was not alone in my suffering. But when the broom wagon caught me again I finally had to accept the reality. It is like the black flag to a car lagging the field in the Indy 500. You don't have a choice. You are disqualified and instructed to get off the course.

My race was over. So with much regret I swallowed my pride, stepped off my bike like a cowboy off his horse, and begrudgingly joined the other riders in the van about seventy miles into the stage. The broom wagon is not a happy place. Riders from different teams stare with blank, sullen faces, worse than the morning subway to work. But it is a good place for general bitching and moaning about how hard the stage was or other grievances. Misery loves company, so I had a lot of company. I had only come three hundred miles for this race. Some of these guys came all the way from South America and Europe.

The winner of this stage was a professional from Colombia, South America, who described the stage as harder than anything he had raced in his homeland and comparable to the mountains of European stage races. The third-place finisher described the stage as the "hardest I have ever done" and another told *Cycling News*, "I was just trying to survive." I know how he feels. At the end of the day I was one of fifty-nine riders who didn't survive this stage, a full one third of the entire field. After three stages only 116 riders remained from the 180 who started stage one.

That night I drove back to South Carolina, and one week later our first child was born, daughter Janna. The feeling of seeing that face was better than any Ironman finish. I could see the handwriting on the wall. I had been preparing for this, and I did not want my wife and daughter home while I tried to squeeze in workouts on mornings, nights, and weekends in addition to being at my law office all day.

With this reduced training I raced the inaugural Ironman Louisville in August later that summer. Fortunately in later years they would move IM Louisville to mid-October because racing there in August is a sweltering death march in the summer heat. My reduced training showed at IM Louisville. I started feeling sick on the last twenty miles of the bike and could not finish the marathon with stomach issues and heat. I spent an hour in the medical tent getting rehydrated. They need a special cot reserved for me in the medical tent. I probably pushed it too hard given my lack of training, but I can't race an Ironman half speed. My mind wants to race it all out like I've done before and it is too long to do that without proper training.

I raced half Ironmans in October and November with decent results despite my reduced training. I placed second out of sixty-four in my division, thirty-seventh out of 450 overall at Half Ironman South Carolina, despite a persistent (and puzzling) high blood sugar of three-hundred that stayed with me throughout the race. I essentially did a half Ironman without consuming any calories or carbs because my blood sugar would not come down. I began fighting a sore throat and sinus congestion that night, which developed into a three-day cold, so that may explain the high blood sugar that never came down during the race. Cold viruses always make blood sugar go up and stay up.

At a half Ironman in Miami in November I enjoyed the warmth and sun and having my wife and baby daughter with me. We stayed at the home of my agent who lived in Miami Beach. The race was a qualifier for the 2008 long-distance national team. I had raced for Team USA in 2004 to 2006 but had taken a year off in 2007 for the birth of our daughter. There was only one slot available, so I would have to come in first against eighty-five competitors to qualify. After the swim I was pleased that my blood sugar in T1 was a lovely 150 to start the fifty-six-mile bike. I had a good bike split, 2:25 averaging 23.2 miles per hour, and a decent half marathon, but unfortunately I finished third so I did not get that one slot available on the 2008 national team.

I used to wonder why dads carried their kids across the Ironman finish line after hours of suffering. This year I knew. I held my daughter on the podium at every race claiming my award for top three, even though at only a few months old she had no idea where she was or what Daddy was doing. I'm pretty sure she didn't even know that I *was* Daddy at that point. I was just somebody picking her up all the time who did not offer any nutrition.

LESS RACING, MORE SPEAKING

Heading into 2008 I was changing a lot of diapers and making a lot more bottles of baby formula than protein shakes. I was thinking about my plan to cut back on racing even more. I decided not to race any Ironmans in 2008 and to just do four half Ironmans. I was following one of the principles discussed in the chapter on work–life balance: to have the time of your life, make it the right time of your life. My time for racing was changing, and I had new goals and priorities with a wife and child—new finish lines to dedicate myself.

One of those new goals was speaking. In the summer of 2008 I attended my second national convention of the National Speakers Association in New York City.

I spent a cool day testing my aerodynamics on my time trial racing bike in a NASCAR wind tunnel in Mooresville, North Carolina, in early 2008. I also raced the 2008 Boston Marathon that April. In May I DNF'd in a hot half Ironman in Macon, Georgia, when I had physical problems. Like Ironman Louisville the year before, I had pushed myself too hard without adequate training and had a bad race. But my results were better in shorter races. That summer I won my division with the fastest bike and run splits and finished tenth overall out of seven hundred in the largest sprint triathlon in South Carolina. I placed top ten overall in an Olympic-distance race in Greenwood, South Carolina (2:17), and fourth in the Georgia State Championship (2:24) on a hilly course in north Georgia. But I did not have the long-distance training in me to do well in longer half Ironman and Ironman races at this point in the year.

I also had bike mechanical failures in two half Ironmans in 2008. My first was a flat tire at mile fifty of Ironman 70.3 Rhode Island in July, the only flat I've ever had in a race. I hit a pothole in the bumpy streets of downtown Providence and it cost me about ten to twelve minutes changing that flat. I had carried a spare tire and CO_2 cartridges in every race for years, like a spare tire under your car, but always brought them in unused. Trying to rip a glued tire off a wheel rim is no easy task in the middle of a race, but Ironman triathletes have to fix their own flats. Even though it cost me too much time changing this flat, in a strange way it gave me satisfaction to finally show that I could do it in a race. I'd practiced it many times, but the pressure and fatigue of a race always makes it harder and slower, so my race in Rhode Island was a disappointing result. My race at the South Carolina half Ironman the next month was only slightly better, finishing a disappointing forty-first out of six hundred in a time that would have placed me fourteenth overall in this same race just three years before. The competition was getting faster and growing, and I was getting older and training less.

My second mechanical problem that year was more devastating than Rhode Island's flat tire. In October I raced the US Long Distance Triathlon National Championship in Boulder City, Nevada, a qualifier for the 2009 national team and the world championship in Australia. We swam in the beautiful waters of Lake Mead, formed by the famous Hoover Dam on the Colorado River. It was only a half Ironman and by mile thirty-five of the bike I was close to the lead, in about twentieth place out of a thousand of the top triathletes in the US. I had finally built up some good training over the summer and fall, and it looked like it was going to be a good day when a hub on the cassette of my disk wheel broke. I had just raced that same wheel in the South Carolina half Ironman two weeks before with no problem. Unlike a flat tire, there was nothing I could do to repair this break. My race was over and so was my season—a disappointing end to racing in 2008.

A NEW FINISH LINE

These disappointing race results were not as significant as other things that happened in late 2008. In August my law firm merged with a much larger regional firm from out of state. Overnight we went from forty lawyers in one office to almost two hundred lawyers in six offices in three states. It was a business decision that I supported with cautious optimism.

That optimism lasted about thirty days. One month after our merger, Lehman Brothers filed for bankruptcy on September 15, 2008. The US and worldwide economy shook and then collapsed.

In early 2009 my wife was pregnant with our second child and we purchased a larger home because my two-bedroom bachelor pad would not accommodate a family of four. I raced the Boston Marathon in April 2009, but I had not trained much, worrying more about the economy and supporting my growing family than hill repeats and interval training.

With the economy in free fall, I knew our new big firm would not like me racing triathlons, speaking, or doing anything other than rowing the firm boat. There was tremendous pressure to generate revenue in 2009. The firm started laying off lawyers and asking partners to leave just like every industry was cutting back. I wanted to continue speaking, but now was not the time for that in the worst financial crisis since the Great Depression. Companies were cutting costs and laying off employees and they were not having meetings. The National Speakers Association was full of experienced speakers who were suddenly sitting at home with no engagements.

I was excited about every speaking engagement I did have in 2009. I spoke several times at regional and national sales meetings for a great international pharmaceutical company, Novo Nordisk, that makes insulin and other medications for patients with diabetes. I also spoke at meetings for Becton Dickinson (BD) Company, which makes syringes, and Insulet Corporation, which makes the Omnipod insulin pump. The world-renowned Joslin Diabetes Center in Boston asked me to speak at their annual black tie gala. At these events I watched the audiences respond enthusiastically and I knew that I helped them in their business and their lives. I wanted to do more of this.

Holding my second baby daughter in early 2010, I thought about how far I had come in just ten years since I ran that first marathon in 2000, worried and wondering if I could even do it. I had achieved everything I wanted to achieve in racing: fourteen Ironman and ultra-distance triathlons and breaking the elite ten-hour Ironman barrier at 9:47; qualifying and racing three years on Team USA at the ITU Long Distance Triathlon World Championships; eighteen half Ironman triathlons; eight individual marathons and three times at the Boston Marathon; cycling the Race Across America (RAAM); and the professional Tour of Virginia stage race—over seventy triathlons of sprint, Olympic, half Ironman, and Ironman and ultra distances.

I was satisfied that I had proven it racing, proven it to the hardest judge—myself—and gone farther and faster and longer than I ever thought was possible. Now I was ready to help others achieve their finish lines.

I have spoken at over sixty events a year—company meetings, associations, conferences, and conventions—any event where the audience wants to be motivated, achieve goals, overcome obstacles, and improve their lives. I have several different presentations on motivation, leadership, work-life balance, health and wellness, and handling change and failure.

If you or someone you love is living with diabetes, I hope this book has helped you realize that you can live a long, healthy life and achieve your dreams as long as you manage your diabetes properly. Respect your diabetes, but don't surrender to it. I didn't know anything about diabetes when I was diagnosed in 1991. I was scared, intimidated, and full of questions and wondering what it meant for me. If someone had told me that I could one day race Ironman triathlons and qualify for the US national triathlon team, I would have been thrilled. But I would want

Respect your diabetes, but don't surrender to it.

some proof. I would want to see someone who did it. I hope that I have been that proof for you. I would not have done that, or even tried that, if I did *not* have diabetes. Diabetes can be the best thing that ever happened to you. Make it that way.

If you are facing another health condition, I hope this has inspired you to keep fighting to overcome it. Reach your health finish line.

If you are a person facing change or challenges at work, thinking about a different position or career, or if you have lost your job, I hope this has inspired you to make that change and keep striving. Reach your career finish line.

If you are a person facing challenges and difficulties in your personal life—divorce, financial difficulties, stress of family and work—I hope this has helped you keep going, pursue a goal that inspires you, recover, and come back stronger. Reach your personal finish line.

If you are a person who wants to improve your health, change your body and physique, get healthy or strong or lose weight, run a race you never thought you could, play a sport and win a championship you dream of winning, I hope this has helped you visualize it. Keep training, sweating, and pushing. Reach your athletic finish line.

If you are the leader of an organization, a CEO of a company, or the coach of an athletic team, I hope this has given you knowledge to perform as a leader and not just as a manager, to create a finish line vision for your company or team that motivates each member to perform their best so that the organization performs its best.

I was speaking recently at a diabetes camp in the beautiful Kings Canyon and Sequoia National Parks in California. I was giving a motivational talk to over 150 kids and staff about racing Ironman triathlons with diabetes. I loved seeing the wheels turning in their head, thinking of obstacles they could overcome and goals they could achieve. But that day a girl about ten years old in the audience surprised me. She raised her hand and asked me a question very politely and quietly. I could tell she had been thinking about this while I was talking about how diabetes had motivated me.

"If you had a magic wand and you could go back and never get diabetes, would you do it?"

Wow. I had to pause for a moment. *What a great question.* No, I would not wave that wand. I do not like having diabetes. It is difficult to live with, expensive, and potentially very devastating. It has frustrated me with lows and highs and made my life more complicated and painful, but it has shaped my life and led to wonderful joy and satisfaction and self-discovery that I otherwise would not have had. It has made me more motivated, disciplined, and determined. It has motivated me to attempt and achieve things I never would have tried or achieved—racing Ironman triathlons and on the US national team, a professional speaking career, health and fitness and world travel, and the incredible honor to motivate and help others speaking and with this book. I would not want to give that up. I have worked to make it the best thing that ever happened to me. If and when you face a similar challenge or obstacle in your life, I hope that you will remember this and one day look back five, ten, or twenty years later and say you made it the best thing that ever happened to you.

It is an honor to influence the lives of people to whom I speak and consult to help them reach their finish lines. I hope I have done that for you with this book.

Keep going.

BIBLIOGRAPHY

Branson, Richard. *The Virgin Way*. Penguin Group, 2015.

Canfield, Jack. *The Success Principles*. HarperCollins, 2005.

Chua, Amy and Jed Rubenfeld. *The Triple Package*. Penguin Press, 2014.

Colvin, Geoff. *Talent Is Overrated*. Penguin Group, 2010.

Covey, Stephen. *Seven Habits of Highly Effective People*. Simon & Schuster, 2004.

Covey, Stephen, Sean Covey, Muriel Summers, and David Hatch. *The Leader in Me*. Simon & Schuster, 2014.

Coyle, Daniel. *The Talent Code*. Bantam, 2009.

Coyle, Daniel. *The Little Book of Talent*. Bantam, 2012.

Duckworth, Angela. *Grit*. Scribner, 2016.

Fitzgerald, Matt. *How Bad Do You Want It?* VeloPress, 2015.

Gielan, Michelle. *Broadcasting Happiness*. BenBella Books, 2015.

Gladwell, Malcolm. *David and Goliath*. Back Bay Books, 2015.

Gladwell, Malcolm. *Outliers*. Back Bay Books, 2011.

Hincapie, George. *The Loyal Lieutenant*. HarperCollins, 2014.

Hirsch, James. *Cheating Destiny*. Houghton Mifflin Harcourt, 2006.

Hsieh, Tony. *Delivering Happiness*. Business Plus, 2010.

Kelly, Megyn. *Settle for More*. HarperCollins, 2016.

McCormick, Chris. *I'm Here to Win*. Center Street, 2011.

McDougall, Christopher. *Born to Run*. Vintage, 2009.

Sandberg, Sheryl. *Lean In*. Knopf, 2013.

Seligman, Martin. *Authentic Happiness*. Atria Books, 2004.

Sinek, Simon. *Start with Why*. Penguin Group, 2009.

Sotomayor, Sonia. *My Beloved World*. Vintage, 2014.

Southerland, Phil. *Not Dead Yet*. Thomas Dunne Books, 2011.

USDA. "Implications of Restricting the Use of Food Stamp Benefits." March 1, 2007. https://www.fns.usda.gov/sites/default/files/arra/FSP-FoodRestrictions.pdf.

ACKNOWLEDGMENTS

I thought about writing this book after being asked several times by attendees at my speaking engagements. I am honored that I inspired them and that they wanted to share it or learn more.

Thank you to Anna for living much of this story with me and the countless hours and times that you helped me with low blood sugar, high blood sugar, and the endless challenges of living with someone with diabetes. Thank you to my mom and dad, who have always supported me as a kid pursuing my goals and taught me to work hard for them, and my brother, Rick, and sister, Camille, for support and fun throughout our lives. To the numerous people who reviewed drafts and excerpts of this manuscript and contributed their wisdom, including Kerri Sparling, Mike Murray, Dr. Bruce Latham, Dr. David Harlan, Dr. Rick Kattouf, and Joe Towson and others who offered advice and content: George Hincapie, Will Knecht, Chuck Gallagher, Dr. Etie Moghissi, and Peter Kotland.

Thank you to the people and organizations of the diabetes community for allowing me to speak and hopefully inspire you and for teaching me, including Jeff Hitchcock and Laura Billetdeaux with www.childrenwithdiabetes.com, the Joslin Diabetes Center, and the staff and volunteers of dozens of diabetes camps around the country. You make kids with diabetes feel great. Special thanks to the people of Novo Nordisk for allowing me to share a message of living successfully with diabetes by speaking to healthcare professionals and patients throughout the country. And thank you to the mom and dad of a child with type 1 diabetes and to the person with type 1 or 2 diabetes at any age who is trying to manage it well every day. It is a challenge, but you can do it. You inspire me.

ABOUT THE AUTHOR

Jay Hewitt is an athlete, attorney, and speaker. After being diagnosed with type 1 diabetes he qualified and raced for the US National Long Course Triathlon Team, racing three years for Team USA at the World Championships in Denmark, Sweden, and Australia. He raced fourteen ultra distance and Ironman triathlons—a 2.4-mile swim, 112-mile bike race, and 26.2-mile marathon run (140 miles total in one day)—all while injecting insulin and managing his blood sugar.

While racing he balanced work and life, practicing business litigation as trial counsel and arguing appeals to the South Carolina Supreme Court and the US Court of Appeals. He now speaks to business groups and the public about health and wellness, diabetes, overcoming obstacles, and achieving goals in work and life. He lives in Greenville, South Carolina, with his wife and three children.

FINISH LINE VISION®

Jay Hewitt's message inspires audiences to overcome obstacles and achieve success. He speaks to business professionals and the general public, students, and athletes on:

MOTIVATION
LEADERSHIP
WORK-LIFE BALANCE
HANDLING CHANGE AND FAILURE
HEALTH AND FITNESS
DIABETES

Contact Jay to speak at your next event:

JAY@JAYHEWITT.COM
WWW.JAYHEWITT.COM
TWITTER: @JAYHEWITTSPEAKS

Printed in the USA
CPSIA information can be obtained
at www.ICGtesting.com
JSHW011546190224
57673JS00019B/583